Stepfam...

THE UNIVERSITY OF
WINCHESTER

brary
'06

This new book reviews the most current global research and highlights the challenges, possibilities, and dynamics of stepfamily households. It describes their formation, their experiences, and the factors that help them thrive. International and cultural differences are highlighted throughout along with issues of class, gender, and religion. Nontraditional stepfamilies such as those headed by same-sex parents are also explored along with clinical and legal issues. Engagingly written with numerous vignettes and examples, each chapter features objectives, an introduction, bold-faced key terms, summary, list of key terms, discussion questions, exercises, and additional text and web resources. The book concludes with a glossary.

Highlights of coverage include:

- The history, diversity, and demography of stepfamilies (Chapter 1).
- Frameworks for thinking about stepfamilies (Chapter 2).
- The impact of race and culture on stepfamily dynamics (Chapter 3).
- Stepfamily formation, including the role of cohabitation and lone parenting (Chapter 4).
- The well-being of adults in stepfamilies, including resident and nonresident parents (Chapter 5).
- Relationships in stepfamilies, including those between adults, between adults and children, and between siblings (Chapters 6 and 7).
- Children's well-being in stepfamilies, and factors that help explain outcomes (Chapter 8).
- The importance of intergenerational relationships (Chapter 9).
- Stepfamilies headed by same-sex couples; well-being, stigma, and legal issues (Chapter 10).
- Factors that promote well-being in stepfamilies such as communication patterns, rituals, and flexibility (Chapter 11).
- Interventions and therapy, and recent legal and policy issues (Chapters 12 and 13).
- New ways of thinking about stepfamily living (Chapter 14).

Intended as a core advanced undergraduate/beginning graduate text for courses on stepfamilies or as a supplement for courses on divorce, family studies, introduction to the family, and/or marriage and the family taught in human development and family studies, psychology, sociology, and social work, the book also appeals to those who work with stepfamilies in a counseling or legal setting.

Jan Pryor, PhD, is ... Wellington, New Zealand.

Textbooks in Family Studies Series

The *Textbooks in Family Studies Series* is an interdisciplinary series that offers cutting-edge textbooks in family studies and family psychology. Volumes can be complete textbooks and/or supplementary texts for the undergraduate and/or graduate markets. Both authored and edited volumes are welcome. Please contact the Series Editor, Robert Milardo, at rhd360@maine.edu, for details in preparing a proposal that should include the goal of the book, table of contents, an overview of competing texts, the intended market including course name(s) and level, and suggested reviewers.

These are the books currently in the series:

Stepfamilies: A Global Perspective on Research, Policy and Practice
written by Jan Pryor (2014)

Serving Military Families in the 21st Century
written by Karen Rose Blaisure, Tara Saathoff-Wells, Angela Pereira,
Shelley MacDermid Wadsworth, and Amy Laura Dombro (2012)

Father–Daughter Relationships: Contemporary Research and Issues
written by Linda Nielsen (2012)

Stepfamilies

A Global Perspective on
Research, Policy, and Practice

Jan Pryor

Routledge
Taylor & Francis Group

NEW YORK AND LONDON

First published 2014
by Routledge
711 Third Avenue, New York, NY 10017

and by Routledge
27 Church Road, Hove, East Sussex BN3 2FA

Routledge is an imprint of the Taylor & Francis Group, an informa business

© 2014 Taylor & Francis

Library of Congress Cataloging in Publication Data
Pryor, Jan.
  Stepfamilies: a global perspective on research, policy, and practice/ Jan Pryor.
  pages cm—(Textbooks in family studies series)
  Includes bibliographical references and index.
  1. Stepfamilies. 2. Stepfamilies—Textbooks. I. Title.
  HQ759.92.P76 2014
  306.874'7—dc23
  2013023833

ISBN 978-0-415-81465-2 (hbk)
ISBN 978-0-415-81466-9 (pbk)
ISBN 978-1-315-88734-0 (ebk)

Typeset in Sabon and Gill Sans
by Florence Production Ltd, Stoodleigh, Devon, UK

MIX
Paper from
responsible sources
FSC FSC® C014174
www.fsc.org

Printed and bound in the United States of America by Sheridan Books, Inc. (a Sheridan Group Company).

This book is dedicated to Duncan, with love

Contents

Figures

Tables

Boxes

Series Editor Foreword

Stepfamilies: A Global Perspective on Research, Policy, and Practice appears in the Routledge Textbooks in Family Studies Series. In each book, our purpose is to pair leading experts with important topics in the field of family studies that are underrepresented in standard textbooks. These experts are active researchers, practitioners, and talented teachers who can write engaging books that can be used in the classroom as standalone textbooks, or paired with additional books.

Jan Pryor is a leading global authority on stepfamilies. She served as Professor of Psychology at Victoria University, Director of the Roy McKenzie Centre for the Study of Families, and Chief Commissioner at the New Zealand Families Commission. Jan brings to the table a rare combination of skills as an experienced social scientist, and sophisticated policy analyst with a long career of advocating for families and children.

The book comprises 14 chapters that provide a comprehensive treatment of stepfamilies. Nearly a third of all children in the US are expected to spend some of their formative years living in stepfamilies, and although this form of family is not new, it is growing in incidence globally and therefore in importance.

Stepfamilies are unique in many ways and this book details how we can best understand this uniqueness. Stepparents and their children face a wide array of issues not represented in ties among biological parents and their offspring. By understanding the unique experiences and challenges of stepparents, their children, grandparents and step-grandparents as well as other family members, we can design social policies that are inclusive and effective in supporting families.

Professor Pryor brings to bear a comprehensive accounting of contemporary research with its practical implications for understanding relationships in stepfamilies across generations. Her perspective is multicultural and sensitive to issues of gender, race, ethnicity, culture, and sexual orientation. Although much of the current research on stepfamilies in based in the US and Canada, she develops a welcome multicultural perspective, and draws heavily on work in Great Britain and Europe,

Australasia, including her home country New Zealand, and parts of Asia and Africa where information is available.

We anticipate that this book will provide students with a diversified understanding of stepfamilies, their special needs and challenges, and a clearer understanding of the basis for effective social policies that are sensitive to the needs of individuals and their communities.

Robert M. Milardo, PhD
Series Editor
Professor of Family Studies
University of Maine

Preface

Stepfamilies are increasing in number, and they are diversifying in ways that most other family forms are not. The fact that nearly one in five children in the United States lives in a stepfamily should in itself alert us to the importance of understanding this family form; the likelihood that one in three will enter a stepfamily during their childhood or adolescence suggests that we should be taking stepfamilies very seriously.

Many colleges in the United States teach family studies; comparatively few of them take a specific focus on stepfamilies. Yet the increasing prevalence of stepfamilies, and their combination of biological and nonbiological kin, means that understanding their dynamics is a way of coming to grips with the reality of much of family life in the twenty-first century. This book is designed to address the gaps in information by providing an up-to-date account of stepfamilies based on research, and on clinical and legal writing. Importantly, it also takes a global perspective, examining stepfamilies across cultures and across countries. The author is a scholar in New Zealand, and discusses research material from many parts of the world, including Europe, the United States, Australasia, and parts of Africa and Asia.

Scholarship about stepfamilies has increased vastly in the last two decades. It has moved from straight comparisons of how children raised in stepfamilies fare, to an examination of the dynamics of stepfamily households. The goal of this book is to bring recent research and thinking about stepfamilies together, and to consider aspects that are not well studied. These include cultural and international diversity, 'nontraditional' stepfamilies such as those headed by same-sex families, communication strategies that work well for stepfamilies, and the nature of stepkin created by stepfamily formation—stepgrandparents, stepsiblings in other households, and other extended stepkin.

Another reason for writing this book is to bring a perspective that both acknowledges the challenges and difficulties of being in a stepfamily, and also points to the factors that help stepfamilies to thrive. Stepfamilies encompass some dynamics that are shared with 'first families', but also some that are unique to them. The combination of biological relationships and 'fictive kin' that characterize stepfamilies means that the ways in which members interact, and in which those interactions change over time, are not the same as in first families. Unless these differences are acknowledged we will fail to support their well-being.

Learning Tools

Each chapter includes opening quotes, an introduction, key terms that are boldfaced when they are first introduced and listed at the end of each chapter (and defined in the end-of-text glossary), chapter summaries, discussion questions, additional text and web resources, and, in some cases, suggested exercises. These tools are intended to help students to focus on the main themes of each chapter, and to promote further discussion and exploration of the topics. It is impossible to cover all the material there is about each topic, so readers are encouraged to discover other material and to think about the often complex areas of stepfamily life that are raised in each chapter.

Intended Audience

The book is primarily intended as a supplementary text for advanced undergraduate and/or graduate courses in family studies, introduction to the family, and/or marriage and the family taught in departments of human development and family studies, psychology, sociology, social work, and education. The book will also serve as the core text for a specialized course on stepfamilies.

It will also be of interest to those who work with stepfamilies such as counselors, social workers, psychologists, and professionals working in family courts. Stepfamily members themselves may find it of interest, since it discusses many aspects of stepfamily living in the twenty-first century in approachable language.

Content

The first chapter is an introduction, addressing history, definition, stigma, diversity and prevalence of stepfamilies. It raises many issues that are taken up in detail in later chapters.

Chapter 2 considers frameworks and theories that are used in understanding stepfamily life. It covers four major theories (Family Systems Theory, Life Course Theories, Family Social Capital, and Evolutionary Theory), and three frameworks that are useful when applied to stepfamilies (parenting styles, boundary ambiguity, and bidirectional effects). This chapter provides a framework for considering research discussed throughout the book.

Chapter 3 addresses cultural and race issues that are vital in thinking about the ways in which stepfamilies function. Although research is sparse outside North America and Europe, information from Namibia, Japan, New Zealand, as well as about Hispanic and Black American cultures is discussed. Throughout the book race and cultural issues are addressed; however, this chapter provides an overall framework for thinking about these.

Chapter 4 addresses the ways in which stepfamilies are formed. It looks at multiple transitions and multipartner fertility as well as the major pathways of stepfamily formation such as lone parenting and cohabitation.

Chapter 5 examines the well-being and roles of adults living in stepfamily households. The three main kinds of adults—biological parents, stepparents, and nonresident parents, are discussed.

Chapter 6 moves on to dyadic, or two-person, relationships by considering those between adults, and those between different kinds of siblings in stepfamilies. Three kinds of relationships for adults, and three for siblings, exist: parent–stepparent, parent–nonresident parent, and stepparent–nonresident parent; and biological sibling, stepsibling, and half-sibling relationships.

Chapter 7 looks at the research on relationships between children and adults in stepfamilies. Children have relationships with three main parenting figures: resident parents, stepparents, and nonresident parents. This chapter also considers the evidence about how children manage relationships with multiple parenting figures.

Chapter 8 focuses on children's well-being. It considers the comparisons in well-being between children in stepfamilies and those in other kinds of families, and looks at the factors that explain the differences that are found. In this chapter the issue of abuse of children is also discussed. The evidence for higher rates than in other families and possible explanatory factors are covered.

Chapter 9 examines what we know about intergenerational relationships in stepfamilies. Step-grandparents are a group that is comparatively neglected by researchers. We look at how they become step-grandparents, and how much contact they have with step-grandchildren.

Chapter 10 addresses stepfamilies headed by same-sex parents. It discusses what we know about prevalence, stigma, well-being, and legal structures.

Chapter 11 approaches stepfamilies as units, and discusses well-being and challenges faced by families as a group. Factors associated with strong stepfamilies are identified.

Chapter 12 describes interventions and therapies for stepfamilies. It notes the lack of evaluation of interventions, and discusses some that have been evaluated. It describes two major therapeutic models used in the United States.

Chapter 13 examines the legal situation for stepfamilies both in the United States and in other countries. It notes the lack of legal support for stepfamilies that continues to exist.

The final chapter, Chapter 14, pulls together main themes from the book and proposes two models for approaching the understanding of stepfamilies that might take us beyond the limitations of the usual focus on nuclear families and family structure.

This book brings together the latest research and thinking about stepfamilies. It emphasizes their diversity, and suggests ways in which they might be best supported to thrive as an increasingly common family form.

Acknowledgments

I want to thank Debra Riegert and the team at Routledge/Taylor & Francis for their help in preparing this book. I am especially grateful to Robert Milardo for his unstinting support and readiness to respond to my slightest queries from the other side of the world. Thank you also to reviewers: Robert Emery, University of Virginia; Valarie King, the Pennsylvania State University; Ross Parke, University of California, Riverside; and Kay Pasley, Florida State University. I would also like to thank my colleagues who were generous in their encouragement and provision of material: Graham Allan, Belinda Baham, Scott Browning, Claire Cartwright, Marilyn Coleman, Larry Ganong, Shinji Nozawa, and Patricia Papernow. And thank you to those who have lived with my psychological absence during its writing—Duncan and Maggie. Without Duncan's love, patience, and encouragement it would not have happened.

About the Author

Jan Pryor

Jan Pryor, PhD is an adjunct professor at Victoria University, Wellington, New Zealand. She recently retired as the founder and Director of the Roy McKenzie Centre for the Study of Families, in the School of Psychology at Victoria University. She was also Chief Commissioner at the New Zealand Families Commission between 2008 and 2010. Her research has focused on the impact of divorce on children and adults, and on stepfamily well-being. She works with family court professionals, providing educational courses and contributing to conferences. She co-authored with Bryan Rodgers *Children in Changing Families: Life After Parental Separation* (Blackwell 2001). She is the editor of *The International Handbook of Stepfamilies: Policy and Practice in Legal, Research, and Clinical Environments* (John Wiley & Sons 2008).

Chapter 1

Introduction to Stepfamilies

The potential for varied and intense emotions shared with related and unrelated human beings brought together in a 'family' produce(d) experiences of fear of failure, of joy, hope, and success . . .
(Curtis-Clark 2012, p. 102)

Objectives of this Chapter

- To understand the history of stepfamilies.
- To become familiar with terminology associated with stepfamilies.
- To appreciate the diversity of stepfamilies.

Introduction

Throughout human history, there have been stepfamilies. They are not a new family form, but they are one that is increasing at an astonishing rate in the twenty-first century. And they are one that we are aware of far more than we used to be. Chances are high that you or someone you know has lived in a stepfamily at some time. It has been estimated that in the United States nearly 30 percent of all children will spend some time in a stepfamily household before the age of 16, and that 40 percent of all mothers will do the same (Bumpass, Raley et al. 1995). Given that this estimate was done nearly 20 years ago, the likelihood of being in a stepfamily is even higher now.

Stepfamilies are, by and large, depicted negatively. In folklore wicked stepmothers and violent stepfathers are common, and are part of the cultural view of stepfamilies that exists in many countries. In some languages there is not even a word for a stepfamily. We can get an impression about how they continue to be seen in modern society from, for example, the terms used for stepmothers and stepfathers in Sweden— literally, plastic moms, and plastic dads. In Germany, the term for stepfamilies is *Patchworkfamilie*. And in Chinese culture second wives and husbands are referred to as *as yee sau for*—used goods. The implications are clear—stepfamily members are insubstantial and tainted.

Despite the fact that stepfamilies have always been a part of human societies, and that they are a rapidly increasing family form, our understanding of how stepfamilies function in the late twentieth and early twenty-first centuries remains remarkably underdeveloped. Fortunately, there is an expanding body of research in the US and other Western countries that is examining the ways in which stepfamilies are formed, the nature of stepfamily dynamics, and how they might be supported to flourish. The purpose of this book is to describe what we know, primarily from a basis of research. It examines key areas of stepfamily functioning, the contexts in which they exist, the diversity of their forms, and the factors that impede or enhance their well-being.

VIGNETTE
A 'typical' stepfamily

Suzie and James were married and had three children, Charlie, Sarah, and Paul. When the children were 4, 6, and 8 years old Suzie and James divorced. The children lived mainly with Suzie, but spent weekends and some weeknights with James. A year later James met Carrie, and they moved in together. Carrie had no children. The children continued to visit James some weekends, but spent most of their time with Suzie. Two years later Suzie started dating Zeb, who was divorced from his wife and had two children who visited him every other weekend. Suzie and Zeb married, and her children continued to live with them. Zeb's children came to stay every second weekend. On many of those weekends there were five children in the household—Suzie's and Zeb's—on others there were none. Suzie's children and Zeb's children are stepsiblings.

Carrie and James had a child of their own two years later. This gave Charlie, Sarah, and Paul a half sibling whom they were with in their other household.

A Brief History of Stepfamilies

In the past in Western societies, stepfamilies were common. They were, however, formed through rather different processes than we see today. They were most likely to be formed as a result of the death of a parent.

Death in childbirth was widespread for women before modern medicine developed techniques and antibiotics to prevent their dying. In these situations fathers were very likely to remarry in order to have someone to help to raise their children, bringing a stepmother into their children's lives. Conversely, if a father died—as many did through infection or accident—his surviving widow would often remarry and hence bring a stepfather into the lives of her children.

It was common in Europe for widows or widowers to marry very shortly after the death of their spouse, although it was frowned on for widows to marry too soon, and to marry someone younger than themselves. In France and England in the sixteenth and seventeenth centuries, remarriage was almost as common as it is today—about one third of marriages involved at least one partner who had been widowed. However, toward the middle and end of the nineteenth century, the rates of remarriage began to decrease as death rates dropped. This was accompanied by a rise in the disapproval of remarriage, since it was no longer based on widowhood and the need for a surviving partner to marry someone in order to help raise children. Remarriage based on divorce was frowned upon, especially by churches. By the mid 1800s, remarriage rates had dropped to between 10 and 14 percent in most European countries.

Today, a common pathway to stepfamily formation is through divorce and remarriage of one or both parents. An important difference for children is that when a stepfamily was formed because of the death of one parent, they lost that parent completely. Where divorce precedes stepfamily formation, children do not literally lose a parent (although they may lose contact); they gain a new parental figure—or even two if both parents repartner.

Defining and Classifying Stepfamilies

The clear defining feature of a stepfamily is that it is a family in which at least one child is not biologically related to both parents. There are, though, many problems when we try to define stepfamilies. First, it is common for the term 'remarriage' to be used (e.g. by the United States census). This restricts the identification of stepfamilies to households where the parents are legally married. In practice, this excludes many stepfamilies, since the majority of stepfamily couples cohabit before they marry, and many remain in cohabiting unions rather than marrying. The emphasis on marriage, then, excludes large numbers of stepfamilies and this is of concern both when we are attempting to understand how many stepfamilies there are, and in research where excluding participant families who are not married means that findings are restricted to an increasingly small proportion of actual stepfamilies.

Households versus Families

Not all stepfamily members live in the same household. In the past when stepfamilies were formed as an outcome of the death of a parent, the new family was likely to live in the same household. Today, with the increased complexity caused by the ongoing presence of nonresident parents and the likelihood that children will live in two different households, restricting the definition to households fails to take into consideration large numbers of stepfamilies. It also gives an unrealistic impression of the real lives that stepfamily members live.

Labeling Stepfamilies

One of the main messages to come in this book is that stepfamilies are extraordinarily diverse. They take many forms, and their forms are fluid. So the terminology used to refer to different stepfamily forms is at best only partly adequate.

There have been frequent attempts to avoid the stigma associated with the term stepfamily, by using other labels—for example, 'reconstituted', 'reformed', 'second-time-around', and 'blended'. Stepfamily members themselves often avoid the term, preferring to see themselves as 'ordinary' families. (The stigma still experienced by some stepfamilies is discussed further later in this chapter.)

Most researchers have now, despite the potential stigma, reverted to using the term 'stepfamilies' to refer to the group of families that fit the broad definition of at least one child in the family being unrelated to one of the parents. In this book, we will use the term 'first family' to refer to family structures that involve the first committed relationship for adults, and often precede stepfamilies. In both first and stepfamilies, parents may or may not be married.

Unfortunately, the terminology used to refer to different kinds of stepfamilies varies among researchers and policy makers, making it difficult to compare findings. For example, the term 'blended' can be used to refer to *all* stepfamilies—e.g. Kreider, reporting on US Census data (Kreider & Ellis 2011). Others use that term to refer to a specific kind of stepfamily. An example of simple classifications is shown in Box 1.1.

Stepmother and stepfather families are examples of 'simple' stepfamilies. Stepfather families are formed when a mother and her children live with her new partner, the children's stepfather. Stepmother families are formed when a father and his biological children live with his new partner, the children's stepmother. Of course, simple stepfamilies can become less simple if the parents have a child of their own, as in the vignette earlier in this chapter. Stepmother households are less common than

> **Box 1.1 Classifications of stepfamily households**
>
> - **Simple stepfamily**: a mother or father and his/her biological children.
> - **Complex or blended stepfamily**: a household in which biological children of both parents live.
> - **Patchwork stepfamilies**: those in which at least two types of children live (biological, stepsiblings, half siblings).
> - **Multifragmented stepfamilies**: those formed from multiple divorces or deaths, and subsequent transitions.

stepfather households, since children are more likely to live with their mothers than their fathers after divorce.

A more complicated stepfamily household is a blended, or 'complex' stepfamily in which biological children of both parents live. Complex stepfamilies may also contain stepsiblings and half siblings, or biological children and half siblings, or sometimes all three.

'Multifragmented' families are those that contain children from several partners of the mother (or less commonly the father). The other parent in the family may not be biologically related to any of them. These families arise from **multipartner fertility**, an increasingly common phenomenon in which either parent has biological children from relationships with more than one other partner.

It is important, then, when reading about or discussing stepfamilies, to check which definitions and terminologies are being used. Other typologies and ways of classifying stepfamilies are discussed in detail in Chapter 4.

Accordion Families

The reality of many stepfamily households is that, unlike first-union families, the membership does not stay the same from week to week. After parents separate, children often spend time in the homes of both parents. If both parents in a stepfamily household have children from earlier marriages, the household expands and contracts as children come and go between households. This leads to the reference to stepfamilies as **accordion families** that expand and contract rather like a piano accordion.

The house in the middle is the stepfamily household, with a mother and her two children, and a stepfather. To the left is the household of the stepfather's previous partner, who lives with their three children.

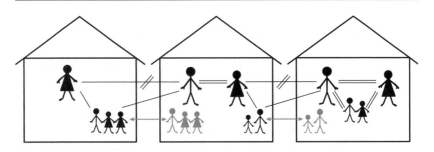

Figure 1.1 Living arrangements for a typical stepfamily

Source: From *Children in Changing Families: Life After Parental Separation*, J. Pryor and B. Rodgers. Reproduced with permission of John Wiley & Sons.

The household on the right contains the previous partner of the mother in the stepfamily household, with his new partner and their two children. However, both sets of children spend some time in the houses of their nonresident parents. So the house in the middle may at times have five children in it, and at others none. Likewise, the two other households vary from time to time in the number of children in them.

You can see why the term 'accordion families' is used; each house expands and contracts depending on how many children are in it at any one time. Typically, stepsiblings will be required to share bedrooms, which may present challenges to both them and to their parents. These arrangements call for flexibility from family members, as well as the ability to accommodate different numbers of children. They also emphasize one aspect of the fluid nature of stepfamilies, a theme to which we will return often in the book.

In summary, defining stepfamilies is fraught with difficulty. Yet definition is needed for census and for research purposes. In Chapter 14 we will suggest a way of avoiding definitions by talking about family practices, rather than using 'family' primarily as a noun.

Incomplete Institutionalization

Early in the history of research that addressed stepfamilies, Cherlin referred to remarriage as an 'incomplete institution' (Cherlin 1978). He suggested that the difficulties faced by stepfamily households were due in large part to the lack of institutional support. This takes the form of lack of definition of roles in Western stepfamilies with lack of agreed language to describe family members, and lack of legal sanction and guidance for stepfamily members. Since Cherlin introduced this term, it has been used widely in reference to multiple aspects of stepfamily dynamics and will be referred to in this book.

Stereotypes and Stigma

From early childhood, children are exposed to stereotypes about step-families—particularly in regard to stepmothers. These stereotypes are overwhelmingly negative—Cinderella's wicked stepmother who tried to poison her, Hansel and Gretel abandoned in the forest to die at the instigation of their stepmother.

Contemporary movies, too, are more likely than not to portray stepfamilies negatively (Leon & Angst 2005); and newspaper headlines tend to portray stepfamilies in adverse ways (Claxton-Oldfield 2000).

Research has shown that the word 'step' in front of terms such as mother and father, leads to adverse perceptions of people's behavior (Claxton-Oldfield 2008). More recent studies suggest, though, that negative stereotypes are reducing, and this is perhaps not surprising given the rapid increase in the numbers of stepfamilies. An example of how attitudes might be changing is shown in a recent study of children's perceptions of families, in which they were given vignettes of varying groupings of people and asked if they were families. Stepfamilies were almost as likely to be seen as a 'real' family as were biological families (Rigg & Pryor 2007). Box 1.2 shows some of the findings.

We might, then, be cautiously optimistic that members of stepfamilies are less and less likely to experience stigma as this family form becomes more common, at least in western societies. Later in the chapter we discuss the prevalence of stepfamilies in more detail.

Factors Contributing to Stepfamily Diversity

As we have seen, stepfamilies are remarkably diverse. There are several factors that are important in contributing to diversity.

Box 1.2 Percentage of 10–14-year-olds who endorsed a grouping of people as a family

Married couple with child	100 percent
Stepfamily of ten years	95 percent
Lone mother + partner (recently married) + child	93 percent
New stepfamily	85 percent

Race, Ethnicity and Culture

As you will see throughout the book, stepfamilies vary according to the culture, race, and ethnicity of their members and of their context. This is true both within the United States, where prevalence and other aspects of stepfamilies vary, and internationally, where variation is found across countries and regions. Cultural difference and diversity is the subject of Chapter 3 in this book.

Class/Socioeconomic Status

Given that there are well-documented class differences in factors such as household income, employment, and social attitudes, it would not be surprising to see diversity in stepfamilies arising from class. However, there is a lamentable lack of research in this area. It has been found in England that working-class families are more likely than middle-class ones to emphasize the importance of the *social* than the *biological* family. Throughout the book class and socioeconomic differences will be highlighted and described where information is available. Unfortunately, most research with stepfamilies focuses on White, middle-class (and often married) families.

Religion and Religiosity

There is also a lack of research that examines the relationship between religion and stepfamilies, yet we can imagine that attitudes to divorce and remarriage held by Churches might predict lower rates of stepfamily formation in those who have a religious affiliation. One study has shown that adolescents in stepfamilies are less likely to attend church than those in first families (Day, Jones-Sanpei et al. 2009). Religiosity is also related to being in first marriages and marital stability in Black families (Cutrona, Russell et al. 2011). Religious practice is comparatively strong in Black and Hispanic families, so there is an apparent contradiction between this and the fact that these groups have comparatively high levels of single motherhood (see Table 1.1, p. 11). However, many Churches now embrace divorced and remarried members (Cherlin 2009), so the contradiction may not be so apparent.

Gay and Lesbian Stepfamilies

Gay and lesbian stepfamilies are increasing in numbers, although it is almost impossible to get accurate estimates of their prevalence. Most commonly, same-sex stepfamily households are formed when a lesbian mother has children from a formerly heterosexual relationship, who live with her and her partner. Gay fathers may also have children in their household whom they had in previously heterosexual relationships. Gay and lesbian stepfamilies are discussed in detail in Chapter 10.

Other Factors Contributing to Diversity

The *age* of children when stepfamilies are formed is another source of diversity in how well the family establishes itself and flourishes. If children are young when they enter a stepfamily, chances are they will adapt readily to the parenting of their stepparent in comparison with adolescents. Adolescents can struggle with the presence of a new potential parenting figure at a stage of development when they are establishing their own autonomy and independence from their family.

The *complexity* of stepfamilies also makes a difference to how a stepfamily functions. In a simple stepfamily children have only a stepparent to encompass into their lives; in a complex stepfamily they will have stepsiblings living in the same household, and may also have half siblings if their biological parent and stepparent have children of their own. This adds to the intricacy of relationships that all stepfamily members need to manage.

There is diversity in all family forms. However, the variation in composition and in dynamics for stepfamilies is particularly striking, making the task of understanding and supporting them complex. Given their increasing prevalence, it is vital that we understand stepfamilies in all their diversity and complexity in order to be able to foster their well-being.

Prevalence of Stepfamilies

Although we know that the prevalence of stepfamilies is rising in most countries, there are formidable difficulties in counting them. First, they

---

Box 1.3 Spotlight on demography

- Demographers study human populations using statistics in order to understand size, structure, and change. They often, as with stepfamilies, focus on a subpopulation.
- Sources of data include census, which are carried out infrequently (4–10 years apart); and vital statistics such as births, deaths, and marriages.
- Analyses can be quantitative (numbers, composition, structure) and qualitative (e.g. well-being, social class).

present a moving target for demographers, the researchers who study their characteristics such as size, growth, and prevalence. Change is a constant feature of stepfamilies as attitudes and behaviors change. Data about prevalence of families gathered in a census, for example, run the risk of being out of date by the time it is analyzed.

Second, stepfamilies vary by race, culture, and ethnicity, making it complicated to look for commonalities across groups. It is also difficult to identify real differences, and to understand the implications of such cultural and geographic variation.

Third, the very definition of who belongs in a stepfamily is complex. Individual stepfamilies themselves often have difficulty in identifying members, whether in the household or outside. In Chapter 2 we discuss **boundary ambiguity**, a term that describes the situation in which individual stepfamily members hold differing perceptions of who is in the family.

Challenges for Demographers

The measurement of stepfamilies is bedeviled by many factors that make it almost impossible to gain accurate counts of their prevalence. Box 1.4 lists some of these factors.

First, overarching other problems, the definition of a family is problematic for measuring stepfamilies (or indeed other kinds of families). Is a family those who are biologically related? Legally related? Living in the same household? Should same-sex parent families and cohabiting families be counted as 'real' families?

Second, the processes by which data, and in particular census data, are gathered leads to the numbers of stepfamilies being undercounted in other ways. The collection of census data in the United States means that the adult in a household who completes the census form may not mention that a child is a stepchild because he or she is not related to his or her partner. Teachman and Tedrow (2008) estimate that only two-thirds of stepfamilies are taken into account using census data. A further problem with data collection is that some countries—for example,

---

Box 1.4 Factors complicating the counting of stepfamilies

- What is a family (and therefore what is a stepfamily)?
- Measurement difficulties (data collection).
- Cross-sectional versus longitudinal data.
- Rapid change.

New Zealand—do not collect data on stepfamilies at all. Estimates then have to be based on other data sets that may not be representative of populations.

Third, cross-sectional data gives a snapshot of who is living in a stepfamily at one time. Taking a longitudinal perspective, many more people will spend some time in a stepfamily at some stage in their lives than is indicated by cross-sectional numbers, since family structures change over time with parents and children moving in and out of stepfamilies and other kinds of households.

Fourth, the astonishing increase in the prevalence in stepfamilies (driven in large part by increases in extra-marital child bearing and cohabitation, as described further in Chapter 4), means that it is almost impossible to obtain accurate current estimates. For example, Teachman and Tedrow show that the number of households containing 'householder, spouse, biological child and stepchild' increased by 9 percent over the decade between 1990 and 2000, and the number of *unmarried* households with stepchildren doubled in that decade. Over that time, 95 percent of new households with stepchildren were cohabiting households, indicating the strong influence of cohabitation on family structures and the dangers in counting only stepfamilies with married parents.

How Prevalent are Stepfamilies?

Despite the problems we have just discussed, it is possible to get an estimate of the prevalence of stepfamilies. Table 1.1 shows the percentage of children reported by the US Census Bureau as living in various family structures in 2010, by race.

These estimates are likely to be low, given the probability that the census data count only two-thirds of stepfamily households. However, Table 1.1 shows that the households in which children were reported as living in 2010 vary considerably by race, and these comparisons are likely to be accurate. Asian children are more likely than any others to

Table 1.1 Percentages of children by presence and type of parents, by race (adapted from US Census Bureau, www.census.gov)

Race	Married/ biological parents	Cohabiting biological parents	Lone mother	Lone father	Step-mother family	Step-father family	Total stepfamily
Asian	84.1	1.4	10.1	2.2	0.7	1.4	**2.1**
Hispanic	60.9	6.0	26.0	2.7	0.9	4.0	**4.9**
White	71.5	3.4	18.3	3.5	1.4	4.5	**5.9**
Black	34.7	4.6	49.7	3.6	0.9	4.2	**5.1**
All	59.0	3.6	23.1	3.4	1.3	4.4	**5.7**

be living with married biological parents, while Hispanic children are most likely of all children to be living with unmarried biological parents. Black children are the most likely to be living with a lone mother or father. Highest rates of stepfamilies are recorded for children in White families.

While the *comparative* levels across race are likely to be accurate, the actual percentages are low. Another source of data about American families is the Survey of Income and Program Participation (SIPP), which uses a comparatively thorough method to collect relationship data by considering the relationship of every person in the household to every other person in the household (the Census takes the perspective of only one adult). SIPP data indicate that in 2009, 8 percent of all children in the United States were in stepfamily households, and 10.4 percent or 5.3 million of those who lived in two-parent households were in stepfamilies.

International Comparisons

There are considerable differences among countries in the prevalence of stepfamilies (again, bear in mind that ways of counting families may differ across countries). The OECD has published the rates of young people living in stepfamily households in 2006; Figure 1.2 shows the comparisons.

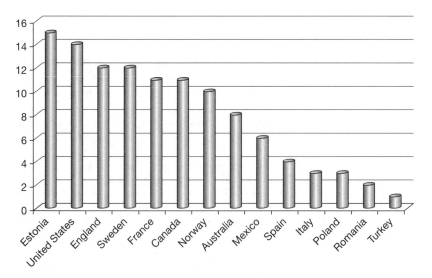

Figure 1.2 Percentages of adolescents aged 11–15 living in stepfamily households

Source: Data taken from OECD Family Database SF1.3: Living arrangements of children, accessed February 2013.

This graph shows that the United States has comparatively high rates of young people living in stepfamilies, well above the OECD average of 9 percent, with only Estonia having higher levels. Southern European and Eastern European countries are comparatively low. Note that these rates are for young people in the 11–15-year age group, not for all children, so they differ from SIPP numbers.

In summary, the United States has comparatively high rates of stepfamily households when compared internationally with other countries. Within the United States, the highest rates are in White families, and the lowest are in Asian families.

Chapter Summary

Stepfamilies are not a new family form, but the pathways by which they form have changed as divorce, children born to lone mothers, and cohabiting families increase. Today, stepfamilies are complex and diverse. They continue to experience stigma although it is probably decreasing as numbers of stepfamilies increase.

Defining stepfamilies is complicated. It varies according to the intended use of the definition—for example, census data gathering, and inclusion of factors such as whether or not the parents are married. Later in the book the complexities of definition will be discussed in more detail (Chapter 4).

Stepfamilies are also remarkably diverse, with factors such as race and culture, class, religiosity, gay and lesbian families, and children's age contributing to differences and to complexity. They are also fluid; children move from household to household, demanding expansion and contraction in individual households. This makes it vital to acknowledge the multiple households for children in stepfamilies.

The prevalence of stepfamilies is difficult to estimate, and many counts are lower than the actual numbers. Approximately 5.3 million children in two-parent households live in stepfamilies. There are higher percentages of White children than other racial groups in stepfamilies, and the lowest proportion is of Asian children. The United States has high rates of young people living in stepfamilies when compared internationally.

Key Terms

- Cohabitation versus marriage
- Stigma
- Households versus families
- Accordion families
- Multifragmented families
- Multipartner fertility

- Diversity
- Boundary ambiguity
- Social families
- Biological families

Discussion Questions

1. How do you think stepfamilies should be defined? How might this differ depending on the purpose of the definition?
2. Why does the US have high prevalence of stepfamily households?
3. Why do stepfamilies continue to experience stigma? Is it deserved?
4. Discuss how stepfamily members might best manage the fluidity of households.

Exercise

Look for media depictions of stepfamilies, in films, TV shows, and advertisements. How are they portrayed? Does their presentation accord with the topics raised in this chapter—for example, stigma, complexity, accordion families?

Additional Readings and Web Resources

Ganong, L. & Coleman, M. (2004). *Stepfamily Relationships: Development, Dynamics, and Interventions*. New York: Kluwer Academic/Plenum.

Kreider, R. & Ellis, R. (2011). Living arrangements of children: 2009. *Current Population Reports* (pp. 70–126). Washington, DC US Census Bureau.

Pryor, J. E. (2008a). *The International Handbook of Stepfamilies: Policy and Practice in Legal, Research, and Clinical Environments*. Hoboken, NJ: John Wiley & Sons.

Stewart, S. D. (2007). *Brave New Stepfamilies: Diverse Paths Toward Stepfamily Living*. Thousand Oaks, CA: Sage.

Teachman, J. & Tedrow, L. (2008). The demography of stepfamilies in the United States. In J. Pryor (Ed.), *The International Handbook of Stepfamilies: Contemporary Issues* (pp. 3–29). Hoboken, NJ: John Wiley & Sons. www.stepfamilies.info

Chapter 2

Frameworks and Theories for Understanding Stepfamilies

The poet shapes a verse; the therapist tries an intervention; the researcher tests or generates hypotheses. But the theorist must be aware of all three possibilities.

(Boss 1999)

Objectives of this Chapter

- To understand the importance of theory and constructs.
- To become familiar with major theories that are relevant to stepfamilies.

Introduction

Theoretical and conceptual frameworks are essential if we are to understand and explain the findings of any research. We use theory to generate questions and hypotheses, and to interpret the data that are a result from our research. In seeking to understand something as complex as stepfamilies it is especially important to have some frameworks or lenses through which to address the data that are gathered. Such frameworks guide the development of questions that might be addressed, and the interpretation of diverse sets of information. It is, however, only in the last few decades that theoretical frameworks have begun to be developed and used in studies of stepfamilies.

There are several conceptual models that are applied in work on families in general, and some of these have been extended and adapted in the study of stepfamilies. Others have been developed specifically for the understanding of stepfamily dynamics. In this chapter we will consider some of the major theoretical perspectives that are used by researchers.

Family Systems Theory

A major framework utilized for understanding and studying both families and stepfamilies is Family Systems Theory. The family, in this view, is seen as an *integrated whole*, a set of individuals and of separate relationships that are all connected and interdependent. From this perspective, a family is a 'system' that is not confined by biological or legal relationships, and especially in stepfamilies family members may not live in the same household. Thus in families there are individuals (parents and children), dyadic relationships (involving two family members—for example, a parent and child or two siblings), triadic relationships (e.g. mother, father, and one child), and the whole wider family system itself. The interdependence of individuals, subsystems, and the wider system can be illustrated in many ways. For example, the individual functioning of a child is closely related to that child's relationships with each parent (dyadic relationships), but also to the relationship *between* the parents. In turn, the larger family system is both affected by, and affects the individual and dyadic relationships within the family.

Box 2.1 Components of a family system

- Individuals (child, parent).
- Dyads: e.g. mother and father; parent and child; sister and brother.
- Triads: e.g. mother, father and child; sister, brother, and father.
- Whole family system: parents and children.

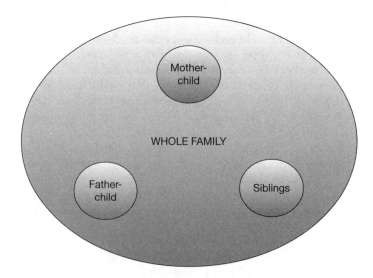

Figure 2.1 A simple family system of dyads, making up the whole family

A key aspect of family systems theory is the capacity for families to *stabilize* themselves in the face of external change. This is managed by the establishment of internal codes and rules, and adherence to them. These rules and the encouragement to follow them enable a family to stay stable when an individual, for example, deviates from the shared family values.

Related to self-stabilization in families is the capacity to *reorganize* themselves in the face of change. When a child starts school or a family member dies, reorganization is called for in order for the whole family to adapt to the change. Thus a balance is needed between stability and flexibility.

For stepfamilies in the early phases, adaptive reorganization is a particular challenge as new relationships and roles have to be negotiated, and existing relationships are renegotiated. The children of the mother in a stepfather family will have to adapt to the fact that their mother is possibly parenting other children (their stepsiblings), and that her attention is divided among several children and her new partner, as well as them. A stepfather who is new to a stepfamily faces the challenge of building a workable relationship with his partner's children, and they must adapt to having another parenting figure in their household. These challenges are discussed in later chapters, and the phenomenon of **boundary ambiguity**, where individual family members have differing views on who is part of the family, is described later in this chapter. Family systems theory gives us an effective framework for examining and understanding stepfamily dynamics.

Life Course Theories

Life Course frameworks focus on the *trajectories* of lives and development, including the cumulative processes that can advantage or disadvantage an individual as experiences build on earlier experiences and are affected by them. They encompass notions of time, agency, and process in suggesting ways in which lives and outcomes can be understood. There are four key principles of Life Course Theory (Elder 1998).

Historical time and place. Families and family transitions take place in a particular time historically, and in specific geographic locations. This principle emphasizes the broad context in which families are living. An example of how this might impact on stepfamilies is how time and place impact on stigma. It is likely that the stigma of being a stepfamily member in the United States has reduced in the last few decades (although it lingers in many places still). And stigma is more prevalent in some cultures than others. In Asia, for example, as we have seen, the word for stepfamily can have negative connotations such as 'used goods'. Both time and place, then, impact on the role that stigma has for families. A child in

Box 2.2 Four principles of Life Course Theory

- Historical time and place: 'The life course of the individual is embedded in the historical times and places they experience over their lifetimes.'
- Timing within lives: 'The developmental impact of a succession of life transitions or events is contingent on when they occur in a person's life.'
- Human agency and individual difference: 'Individuals construct their own life-course through the choices and actions they take within the opportunities and constraints of history and social circumstances.'
- Linked lives: 'Lives are lived interdependently, and social and historical influences are expressed through this network of shared relationships.'

a stepfamily in Japan will endure more stigma than one living in New York City. Legal frameworks within which stepfamilies have to operate are also subject to historical time and social context. In a few jurisdictions stepparents and stepchildren are able to have a legal relationship; in others it remains difficult.

Timing within lives. The points in a person's life when events occur are centrally important in understanding their impacts. The ages at which separation and stepfamily formation happen in children's lives have ongoing effects on how those experiences affect them. A particular example for stepfamilies is the age of children when their parents repartner. A young child is likely to find this transition comparatively easy because they are more likely to accept the presence of a stepparent in their family. In adolescence, on the other hand, the intrusion of another parenting figure is difficult when a young person is trying to establish autonomy and independence from parents. This difference has ongoing effects for the stepfamily as a whole, since the stepchild–stepparent relationship is pivotal to its well-being. If the relationship is conflicted, it can impact on the parents' relationship in the family and in turn contribute to the dissolution of the stepfamily. Hence, age can have cumulative effects on both individuals and whole families.

Human agency and individual difference. Individual differences are diverse. They include appraisals of events, patterns of behavior as a result of earlier experiences, and personality and temperament factors. There is some evidence, for example, that suggests that there are personality factors that are associated with stepfamily formation that lead to

difficulties in sustaining relationships. Another example is the temperament of children. Temperament can be identified relatively early in life,
and includes categories of being 'easy', 'slow to warm up', and 'difficult'.
Depending on a child's temperament, he or she will have different ways
of adapting to the changes involved in stepfamily formation. These are
examples of individual differences that interact with contexts and timing
in determining life course trajectories.

Linked lives. Every individual's life is interlinked with those of others,
and this is especially relevant when we are considering families. Links
exist through time and across contexts, and it is simply not possible to
consider stepfamily well-being and functioning without focusing on the
relationships within and outside them.

In summary, Life Course Theory offers a framework within which the
complexities of development and context are taken into account from a
longitudinal perspective. The emphasis on cumulative events and processes
focuses us on the fact that there is constant change, but that previous events
can have a strong impact on subsequent events and well-being.

Family Social Capital

Social capital is a widely used framework that arises originally from
economic theory. Its emphasis is on the existence of networks that supply
the resources needed for optimal functioning in families. And analogous
with economic models, family social capital relies on investments—in
relationships that provide resources from which individual family
members can draw as needed.

Family social capital exists as a resource, but also important is the
ability to manage and use capital, to exercise the use of resources available.
A useful definition of social capital has been given by Furstenberg: '[Social
capital is] the stock of social good will created through shared norms
and a sense of common membership upon which members may draw
in their effort to achieve collective or personal objectives' (Furstenberg
& Kaplan 2004).

The analogy with banking is obvious. First, families must have or
acquire a stock of capital in order to thrive—they need capital in the
bank. Second, and just as important, they need a sense of identity and
common membership in order to access the capital held by them as a
group. They need check books or credit cards.

Generation of Family Social Capital

In first families in Western societies, family social capital is built primarily
by the couple that forms the family. Commonly, couples engage in a

process of 'nomos building'—they construct rules, expectations, rituals and, as time passes, shared memories that constitute the value system or mini-culture of the family. 'Nomos' is defined as a socially constructed ordering of experiences, and includes the normal rules and guidelines for day-to-day activity. A crucial aspect of this process is the establishment of trust and reciprocity, which in turn leads to a sense of belonging and family identity, and of family cohesion.

Another source of capital is its intergenerational transmission; family-based values and beliefs are transmitted down generations, from grandparents and other extended family members, and adapted to the developing identity for the family. There are likely to be cultural and racial differences in the extent to which capital is transmitted from an older generation and accepted by the next. Asian families, for example, hold elders in greater veneration than do White families. Similarly, Mexican-American families embrace the concept of **familism** in which the needs of the family as a collective override those of the individual. African-American and Polynesian societies have specific cultural practices for intergenerational transmission of family norms and beliefs (see Chapter 3).

The Extension of Social Capital Beyond Family Boundaries

Connections with other households and with communities is a potent source of social capital for families. Schools, workplaces, and community groups are rich sources of knowledge and connection that can be appropriated for the well-being of the family and its members. To the extent that a family is integrated into its community, it is able to call on those external resources. The stability of the family is a crucial factor in its ability to access community-based capital; movement out of communities and into new ones makes uptake of community and neighborhood capital harder to achieve.

Management and Utilization of Social Capital

Families may have high levels of capital 'in the bank', but not be able to utilize them. Trust and reciprocity among family members are central to efficient utilization of the resources held. Individual differences in how stock of capital is approached may exist. For example, an outgoing person with a sense of entitlement to resources such as help or advice is more likely to use family capital than one who is shy and feels that resources are not deserved.

Stepfamilies face specific challenges in generating and utilizing family social capital. Couples do not have the opportunity to 'nomos build' before they have children, because they come to the family with children and with two sets of family values that may differ. They are faced with establishing trust and reciprocity, a sense of belonging and identity, in the face of already existing rituals and beliefs that may contradict each other. The question of who belongs in the family is often contested, and the rituals and meanings associated with events such as celebrating Christmas and birthdays may be sources of conflict. Stepfamilies are faced with the task of combining elements of two sets of rituals into new, shared understandings.

They may live, too, in a new neighborhood or community where links that foster social capital have to be re-established. Children go to new schools, the family may attend a new church or join an unfamiliar sports club.

External sources of capital for children include relationships with nonresident parents and accessing that resource is not straightforward. Both biological and stepparents in the family may resent the involvement of nonresident parents in the lives of the children.

In summary, the framework of Family Social Capital provides a powerful way of examining the well-being of stepfamilies that focuses on relationships and on the family as a whole unit.

Evolutionary Theory

Evolutionary Theory takes the view that human behavior and psychological processes have evolved over time as adaptive for survival. Natural selection has ensured, from this perspective, that psychological aspects of human beings today reflect the ability of our ancestors to invest in their own biological children in preference to nonbiological kin. This ensures genetic continuity, analogous to the propensity for male lions to kill cubs that are not theirs that have been born to a lioness they are now mating with. In relation to stepfamilies, Daly and Wilson have argued that having a stepparent is a strong risk factor for children because it is in the interests of stepparents to abuse or even kill their stepchildren and to invest instead in biological children (Daly & Wilson 1998). Stepparents are programmed to provide material and emotional resources preferentially to those children who are related genetically to them.

At a benign level, this framework might be used to explain the difficulties that stepparents have in engaging with their stepchildren, and in turn the resistance sometimes seen in stepchildren to engaging with stepparents.

The more controversial claim, made by evolutionary theorists, that stepparents are a danger for children, is counteracted by the fact that children are more likely to be killed by biological parents—usually mothers—than by stepparents. Furthermore, to the extent that stepparents are disengaged from their stepchildren, this is likely to be because they have not known the child from infancy and therefore have neither formed a strong attachment nor established the incest taboo that usually occurs when adults parent young babies.

Boundary Ambiguity

Although it is not a fully developed theory, Boundary Ambiguity is a conceptual framework that helps in understanding stepfamily dynamics. It exists when family members are not clear, or disagree about, who is in and who is out of the family. For stepfamilies this is a particularly acute issue. In first families, relationships and boundaries are relatively simple. Figure 2.2 shows a typical first-family system.

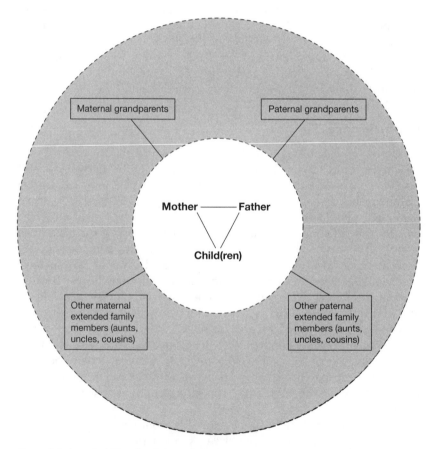

Figure 2.2 A typical 'first-family' system

Source: Reproduced with permission of John Wiley & Sons.

For stepfamilies, however, the network of possible and actual relationships is far more complex. Figure 2.3 shows a typical stepfamily system.

Within the household there are relationships that are both biological and nonbiological; outside the household there are numerous possible relationships and family configurations, many more than in a first family. It is not surprising, then, that lack of agreement among family members is common, and leads to ambiguity about who is a family member.

Boundary Ambiguity can be both physical and psychological. If there is disagreement about who actually lives in the household, this is physical ambiguity, and happens more often than we might think. For example, a stepchild who spends some of her time with her nonresident parent may not agree that she is a member of the stepfamily household, whereas her mother considers that she is.

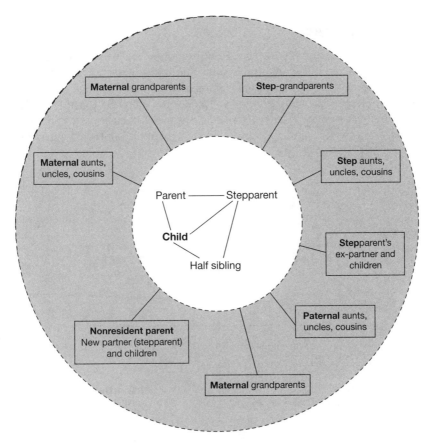

Figure 2.3 Family boundaries in a typical stepfamily

Source: Reproduced with permission of John Wiley & Sons.

If the lack of agreement is about whether or not an individual is a member of the family, psychological ambiguity exists. For example, a stepchild in a family may not consider her stepsibling who visits the house regularly to be a part of the family, although the adults in the family do.

Boundary Ambiguity has important implications for counting step-families. In a recent study using data from the Adolescent Health Study, it was found that reports about who lived in the household (physical Boundary Ambiguity) differed markedly between adolescents and their mothers (Brown & Manning 2009). Furthermore, the more complex the family the less likely parents and their teenagers were to agree. The lowest levels of agreement were found for cohabiting stepfamilies, where only 30 percent agreement was found between teenagers and their mothers. This has serious consequences for demographers when they try to estimate the number of children living in stepfamily households.

Parenting Styles

The conceptual framework of parenting styles has been well studied, and is important for stepfamilies since parenting tends to change when a transition such as divorce or stepfamily formation happens. A widely used typology is that of parenting styles, developed by Baumrind (1971). This involves four styles characterized along two dimensions. The dimensions are warmth–rejection, and low control–high control. Figure 2.4 shows how the styles are conceptualized.

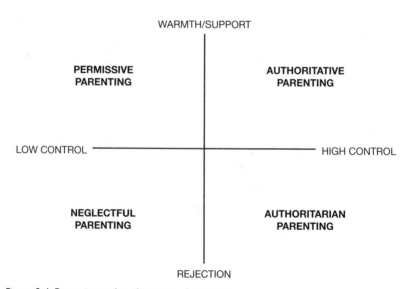

Figure 2.4 Parenting styles along two dimensions

Authoritative parenting is generally associated with optimal outcomes for children. It encompasses warmth and support, as well as monitoring. There is also a third dimension of authoritative parenting, not depicted in the figure, which is the encouragement of psychological autonomy. This means that parents involve their children in decision-making at appropriate levels as they develop.

Authoritarian parenting is low on warmth and high on control and monitoring. Generally it is associated with adverse outcomes for children, including depression.

Neglectful parenting is low on control and on warmth and support. It is associated with a raft of poor outcomes, including externalizing behavior and low self-esteem.

Permissive parenting is high on warmth and support but low on control.

Many studies have concluded that authoritative parenting is optimal in stepfamilies, as it is in first families. However, very few have examined the impact of permissive parenting, which encompasses the features suggested by children's views of the stepparent role that stepparents should be friends rather than authority figures. One study that did include permissive parenting styles by stepparents found that in these families where stepparents were warm and supportive but low in control and discipline, not only was the relationship reported as being of high quality but also the levels of family happiness were high (Crosbie-Burnett & Giles-Sims 1994).

Bidirectional Effects

Although most research and clinical writing tends to focus on the impact that adults have on children, it is likely that the direction of effects may also be the other way—that characteristics of children can influence adult

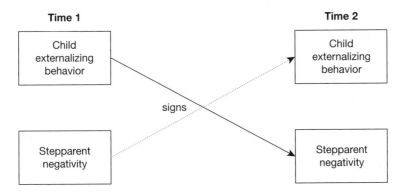

Figure 2.5 Predictiveness over time of child and stepparent behavior

behavior and, in turn, family well-being. Hetherington and colleagues, for example, have shown that child negativity at time 1 has an impact on stepparent behavior at time 2, but that the opposite is not the case—stepparent behavior at time 1 does not predict child negativity at time 2 (Hetherington, Henderson et al. 1999).

Thus, although this is not strictly a conceptual framework, it is included here as an indication that we need to think about causality in both directions—adult to child and child to adult—especially in stepfamilies where children have a greater influence on adult behavior than they do in first families.

Chapter Summary

In this chapter we have considered three major theoretical positions (Family Systems Theory, Life Course Theory, and Family Social Capital), and one less frequently utilized theory (Evolutionary Theory), that all apply to the understanding of stepfamily dynamics. We have also examined three important constructs that are key aspects of stepfamilies: boundary ambiguity, parenting styles, and **bidirectional effects**.

The first three can be considered broadly as ecological frameworks in which the individual is seen as a part of the wider context of family and society. They are sufficiently complex that they can encompass the diversity and complexity of stepfamilies by taking into consideration the external impacts on the family as well as the internal dynamics.

As you will see in the following chapters, theoretical and conceptual frameworks are crucial in understanding and explaining stepfamilies. You will also see, however, that much work is done that does not have theoretical underpinnings.

Key Terms

- Self-stabilization
- Reorganization
- Family Social Capital
- Family systems
- Nomos building
- Familism
- Boundary Ambiguity
- Evolutionary Theory
- Life Course Theory
- Parenting styles
- Bidirectional effects

Discussion Questions

1. Why is it important to have conceptual frameworks in order to understand stepfamilies?
2. Do these frameworks overlap? If so, which ones do and how?
3. Do you think any one of them might explain family dynamics the best? If so, which one?

Exercises

Think about your own family and the 'nomos' that has been built to form the values and beliefs your family holds. Are any of them unique to your family? How do they differ from and overlap with other families you know?

Additional Readings and Web Resources

Baumrind, D. (1971). Current patterns of parental authority. *Developmental Psychology Monograph*, 4 (Pt. 2), 1–103.

Carroll, J. S., Olson, C. D., & Buckmiller, N. (2007). Family Boundary Ambiguity: a 30-year review of theory, research, and measurement. *Family Relations*, 56 (April), 210–230.

Cox, M. & Paley, B. (1997). Families as systems. *Annual Review of Psychology*, 48, 243–267.

Daly, M. & Wilson, M. (1999). *Darwinism Today: The Truth about Cinderella*. New Haven, CT: Yale University Press.

Elder, G. H. (1994). Time, human agency, and social change: perspectives on the life course. *Social Psychology Quarterly*, 57, 4–15.

Elder, G. H. (1998). The life course as developmental theory. *Child Development*, 69, 1–12.

Furstenberg, F. F. (2005). Banking on families: how families generate and distribute social capital. *Journal of Marriage and Family*, 67(4), 809–821.

Furstenberg, F. F. & Kaplan, S. (2004). *Social Capital and the Family. The Blackwell Companion to Sociology*. J. Scott, J. Treas, & M. Richards (Eds.), Malden, MA: Blackwell.

Chapter 3

Contexts of Stepfamilies
Culture and Race

Information about healthy and adaptive family structures and functioning ... has flowed in one direction traditionally—from the dominant European-American culture to populations of color.
(Crosbie-Burnett & Lewis 1993)

Objectives of this Chapter

- To describe cultural differences in attitudes in the United States.
- To examine cultural differences in a global context.

Introduction

Families of all types are deeply affected by the contexts in which they are living. Contexts include time and place, employment rates and opportunities, societal attitudes to 'nontraditional' families, and the legal environment in which they organize their relationships at a formal level. In this chapter, we focus on the contexts provided by culture and race.

The majority of research on stepfamilies has focused on White middle-class families. Yet ethnic minority groups comprise the largest proportion of stepfamilies in the United States, so it is important that we examine the factors associated with culture and race that impact on their well-being and functioning. It is, though, only recently that scholars have started to address the formation and well-being of African-American, Hispanic, and Asian stepfamilies.

As well as considering ethnic minorities within the United States, in this chapter we will also examine the comparatively small body of research that addresses stepfamilies in cultures outside the United States and other Western countries of the world. Studies are sparse, and in many instances we can only speculate on how cultural differences, especially with regard to attitudes to families, have an impact on stepfamilies.

Stepfamilies in Asian Cultures: Chinese and Japanese Families

In both the United States and in their countries of origin, Asian stepfamilies are comparatively uncommon. This is mainly because rates of divorce and remarriage remain lower in Asian than in Western cultures, although they are rising. In this section we will consider stepfamilies in Chinese and Japanese cultures.

Chinese Stepfamilies

Chinese culture is diverse, encompassing vast regions and subcultures in the Asian continent. In general, it is characterized by being comparatively both traditional and **hierarchical**. These features mean that there is a line of power downward between generations by means of which grandparents have a strong influence in families in comparison with Western cultures. In turn, men and women occupy traditionally gendered roles in families, with women focusing on child rearing and housekeeping, and men on their roles in the workforce outside the home.

These traditional attitudes to families mean that stepfamilies in Chinese culture experience considerable stigma and lack of acceptance. This is reflected graphically in the terminology used to describe a stepparent, who is referred to as *yee sau for*, or used goods. In turn, stepchildren are called *yau ping chai* (boys) and *yau ping nui* (girls)—literally, boy or girl of a greasy bottle, implying that they will never lose the 'dirtiness' of living in a stepfamily.

Shame is a strong aspect of socialization in Chinese societies, acting as a deterrent to behavior that is nonconforming and nontraditional. Shame is attached to being a stepfamily member as evidenced by the terminology used, and the fear of it contaminating extended family members may lead to their disapproval and rejection of the stepfamily.

Box 3.1 Characteristics of stepfamilies in Chinese culture

- The importance of hierarchical blood relationships inhibits the acceptance of nonrelated family members.
- The input and influence of grandparents on children causes conflicts between them and stepparents.
- Traditional attitudes pressure stepmothers to fully adopt a mothering role with little support from children's biological fathers.
- There is little contact with nonresident parents because of the focus on the traditional nuclear family, which stepfamilies try to emulate.

However, remarriage is increasing. In mainland China, remarriages have increased from 0.33 percent of all marriages in 1979 to 10.24 percent in 2007 (Wang & Zhou 2010). This is one third or less of the rates in the US, but the increase is significant. It is likely to contribute to a decrease in the stigmatization of stepfamilies and an increase in acceptance as they become more common.

Japanese Stepfamilies

Japanese society has been characterized traditionally by **stem families**—the coexistence of three generations in one household. One impact of this is that, as with Chinese families, grandparents have a strong influence on children and their parents. It is so strong, in fact, that until recently arranged marriages outnumbered 'love' marriages. It was only in the 1960s that the number of love marriages, initiated by the couples themselves, equaled and then surpassed the number of arranged marriages (Nozawa 2008). Traditional attitudes and strong emphases on biological relationships have led to the stigmatization of stepfamilies, and lack of acknowledgment of their existence. For example, a word for 'stepfamily' has only recently entered Japanese vocabulary. *Suteppufamiri* appeared in the Japanese dictionary in 2006 for the first time.

Even in love marriages in Japan, gender roles are rigid, with women expected to focus on child rearing and men to be 'salarymen' (Nozawa 2008). The existence of stem biological families and strict gender roles means that there is pressure from both within and without the stepfamily to emulate a nuclear family. At the same time, the existence of the stem family encourages grandparents to exert influence over the new stepfamily. This is exacerbated by the fact that high proportions of Japanese single mothers live with their parents after separation—25 percent in comparison with only 2 percent in the United States. Grandparents who have been in a quasi parenting role with their grandchildren are, therefore, particularly likely to resent the involvement of a new partner.

Nozawa (2008) refers to the 'scrap and build' model in which the new family does not refer to earlier families, and rebuilds as if it is a nuclear family. However, the tension between grandparents and parents, arising from stem families, and the pressure on stepmothers in particular to be perfectly devoted mothers to their stepchildren, leads to conflict. The expanded network of family members, which comes into existence in Western countries when a stepfamily is formed, is emerging only slowly in Japanese society. Nozawa (2011) says:

> if we turn down the '*scrap and build*' assumption, we might be able to construct an intergenerational co-operation in child-rearing without having stepparents in the center of them. It might be beneficial for children to have multiple places to be at home.

Box 3.2 Characteristics of Japanese stepfamilies

- The continuing existence of stem families (influence of grandparents).
- Strongly traditional gender roles leading to unrealistic expectations on stepmothers from fathers.
- High rates of coresidence by single mothers with their parents, leading to conflict between grandparents and stepparents.

In summary, both Chinese and Japanese stepfamily life is characterized by traditional and strict gender roles and a strong intergenerational influence that can contribute to stigmatization of stepfamilies.

Stepfamilies in Africa: The Case of Namibia

Information on stepfamilies in Africa is almost nonexistent. However, a recent report was published in Namibia that provides some valuable information about families and stepfamilies in that country (Beninger 2011). This section considers Namibian stepfamilies specifically, noting that Namibian society may bear both similarities to and differences from other African cultures.

In Namibian society, children are often raised by social rather than by biological parents. The emphasis is on extended families as the *primary* social institution, rather than a two-parent household. Children are as likely to be raised by female family members such as grandmothers and aunts, as by biological parents. Nuclear families are probably not seen as the norm against which other family structures are compared, to the extent that they are in Western cultures.

The diversity of family forms in Namibia is considerable; only one quarter of children live with both biological parents, and over a third live with neither parent. One in twenty live with their father and nearly a third with their mother. Either of these parents may have a partner who takes the role of stepparent. Moreover, over two-thirds of Namibian adults are not in formal relationships. Cohabitation is therefore a common aspect of families.

Several factors have been identified that contribute to the likelihood that children will live outside a nuclear family, and possibly in stepfamilies, in Namibia.

Migration Patterns

Under apartheid a migrant labor system existed in which men left their families in villages for work, leaving children to be cared for by extended family members and nonrelated adults. This practice continues outside formal apartheid, as men continue to leave their homes for work.

Informal Polygamy

Informal polygamy is partly an outcome of migration patterns where men form 'second house' relationships, although it seems to be quite widely practiced in general. Stepfamilies are set up when this happens, and wives left behind may enter new partnerships as well.

HIV/AIDS Epidemic

HIV/AIDS infects about 20 percent of Namibian people, and most AIDS-related deaths are in the 19–49 year age group. This leaves many children with one or no parents, meaning that they are very likely to be raised by a stepparent or by extended family members or nonkin.

These factors lead to a great deal of fluidity in families and, combined with a focus on extended families as networks of care, it seems that stepfamilies in Namibia are relatively common. The likely frequency of stepfamilies, and the lack of emphasis on nuclear families, probably means that they are less likely to encounter stigma and rejection. However, the report suggests that there are significant problems of abuse and neglect of children in stepfamilies, and that a lack of legal relationships exacerbates this situation.

Box 3.3 Characteristics of families and stepfamilies in Namibia

- Fluidity of family and household composition.
- A lack of emphasis on the nuclear family as the 'norm'.
- Lack of structures, especially legal.
- High levels of death of parents and abuse of stepchildren.

Stepfamilies in Hispanic Cultures

In the United States, the proportion of Hispanic peoples is 14 percent, and it is the largest and fastest-growing minority group. Of these, a significant proportion is made up of immigrants and there are cultural differences between those born in the United States and those who are new immigrants. For example, parents born outside the United States hold more traditional views of families and gender roles. Two-thirds of the Latino population in the United States are Mexican-Americans.

A prominent feature of Hispanic culture is familism. The family, including the extended family, takes priority over the individual, and the family is seen as an extension of the self. Loyalty, reciprocity, and family solidarity are highly valued. Hispanic peoples value **collectivism**, and the extended kin network is central to family life. Collectivism is the practice or principle of giving a group priority over each individual in it. It is relatively common, for example, for extended family members to live in a household together. The extended family system is a key source of both material and emotional support to family members.

Alongside collectivism, the parental relationship is considered central to families. Hispanic culture, then, tends to foster the quality and stability of parental relationships within the network of extended kin, and gender roles are comparatively traditional.

Also important in Hispanic culture are *padrinos* and *madrinos*—godfathers and godmothers, who constitute the *compadrazgo* or coparenting system (Coltrane, Gutierrez et al. 2008). These godparents are providers of economic and emotional support for children and are considered members of the extended family. Hence Hispanic families are focused on both extended family and internal family relationships, with a semi-formal coparenting structure very common.

Another key feature of Hispanic culture is religion. In one survey 94 percent of Latinos said they had a religious affiliation, and the majority of these are Catholic (Espinosa, Elizondo et al. 2003). Paradoxically, there are comparatively high levels of cohabitation rather than marriage, and of lone parents raising children (see Table 1.1, p. 11). Nonetheless, families—including stepfamilies—function in a microculture of religiosity.

Because of these two factors, the prevailing sense of familism, and the ubiquity of religiosity, Hispanic stepfamilies face some stigma. This, alongside the traditional roles that are prevalent, mean that stepfamilies tend to emulate nuclear families, rather like the Japanese model of 'scrap and rebuild'. Nonresident parents tend to be less involved with children than in other cultures and stepfathers report close and involved relationships with stepchildren (Coltrane, Gutierrez et al. 2008). The centrality of the parental relationship thus influences both the comparative stability

---

Box 3.4 Characteristics of Hispanic families and stepfamilies

- Familism and collectivism (emphasis on group rather than individual).
- Traditional attitudes to gender roles (emulating first families).
- Impact of semi-formal coparenting on ease of including a new parenting figure into the household.

of Hispanic families (both first and step), and the tendency to emulate first families. Formal marriage seems not to be as salient to family well-being as in other cultures.

Black American Culture and Stepfamilies

Many aspects of family life in contemporary Black American families are rooted in slavery when family members were separated, as adults were sent to work in other places or sold. One major outcome of this, and of other historical factors, is a strong reliance on the broad family unit or extended family. This broad family was very likely to encompass both biological, and social or fictive kin; indeed, in a study of low-income African-American mothers, 70 percent named fictive kin as members of their family (McCreary & Dancy 2004). In turn, extended family members are relied upon for support —especially practical support such as childcare. **Reciprocity** is a key aspect of extended family life with members expected to exchange both emotional and material support. And because the distinction between biological and nonbiological kin is blurred, those who are not related through bloodlines are easily integrated into family systems.

As a result of their history, Black women have been and are today relatively independent. This is also related to the tendency for Black culture to put less emphasis than others on the couple bond and on marriage. Cohabitation is common, and two-thirds of African-American babies are born outside marriage. Of these, 80 percent are born to lone mothers (in comparison to White births where 50 percent of those born outside marriage are born to mothers who are by themselves). Divorce is also common, and is often a result of infidelity, suggesting again that the couple relationship is more fragile than in some cultures.

As well as the comparatively diffuse nature of families, Black American culture has two other features that are of relevance to stepfamilies. The first is the practice of informal child rearing, which does not encompass legal adoption. **Othermothers** are women who actively mother both biological and nonbiologically related children (Burton & Hardaway 2012). They may be neighbors or other unrelated women, or they may be aunts, sisters, and grandparents. They provide nurturance and guidance for other women's children with no expectation that they will usurp the role of biological mothers. The practice of *othermothering* may well have originated from slavery where mothers were forced to labor apart from their children and often had no partner to coparent. Today, other-mothering continues to exist as a form of informal coparenting.

The second key feature of Black culture is the intergenerational trans-mission of culture by means of **kinscripts**. Kinscripts are a form of racial socialization whereby family history and cultural norms are conveyed between generations, especially by grandparents (Stack & Burton 1993). Kinscripts transmit, among other knowledge, pride in being Black and in belonging to one's families. This practice may assist younger generations to both survive and thrive as members of a minority culture.

African-American family systems overall are '**pedi-focal**', focusing on children and having permeability of family boundaries rather than the inflexible boundaries that are common in White families. The impact of a pedi-focal focus on families is discussed further in Chapter 14.

Thus there are four key features of African-American culture that are salient for stepfamilies. The comparative *fluidity* of families and households means that for children, changes in family composition when stepfamilies form may not be as disruptive as it is for children in White stepfamilies. The entrance of nonrelated adults and children may not be unusual and nor will the changes in relationships be as troubling.

The *extended family networks* are likely to buffer changes for both children and adults as stepfamilies form. In particular, material, instrumental, and childcare support may be freely available through the transitions the family members are experiencing. However, given the high levels of involvement of family members outside the household there might also be conflict between new stepparents and grandparents and others, about parenting and disciplining children.

The practice of othermothering and parenting by nonrelated or extended family members may mean that the establishment of stepparent–stepchild relationships is less fraught for Black stepfamilies than for others where this tradition does not exist. The resistance to a stepmother, for example, is likely to be less if a child is familiar with parenting by nonrelated women. In turn, a stepmother may find it comparatively easy to parent the children of her partner.

Kinscripts, the transmission of cultural and family beliefs and values, fosters the involvement of grandparents and step-grandparents in the lives of children in all families, including stepfamilies. It is a way in which family rituals and beliefs are conveyed, and nonresident fathers may play a crucial role in the lives of their children by the use of kinscripts. Black American fathers are, for example, likely to teach their children about moral and spiritual issues. Furthermore, over half of Black stepfamilies have a step-grandparent living in the household (Szinovacz 1998).

Most research suggests that living in a stepfamily does not disadvantage Black children in comparison with those living in first families. This is in contrast to White children who, on average, do less well in stepfamily households (this is discussed further in Chapter 8). It may be that the factors outlined here buffer the possible risks of stepfamily living. Also, an **attenuation hypothesis** has been suggested, which proposes that family transitions are some of many challenges faced by African-American families and so do not have the impact that they do for White children (McLloyd, Cauce et al. 2000).

> **Box 3.5 Characteristics of African-American families and stepfamilies**
>
> - Permeability and fluidity of family forms and boundaries.
> - Strong extended family networks.
> - Othermothers.
> - Kinscripts.

Maori Culture and Stepfamilies: An Example of Polynesian Culture

Maori are the indigenous peoples of New Zealand. They are related to other cultures of the Pacific region, Polynesian societies. Like Native Americans and the Aborigines of Australia, they have experienced colonization by Western peoples, in particular from the United Kingdom. Unlike Native Americans and Australian Aborigines, they have intermarried extensively with Europeans and do not live in reservations or other designated areas. Nonetheless, their culture has suffered through the imposition of a majority Western population. Today, however, there is a significant re-emergence of Maori cultural awareness and practice, and Maori is the second official language of New Zealand.

In common with African-American culture, Maori have a collective approach to child rearing. *Whanau* is a term that describes multiple relationships with people considered to be family. The wider *whanau* is responsible for children's well-being, although intermarriage with Europeans means that there is considerable variation in the relevance of this aspect of Maori culture.

Also in common with African-Americans, Maori rely on extended family support, and reciprocity is a key part of the culture, with active participation expected in gatherings such as *hui* (meetings), meeting-house activities, and funerals.

There are two aspects of Maori culture that are particularly relevant to the formation of stepfamilies.

First, *whangai* is a customary practice in which a child is raised outside the family, by someone who is not their birth parent. The child is not formally adopted, but *whangai* is more than fostering. It is usually an open process whereby children know both their biological parents and those who raise them (social parents)—although there is variation in this. Children who are *whangai* children vary in the length of time they stay with social parents. A typical situation is where a child is raised with an older sister who is, in fact, his or her mother.

The familiarity of many Maori with *whangai* suggests that boundaries in stepfamilies are blurred. *Whangai* can include all children outside the nuclear family, whether or not they are biologically related. Stepchildren may have known *whangai* sisters and brothers, so that stepsiblings seem little different. As one stepchild said: 'For me it's never been 'stepsisters'. Always whanau. We don't have labels, we are all family, we are all one' (Curtis-Clark 2012, p. 53).

Nonetheless, the practice of *whangai* can engender jealousy if an adult who has had a *whangai* child feels usurped when a stepparent enters the family and takes over a parenting role.

The second concept of relevance to stepfamilies is *manaakitanga*. It is a broad concept that encompasses acceptance, hospitality, nurturing, respect, kindness, and making someone feel at home. *Manaakitanga* eases the acceptance of new partners and children into a family, to help them to feel 'as one' with the family.

To date, there is only one study of Maori stepfamilies (Curtis-Clark 2012). The author notes that for Maori the word 'step' is rarely used, reflecting the fluidity and permeability of families and households. Curtis-Clark concludes:

> the cultural meaning of stepfamily for Maori appears to be fluid and changing. Where there is the expectation that perhaps Maori families and stepfamilies are moving away from Maori cultural normative practices and becoming more 'individuated', a younger generation of Maori are becoming acquainted with . . . principles of Maori family life such as manaakitanga. Therefore, the shape and future of Maori stepfamilies is uncertain.
>
> (p. 102)

Box 3.6 Characteristics of Maori families and stepfamilies

- *whangai*—informal coparenting;
- *whanau*—extended family networks;
- *manaakitanga*—acceptance, nurturing of kin and nonkin;
- *whakapapa*—basis for establishing lineage and geneaology;
- fluidity of family structure.

A Comparison of Cultures

There are significant overlaps and differences among the cultures we have considered in this chapter. Table 3.1 brings together some of the key features we have discussed.

Table 3.1 A comparison of features of families across cultures

Culture	Traditional gender roles/focus on couple	Hierarchical power structure	Extended family importance and support	Fluid family composition	Stigma	Formal or semiformal coparenting practices	Strong inter-generational transmission of culture
Chinese	✔	✔			✔		
Japanese	✔	✔			✔		
Namibian			✔	✔			
Hispanic	✔		✔		✔	✔	
African-American			✔	✔		✔	✔
Maori (Polynesian)			✔	✔		✔	✔

There are obvious similarities between Black American and Maori cultures. First, they both have semiformal coparenting systems—other-mothering and *whangai*, as do Hispanic cultures with the *compadrazgo* system. These coparenting practices are likely to make the acceptance of stepparents by stepchildren easy in comparison with other cultures.

Second, Maori and Black American cultures share a strong inter-generational transmission of culture, through kinscripts and *whakapapa*. In both cases this enables children to gain knowledge of their cultural and genealogical inheritance. This differs, however, from the hierarchy of power seen in Asian cultures, as kinscripts and *whakapapa* focus on the transmission of knowledge more strongly than on the exertion of influence.

The fluidity of family composition that characterizes Namibian, Maori, and Black American cultures is likely to make acceptance of stepfamily households comparatively easy and to reduce stigma in these cultures. Similarly, strong extended family systems will buffer stepfamily households and help to normalize multihousehold families such as stepfamilies.

In contrast, Asian cultures focus on traditional roles and hierarchical power relations. These factors contribute to stigma and difficulty for stepfamilies, making adjustment to stepfamily living comparatively challenging. As Asian families become more Westernized and rates of divorce and remarriage increase, however, difficulties such as stigma are likely to reduce.

Hispanic culture has features of both these groups, with religious affiliation an added factor. Hispanic stepfamilies, then, may benefit from the *compadrazgo* system and the importance of extended families, but may face difficulties because of traditional gender roles and religiosity.

Chapter Summary

Cultural values and attitudes, particularly to family life, impact on the formation and well-being of stepfamilies. In this chapter we have considered several cultures that vary among themselves, and form a contrast with Western family attitudes and values.

Without having research on which to base conclusions, we can only speculate on the impact of these differences on stepfamilies. It seems that Asian characteristics of hierarchical power structures and traditional attitudes may make stepfamily life comparatively challenging. The result is that stepfamilies base themselves on the nuclear model, with little input from nonresident parents and pressure on stepparents to behave like biological parents.

In contrast, features of Namibian, Black American, and Polynesian cultures may contribute to relative ease of stepfamily formation and acceptance. Coparenting, extended families (both kin and nonkin), and fluidity of family forms mean that a stepfamily is not particularly different from other family structures in those cultures.

Hispanic culture resembles Black and Maori culture in its focus on extended families; however, traditional gender roles and the emphasis on the importance of the parental couple may modify the extent to which stepfamilies are easily assimilated into Hispanic culture.

We have little data with which to compare the outcome of these differences. We do know that Black American children tend not to be as adversely impacted by stepfamily living as are White children. Beyond that, more research is needed to explore the significance of cultural differences. It is important, when considering stepfamilies, to keep in the front of our minds the impact that cultural and racial differences are likely to have on their formation, acceptance, and functioning.

Key Terms

- Traditional families
- Hierarchical families
- Stem families
- Familism
- Collectivism
- Reciprocity
- Kinscripts
- Othermothers
- Pedi-focal families

- Attenuation hypothesis
- *Whanau*
- *Whangai*
- *Manaakitanga*

Discussion Questions

1. How might involvement of extended family members help or hinder stepfamilies?
2. How do you think Hispanic families reconcile religiosity with nontraditional families?
3. How might the fluidity of families in Black American and Maori cultures impact on children in stepfamilies?

Exercise

Talk to a person from a culture that is different from yours. Discuss the awareness of stepfamilies and attitudes toward them. See if you can link attitudes to families generally to those of stepfamilies.

Additional Readings and Web Resources

Beninger, C. (2011). Stepfamilies in Namibia: A Study of the Situation of Stepparents and Stepchildren and Recommendations for Law Reform. *Gender Research and Advocacy Project*. Windhoek, Namibia, Legal Assistance Centre, p. 167.

Bulanda, J. R. & Brown, S. (2007). Race-ethnic differences in marital quality and divorce. *Social Science Research*, 36, 945–967.

Nozawa, S. (2008). The social context of emerging stepfamilies in Japan. In J. Pryor (Ed.), *The International Handbook of Stepfamilies: Policy and Practice in Legal, Research, and Clinical Environments* (pp. 79–99). Hoboken, NJ: John Wiley & Sons.

Chapter 4

Stepfamily Formation

Pathways and Processes

The modern stepchild . . . arrives by very diverse paths into a family form that is not merely inherently complicated and diverse . . . but also, at both a public and a popular level, suffers from a disputed model of how it ought to function.
(Gorrell Barnes, Thompson et al. 1998)

Objectives of this Chapter

- To describe the pathways to stepfamily formation.
- To describe typologies of stepfamilies.
- To describe processes of stepfamily formation.

Introduction

In Chapter 1, a simple classification of stepfamilies was described. Stepfamilies are, in fact, much more complicated than these typologies suggest. There are multiple factors that contribute to the fact that the word 'stepfamily' denotes a diverse group of families that can be defined as stepfamilies, on the basis that a child or children are not biologically related to one of the adults. And just as their characteristics are varied, so too are the ways in which they are formed. There are many roads to becoming a stepfamily.

In this chapter we will consider the pathways and trajectories that lead to stepfamily formation. We will discuss the main factors that contribute to ongoing change in how they are formed. We will look at *typologies* of stepfamilies—the ways in which they vary in structure—and consider multiple transitions that often occur in the lives of stepfamily members.

Pathways to Stepfamily Formation

In the past, as we discussed in Chapter 1, stepfamilies were formed primarily as a result of the death of a parent. Surviving parents were very

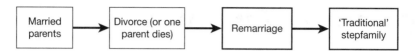

Figure 4.1 Typical pathway to a 'traditional' stepfamily

likely to repartner, leading to what we know as the basic characteristic of a stepfamily—the presence of a parent and child or children who are not related biologically.

Rates of divorce have increased in the Western world, the rise starting mainly in the second part of the twentieth century. This rise has led to an increase in the prevalence of remarriage following the dissolution of a first marriage. What we might think of now as 'traditional' stepfamilies were (and are still) formed via the pathway of marriage, parenting, divorce, and remarriage. A traditional stepfamily is considered to be one in which the parents are married, and in which the pathway to formation is via a first marriage followed by divorce and marriage.

In the twenty-first century, however, two rather dramatic demographic changes have led to the traditional pathway becoming less and less common.

Contributing Factors to the Changing Formation of Stepfamilies

Births outside Marriage

There has been an extraordinary rise in the numbers of births outside wedlock in most Western countries. In the United States, for example, between 1980 and 2000, the percentage of births to unmarried mothers rose from 18 percent to 32 percent. In 2007 40 percent of children were born out of wedlock (Ventura 2009). In other countries this rate is even greater, as Figure 4.2 shows, with Iceland and Mexico recording the highest rates. It is not always possible to tell, however, whether children born outside marriage are born into a cohabiting household, or to a mother living alone.

Rates of extramarital birth also vary by race and ethnicity within the United States. Figure 4.3 shows some differences.

Hispanic children have the greatest likelihood of being born outside marriage, despite a cultural focus on religion and partnership (see Chapter 3). Black children are next most likely, with Asian and Pacific Island children least likely to be born outside wedlock. Remember, though, that being born outside marriage can mean either being born to a lone mother or to a cohabiting couple.

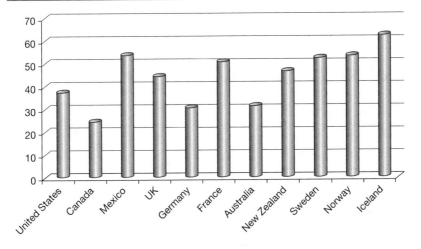

Figure 4.2 Proportion of births outside wedlock, 2009

Source: OECD Family Data Base Data taken from SF2.4 Share of births out of wedlock and teenage births, downloaded January 2013.

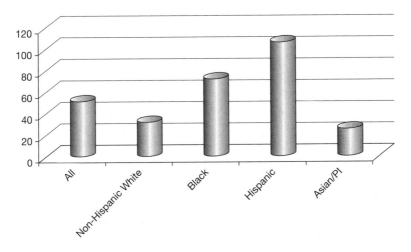

Figure 4.3 Births per 1,000 unmarried women in the United States

Source: NCHS data brief No. 18, Ventura 2009; adapted from Figure 3.

It used to be the case that most births outside marriage were to teenage mothers. This has changed dramatically; the majority of ex-nuptial births are to women in the 20–29-year age group (Ventura 2009). The rate for women over 30 years old has increased from 8 percent in 1970 to 17 percent in 2007, possibly reflecting the increase in rates of cohabitation.

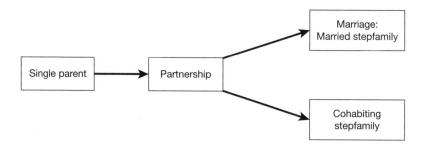

Figure 4.4 Pathways to stepfamilies via nonmarital birth

The birth rate of unmarried women (the percentage of unmarried women who give birth) has increased from about 22 percent to 44 percent over the same period. One third of children enter a stepfamily via a nonmarital birth; nearly two-thirds of Black children do so. Cohabiting stepfamilies formed via nonmarital birth are likely to be comparatively vulnerable, since they are doubly deinstitutionalized—lone parenthood and cohabitation are major risk factors for children and families.

Lone parenthood is usually a relatively temporary phenomenon. For example, in England 50 percent of lone mothers remain alone for four and a half years or less, and 80 percent of those enter cohabiting stepfamilies. Of those cohabiting, however, 25 percent separate within a year—cohabiting stepfamilies are more unstable than those that start with marriage (Ermisch & Francesconi 2000). However, those stepfamilies formed through marriage are likely to be more similar to first families than to traditional stepfamilies, because the children have not experienced the divorce of their parents and the attendant distress that goes with that transition.

Cohabitation

Cohabitation, rather than legal marriage or civil union, is increasingly characteristic of couple households who have children. In the US, for example, while the number of married-couple households has stayed stable since 1970, the number of unmarried-couple households has increased steadily to about 17 percent of all households (Teachman & Tedrow 2008).

Figure 4.5 shows an international comparison among countries for percentages of those living alone, married, and (of those who are couples), cohabiting, for all people over 20 years of age. (Marriage rates are shown for comparison.)

Marriage rates are comparatively high for the United States, and for Italy and Ireland (the latter two of which are predominantly Catholic

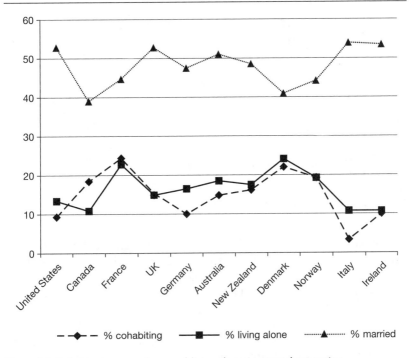

Figure 4.5 Cohabitation, marriage, and living alone in several countries
Source: OECD data taken from OECD Family database SF3.3, downloaded January 2013.

countries). Conversely, cohabitation and living alone are relatively uncommon for those three countries. Cohabitation is high in France and Denmark (and Sweden, not shown here).

There are several ways in which cohabitation impacts on stepfamily formation. First, a couple may have a child or children outside marriage, separate, and repartner. In this trajectory, a stepfamily (or two) is formed without marriage being involved at either transition. Second, a single mother may move into a cohabiting relationship, forming a stepfamily. Again, marriage is not involved in this trajectory toward stepfamily formation. Third (and commonly) a previously married mother or father may cohabit with a partner who is not related to her or his children, in which case divorce but not remarriage is involved.

Whichever of these pathways occurs, two-thirds of children in the United States enter a stepfamily via cohabitation rather than marriage. Figure 4.6 shows the pathways that typically lead to cohabiting-stepfamily formation.

It is likely that many of these cohabiting stepfamilies become married stepfamilies, since one in four stepfamilies at any one time are cohabiting

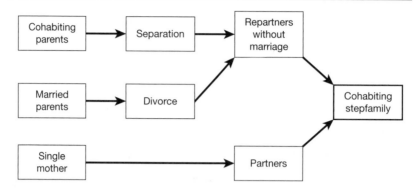

Figure 4.6 Pathways to cohabiting stepfamilies

households. Cohabiting relationships generally tend to be short-lived; half end within a year, with half of those that end dissolving and the other half turning to marriage (Bumpass & Lu 2000).

Why are cohabiting stepfamilies unstable? First, cohabitation is associated with fewer economic resources than marriage, and the stress associated with low economic well-being is predictive of relationship breakdown. Second, the role of a cohabiting stepparent is less defined than that of a married parent; marriage communicates commitment to the other parent and the family. So although the stepparent role is ambiguous in all stepfamilies, it is even more so in cohabiting households and because of the uncertainty of the stepparent role, stress is likely.

A third possibility is that mothers cohabit with a partner when they are not sure that the person is a suitable partner for marriage. In this case, stability of the relationship is also likely to be precarious.

In summary, the majority of stepfamilies are now formed via nonmarital birth and cohabitation, in contrast to 'traditional' stepfamilies formed through divorce of married parents and remarriage. Both these factors potentially bestow vulnerability on stepfamily living.

Multiple Transitions

We have discussed the fact that by the time a child moves into a stepfamily he or she is likely to have experienced at least one former family transition, usually out of a two-parent household. Because stepfamilies are less stable than first families, there is a heightened risk for a child of experiencing further transitions. In Australia, for example, 60 percent of second marriages dissolve, compared with 32 percent of first marriages. The figures are similar for the United States, although the rate of first marriage breakdown is higher than most other countries—50 percent for first marriages.

Box 4.1 Rates of marital breakdown in the United States

- 50 percent of first marriages break down.
- 70 percent of second marriages (with children) break down.
- 75 percent of third marriages break down.

It is estimated that when children are involved in a remarriage, the rate of dissolution of that marriage is as high as 70 percent (Hetherington & Jodl 1994). Remarriages that do not involve children are more stable. The breakdown rate for third marriages is even higher—around 75 percent. Another way of looking at the prevalence of family transitions is that more than 10 percent of remarriages (remember that 75 percent of divorced adults remarry) are a third marriage for one or both of the partners.

Why do second marriages fail more often than first? One theory is that those who marry or partner for a second time are desensitized to divorce, see it as a solution to relationship difficulties, and therefore have a weaker commitment to the marriage. As we will discuss further in Chapter 6, partners in second marriages report similar levels of marital quality to those in first partnerships. However, a recent study found that remarriage couples reported positive attitudes to divorce and higher divorce tolerance (thinking about divorce) than those in first marriages (Whitton, Stanley et al. 2013).

Another possibility is that the stresses inherent in stepfamily living when children are present contribute to the likelihood of the marriage or partnership ending, and this is indicated by the fact that remarriages without children are comparatively stable.

A third explanation is that adults who are not good at relationships are *selected* in to second and subsequent marriages. They have characteristics that are likely to lead to failed partnerships. We will discuss the selection hypothesis later in the book.

It is important to note that these figures are for *marriage and marital transitions*. The instability of cohabitation means that cohabiting stepfamilies are even more likely to dissolve. It has been found that when cohabitation transitions, as well as marital transitions, are taken into account, the number of transitions for children increase by a third for White children, and 100 percent for Black children (Raley & Wildsmith 2004). In a study of young people who were part of the National Longitudinal Study of Adolescent Health, Brown found that 61 percent of cohabiting stepfamilies changed in a one-year period. Of these, over half reverted to single parent families and under half converted from a cohabiting to a married stepfamily (Brown 2006).

Similarly, in an English community sample of stepfamilies, one third of the fathers had had more than one previous committed relationship (marriage or cohabitation). Some had had ten or more. Half of the children in that study had lived in a previous stepfamily (Robertson 2008). A first transition is, then, liable to set in place a trajectory of subsequent changes in family structures.

Multiple transitions introduce a bewildering number of new relationships into the lives of children, as well as bringing losses. Figure 4.7 depicts a child whose mother partners three times, bringing (at a conservative estimate) 20 adults and nearly 9 cousins into her life. What the figure does not show is the likelihood that she will also gain step- and half siblings, in a process known as multipartner fertility.

In summary, the relative instability of second partnerships means that children in stepfamilies are liable to experience multiple family transitions. These changes bring with them losses of some relationships and the establishing of new ones. The **accumulation** of kin may be of advantage to children, or the stress of changes may put them at risk. We discuss outcomes for children who experience multiple transitions in Chapter 8.

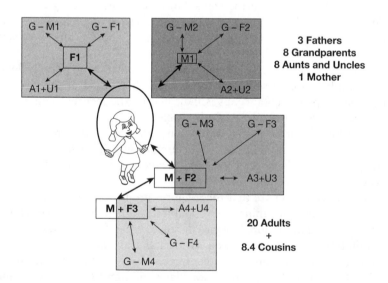

Figure 4.7 Hypothetical accumulation of relationships in a child's life as a result of multiple transitions

Source: Figure produced by author.

Multipartner Fertility

Multipartner fertility refers to the growing incidence of adults having children with more than one partner. The factors considered earlier in this chapter—nonmarital child birth and cohabitation—as well as changing attitudes to marriage and sexual activity, contribute to the likelihood that increasing numbers of parents are raising children across households, and that children have step- and half siblings in their lives.

Multipartner fertility in women usually leads to the situation where children living in households with their mothers will have different fathers. Multipartner fertility in men brings risks that their resources are spread across households and that there are likely to be fewer resources for each household than if they were concentrated in one.

Research into this family trajectory is recent, and most has come from the Fragile Families Project, which focused on unmarried parents, although it included married parents as well. It is a nationally representative sample of urban families. Box 4.2 shows the factors that predict multipartner fertility in men and women (Carlson & Furstenberg 2006).

Box 4.2 Factors associated with multipartner fertility in women and men

Risk factors for multipartner fertility in women:

- cohabitation;
- living with lone parent at age 15;
- young age at first birth;
- no religious affiliation;
- Black;
- in mixed-race relationship.

Risk factors for multipartner fertility in men:

- older;
- living with one parent at age 15;
- Black;
- poor health
- no college degree;
- incarceration;
- unmarried.

It was found that in over one third of the couples in the sample either one or both parents had children with another partner. The rate was higher for unmarried (59 percent) than for married (21 percent) couples.

Other research suggests that multipartner fertility has an adverse impact on parental relationships and parenting (Carlson & Furstenberg 2007), and that social support from kin is less for mothers who have children by more than one partner (Harknett & Knab 2007). Men's but not women's multipartner fertility is associated with subsequent relationship dissolution (Monte 2011). It may be that the obligation to pay child support to children from previous unions puts financial strain on the relationship, contributing to its dissolution. It is difficult, however, to separate the potential consequences of multipartner fertility itself from those of associated factors such as cohabitation, low levels of education, being Black, and other markers of disadvantage.

In summary, the subset of stepfamilies that involve multipartner fertility are those that are otherwise described as complex, and which include children of the current partnership. The pressures on the family that come from the existence of men's children in previous unions is a recent finding. Research into multipartner fertility and its implications is continuing.

Typologies

A typology is a classification of stepfamilies that helps us to consider them more simply than if we had to approach them as individually different family units. In Chapter 1 we introduced the rather basic classifications of simple, complex, patchwork and multifragmented stepfamilies —although these groupings overlap to a considerable extent. There are other ways in which stepfamilies have been classified that arise from the perspectives of stepfamily members themselves.

Children's Typologies of Stepfamilies

In a study of Australian children whose parents had repartnered, Funder and her colleagues interviewed children about who they considered were members of their families (Funder 1996). They found a continuum, ranging from the original nuclear family (ignoring stepparents and stepsiblings), to inclusion of a wide range of people—some not related—and pets. Funder identified the criteria children were using to identify family members:

- original nuclear family;
- biological kin;
- those resident in the household;

- inclusion of the nonresident parents' household;
- extended stepkin;
- key nonrelated others ('fictive kin'), including pets.

In another study, in Canada, in which adolescents were asked to describe their families, Gross identified four typologies (Gross 1987):

- retention—just the original nuclear family (33 percent);
- **substitution**—resident parent and stepparent, not nonresident parent (13 percent);
- reduction—just one biological parent (25 percent);
- augmentation—both biological parents and a stepparent (28 percent).

There are some similarities to these two typologies. Box 4.3 shows the links between them.

The Australian model is more extensive. There are probably two reasons for this. First, the children were younger than the Canadian adolescents, and young children tend to be more flexible and inclusive about who is in their families; and second, the Australian study was done more recently than the Canadian one. It is likely that in the early 1980s when the Gross study was carried out, stepfamilies were both less common and more stigmatized.

Box 4.3 Similarities between typologies of stepfamilies

Australian children		Canadian adolescents
Original nuclear	=	Retention
Biological kin	=	Just one biological parent
Household	=	Substitution
Nonresident parent	=	Augmentation
Extended stepkin		
Fictive kin		

Overarching Typologies

Lawrence Ganong and Marilyn Coleman have identified common features of typologies that have been suggested by earlier writers (Ganong & Coleman 2004). They focus on dynamics within the household. Box 4.4 describes their categories.

> **Box 4.4 'Typologies of typologies'**
>
> - 'Brady Bunch': stepfamilies who think of themselves as no different from first families.
> - Stepfamilies with engaged parents and disengaged stepparents. This can happen when parents act as 'gatekeepers' between their children and their partners, or when stepparents feel rebuffed by stepchildren and withdraw.
> - Couple-focused stepfamilies who focus on the parents' relationship. Couples who partner when children are older and have left home are more likely to fit this description.
> - Progressive stepfamilies, who embrace being different from first families and tend to be flexible and adaptive in their attitudes to roles and behaviors.
>
> Source: Ganong & Coleman 2004

Other Issues in Thinking about Stepfamilies

There are several other factors that are important in how we approach the study and understanding of stepfamilies.

Families versus Households

In Chapter 1, in considering stepfamilies, we identified the distinction that is between families and households. Most stepfamilies are multi-household families, since children commonly divide their time across the homes of their resident and nonresident parents (see Figure 1.1, p. 6). Children are very likely to have both nonresident parents and nonresident *stepparents*.

This distinction between households and families is very important. To focus only on households is to miss the importance of the family members who do not, or only sometimes, live in the same house. We need, then, to consider both the *internal* dynamics of a stepfamily household and the *external* family relationships that are a vital part of a stepfamily.

From another perspective, many adults in stepfamilies also have children and stepchildren living in other households; in one study nearly half of stepparents had children living outside their household (Stewart 2001). A real understanding of stepfamilies, then, needs to take into account these residential complexities. Unfortunately, much research,

Box 4.5 Factors in the consideration of multihousehold stepfamilies

- Children are mobile in their residence.
- Nonresident parents increasingly stay in touch with their children.
- Adults in stepfamilies are very likely to have nonresident children and stepchildren.

and the majority of census databases, takes as their stepfamily unit the household.

Biological versus Social: Class Issues

Another dichotomy that influences perspectives on stepfamilies is the tension between the view that 'children need biological parents' versus 'children need social families'. The first view holds that genetic or biological relatedness is the most important, that parenting is a 'natural' process, and that children need above all to be close to biological relatives such as parents and siblings. The second position states that what is most important for children is the social family in which they live, not biological connections. In this view, close relationships do not depend on biological relatedness. Rather, a family unit constructed on the basis of belonging and stability, regardless of biological ties, provides the needs of children. For first families, these two positions are usually in harmony —children live with people who are both biologically related and who form their social family.

Stepfamilies are clearly an exception to this, since some biological family members are likely to live in other households, while nonrelated kin live in the same household as children. Some English researchers have found that there is an identifiable class difference in the weight that family members put on the two positions (Edwards, Gillies et al. 1999). It is far more likely in working-class families that the social family will be paramount. One stepfather in the study said: 'I think and feel of 'em as my own, not as nothing else . . . and I feel of 'em as me own, take 'em as my own, and that's just it' (p. 91).

Middle-class families, on the other hand, are more likely to favor the view that biology is the most important factor for children. One mother is quoted by Edwards as saying, 'There is a big difference between your natural children and others you take on board. . .things just happen naturally with flesh and blood that don't happen when it's not' (p. 90). These differences have implications for how family members see their stepfamily in terms of membership, and are in part related to cultural as well as class differences.

Chapter Summary

The 'traditional' pathway to stepfamily formation via divorce and remarriage is now the way in which a minority of stepfamilies is formed. Instead, the increase in two major demographic factors—ex-nuptial birth and cohabitation—has led to these being major ways in which children and adults enter stepfamilies. Hispanic and African-American women are the most likely to have babies while they are lone parents. However, lone parents usually remain by themselves for only a short time before partnering or repartnering.

Cohabitation is a relatively unstable family form, both in first unions and in stepfamilies. However, many cohabiting stepfamilies go on to marry. Those marriages that dissolve contribute to the experience for children and adults of multiple transitions, that confer increased risk for children via the losses and disruptions these changes bring.

Many multiple transitions are accompanied by multipartner fertility, where both women and men have biological children with more than one partner. Multipartner fertility is associated with several markers of disadvantage, making it difficult to disengage its potential impact from that of poverty, low education, and other factors. Multipartner fertility in men predicts dissolution of partnerships in this group of stepfamilies, although multipartner fertility in women does not.

Typologies of stepfamilies have been constructed from the perspectives of children and adults. An overarching typology has been developed that focuses on dynamics within the family. Other factors that are important to consider are the distinctions between families and households, and between biological and social families.

Key Terms

- Typologies
- Lone parenthood
- Cohabitation
- Multiple transitions
- Multihousehold stepfamilies
- Multipartner fertility

Discussion Questions

1. Why do you think so many stepfamilies cohabit rather than marry when they form?

2. How might multipartner fertility in women affect the membership of a stepfamily? What kind of stepfamily is formed when a woman has all her children living with her but no partner?

Exercise

Talk to two or more people you know who have lived in stepfamilies. Ask them to identify who they consider to be 'family'. Do they fit any of the typologies discussed in this chapter?

Additional Readings and Web Resources

Carlson, M. J. & Furstenberg, F. F. (2006). The prevalence and correlates of multi-partnered fertility among urban U.S. parents. *Journal of Marriage and Family*, 68 (3), 718–732.

Tach, L., K. Edin, & McLanahan, S. (2011). Multiple partners and multiple partner fertility in fragile families, Princeton University: 15 (http:// crcw. princeton.edu/workingpapers/WP11-10-FF.pdf).

Teachman, J. & Tedrow, L. (2008). The demography of stepfamilies in the United States. In J. Pryor (Ed.), *The International Handbook of Stepfamilies* (pp. 3–29). Hoboken, NJ: John Wiley & Sons.

Chapter 5

Adults in Stepfamilies

Individuals who need immediate gratification may not enjoy being a stepparent.

(Ganong & Coleman 2004, p. 120)

Objectives of this Chapter

- To describe the roles of adults in stepfamily households.
- To describe the well-being of adults in stepfamilies.
- To discuss the challenges faced by adults in stepfamilies.

Introduction

Adults who live in stepfamilies have come to their families by various pathways, as seen in Chapter 4. In many cases these trajectories include transitions into and out of other relationships. Life Course Theory suggests that these transitions are likely to have a cumulative impact on them, both as individuals and in the ways in which they approach relationship formation. Alongside the impacts of previous transitions, they bring with them patterns of relating in previous families and intimate relationships. In this chapter we consider the well-being and roles of individual adults who are members of stepfamilies. These include biological mothers and fathers, stepmothers and stepfathers, and nonresident parents (both mothers and fathers). We approach stepfamilies as multihousehold families. If we were to consider stepfamily adults in an even wider perspective we could include also grandparents and step-grandparents. They are, however, discussed in detail in Chapter 9.

Resident Mothers

The most common two-parent stepfamily form is a stepfather household. In England and the United States, between 80 percent and 90 percent of stepfamily households with two parents comprise a mother, a stepfather, and the mother's children. (It is important to note, however, that this count does not include blended family households in which there is only one parent and no stepparent—see Chapter 8.)

Comparatively little attention has been given by researchers to the experiences and well-being of resident biological mothers. Yet their position is pivotal to the stepfamily's development and functioning. A biological mother in a stepfamily faces the challenges of balancing her relationships with her own children and with her new partner. She facilitates the relationships between her children and their stepfather, and the relationships of both with her ex-partner, the nonresident parent. Her role has been described variously as broker, mediator, facilitator, and lynchpin in the stepfamily.

Commonly, mothers have had some time as lone parents with their children. They are likely to form close relationships during this time, especially with daughters, and the intensity of these parent–child bonds is by necessity diluted when mothers form a relationship with a new partner. At the same time, they are building a new relationship without the opportunity to have a leisurely courtship free of the responsibilities, and possibly the disapproval, of children. Resident mothers, then, are faced with the currents and undercurrents of these loyalty issues and tensions between children, new partners, and themselves.

VIGNETTE
Difficulties in courtship in stepfamily formation

Jenny and her husband George separated amicably, and their three children lived mainly with her. They coparented well for two years, until Jenny met Joe. She and Joe dated for six months, although it was difficult to get time by themselves as the children were usually at home when he visited. They then decided to move in together. Joe did not know her children very well, and had none of his own. Once he moved in her relationship with George deteriorated, with George accusing her of finding another 'father' for the children. She and Joe had even less time to themselves, and she realized that she didn't know him very well. The children's behavior changed for the worse. She found herself mediating between her new partner and the children, trying to reassure her ex-husband that he was not being replaced, and attempting to establish the kind of relationship she wanted with Joe.

Box 5.1 Spotlight on resident mothers in stepfamilies

- Resident mothers are the lynchpins of the new stepfamily.
- They facilitate the adaptation of their children and their new partner to each other and to themselves.
- They are more likely than women in other families to be depressed and to have other mental health problems.
- They are likely to come to the stepfamily with a history of depression, and to have entered partnerships and parenthood comparatively young.

It is common that when a mother repartners, the relationship with her ex-partner also changes. The presence of another potential father figure in her children's lives presents challenges for their father, including the fear that the children might become less close to him. He may worry that he will be replaced in their affections, and he might, too, disapprove of the new partner's attitudes to parenting.

The Well-being of Resident Mothers

Longitudinal studies show us that there is a **selection effect** in regard to who becomes a mother in a stepfamily. Selection effects are defined as the nonrandom incidence of people with particular characteristics in a situation or group. In a New Zealand study that followed 1,000 children for over 30 years, for example, it was found that women who entered stepfamilies were more likely than those who did not to be younger at the time of their first birth, and to have a history of depression and early partnership (Nicholson, Fergusson et al. 1999). There was also an **intergenerational effect**—if they had lived in stepfamilies in their childhood, they were more likely themselves to form a stepfamily.

Studies that examine the current well-being of biological mothers in stepfamilies find that they are in comparatively poor health in a number of ways. In the UK Study of New Stepfamilies, resident mothers showed higher levels of depression, alcohol abuse, antisocial behaviors, and social phobias than mothers in first families (Smith, Robertson et al. 2001). Nearly half of these mothers (who were from a broadly representative sample of stepfamilies in England) had a history of depression, and their current mental health was twice as bad as mothers in first families.

Another British study also reported low levels of life satisfaction, and comparatively high levels of depression and unhappy partnerships in resident mothers (Ferri & Smith 1998). They were more likely than women in blended families and first families to report unhappy partnerships, and they were more likely than men or women in any other group (stepmother, blended, and first families) to report depression.

These findings raise the question: is it that women prone to depression, antisocial behavior, and poor relationship skills are more likely to enter stepfamilies (selection effect)? Or does living in a stepfamily cause these problems? The answer is that it is probably a complex mixture of both factors.

Roles for Mothers in Stepfamilies

Sometimes mothers in stepfamilies take on a **gatekeeping** role in relation to their children, especially in the early stages of the new relationship. This involves taking primary responsibility for the care and discipline of their children, and not allowing their new partner to be involved in decisions regarding the children. As Ganong and Coleman (2004) point out (p. 113), in a first-time relationship a woman has the chance to focus first on the partnership and later on parenthood. In a stepfamily she is likely to reverse that order and maintain the primacy of her mothering role as the relationship develops.

In one study, Weaver and Coleman interviewed 24 remarried women about their roles in stepfamilies, and derived four role functions from the interviews (Weaver & Coleman 2005). They were:

- Gatekeeper: controlling stepfathers' access to their children both before and after the marriage.
- Defender: protecting children from real or perceived threats to their well-being.
- Mediator: mediating potential or actual conflicts between their children and their partners.
- Interpreter: educating children and partners about the others' perspectives.

These roles are strong evidence for the pivotal position mothers play in stepfamilies as they mediate, facilitate, and foster adjustments in existing relationships and the establishment of new ones.

In summary, we need to know more about resident mothers in stepfamilies. The little information we have indicates that their roles are both difficult and delicate. They balance and moderate relationships among stepfamily members, and are likely to suffer from depression and other health issues. Their comparative lack of well-being is likely to be in part a result of the impact of previous separation and divorce, in part arising from the challenges of establishing a second family with a new partner, and in part the effects of selection.

Resident Fathers

Comparatively few men are resident fathers in stepfamilies—only about 10 percent of two-parent stepfamily households include a resident biological father. There has been very little research that has focused on these fathers; more often they are considered in the context of resident stepmothers (see the next section).

Resident fathers in stepfamilies have custody of their children after a divorce (unless the mother of their children has died). Often this is because their children's mother is unable or unwilling to take primary care of them. Like lone mothers, fathers are likely to have developed close relationships with their children while parenting them alone. When they repartner they commonly relinquish the main parenting role in favor of their children's stepmother, their new partner.

In an English study of stepfamilies, men in stepmother families reported the highest levels of unhappy partnerships and lowest levels of life satisfaction (Ferri & Smith 1998). However, and perhaps surprisingly, they reported high levels of agreement about discipline for their children and low levels of depression compared with stepfathers, and with women in stepfather and stepmother families. This paints a picture of fathers who are happy to let their new partners take a major parenting role and to make decisions. However this does not necessarily mean they are happy with their relationships or with life in general.

Box 5.2 Spotlight on resident fathers in stepfamilies

- Resident fathers are comparatively uncommon.
- We know little about their well-being.
- They are likely to take a secondary parenting role, letting their new partners take the primary role.
- They report being comparatively unhappy with their lives.

Nonresident Fathers

Nonresident fathers are usually discussed in regard to the contact and relationships they have with their children. Their roles vary according to many factors, including the kind of relationships they have with their ex-partners and the distance they live from their children.

We know little about their well-being as individuals. Some research suggests that they are more likely than nonresident mothers not to live in family situations, so that it is more difficult for them to have children to stay with them. There is also some evidence that contact with their children is good for their well-being with more frequent contact being associated with feelings of competence and high self-esteem (D'Andrea 1993).

The well-being of nonresident fathers will depend to some extent on the circumstances of their separation from their children's mother. It is found generally that women recover better than men from the stresses of separation and divorce, for several reasons. First, women are more likely to seek and find social support from friends and family. Furthermore, because they usually have children continuing to live with them they obtain some kind of support from children whereas nonresident fathers do not. Men are more likely than women to use harmful means of coping, including alcohol and substance abuse.

Second, women are more likely than men to initiate separation and divorce. This means that nonresident fathers have more to cope with because they did not have the opportunity to prepare. Related to this, having a feeling of control over events is associated with coping well and the person who does not initiate the separation will be left feeling out of control.

Third, and related to the first factor, nonresident fathers do not have day-to-day contact with their children. For most this is a painful fact of separation.

Finally, for some men separation brings with it a loss of status. They are no longer continuous fathers to their children, and, because of the economic consequences of divorce, they may have less income and possibly lower-status jobs.

In summary, the roles and well-being of nonresident fathers vary according to several factors. The circumstances of their separation from their children's mother, the amount of contact they have with their children, and their economic circumstances, all contribute to their well-being and the roles they play in the lives of their children.

Nonresident Mothers

Almost no research addresses the well-being of nonresident mothers. It is generally assumed that women do not have their children living with them after separation because problems exist. These include physical and mental health issues, and alcohol and substance abuse. However, there are mothers who choose for other reasons not to be primary parents for their children; we know nothing about them.

The other aspect of nonresident mothers that is known is that they are more likely than nonresident fathers to have regular contact with their children (Gunnoe & Hetherington 1995; Stewart 1999).

From the two general facts noted here, we can assume that relationships with their children and with fathers and stepmothers in stepfamilies might be vexed. The lack of information about nonresident mothers is lamentable, and it might be especially important to know something about women who choose not to parent their children.

Stepmothers

In discussing stepmothers, it is important to distinguish between *resident* and *nonresident* stepmothers. Resident stepmothers live in the household with their partners' children, and so need to build relationships with the children that work on a daily basis. In contrast, nonresident stepmothers see their stepchildren only when they visit to spend time with their biological father. There are more nonresident stepmothers than resident stepmothers, because children usually live with their mothers after their parents separate.

Stigma

What nearly all stepmothers suffer in common is the stigma surrounding their role, arising from stereotypes that are deeply embedded in Western cultures. Children learn early in their lives about the sufferings of Hansel and Gretel and of Cinderella at the hands of their wicked stepmothers. There is an unfortunately common saying, 'cold as a stepmother's kiss', that conveys this stereotype. Television and movies also often depict stepmothers as unfriendly, cold, and withdrawn. All stepmothers, then, have to overcome this pervasive stigma to some extent, at least in the eyes of their stepchildren, if they are to succeed in their roles. These myths uphold the evolutionary perspective on stepfamilies, which predicts that because they are not biologically related, stepmothers mistreat their stepchildren. In practice, the majority is successful in the face of considerable difficulties.

The 'Motherhood Mandate'

Social and cultural ideals of how mothers should behave are pervasive. The 'motherhood mandate' (Ganong & Coleman 2004) means that all women in all families are, to a greater or lesser extent, expected to be self-sacrificing, to put the needs of children and partners before their own, and to nurture children whether or not they are their own. For both resident and nonresident stepmothers, these expectations can be in conflict with the involvement of their stepchildren's biological mothers. They may have differing styles of parenting, and there may be a sense of competition set up between them. Stepmothers are likely to feel

Box 5.3 Spotlight on challenges faced by stepmothers

- Stereotype of 'wicked stepmother'.
- Possible conflict with biological mother.
- Mothering mandate (expectation they will be good mothers to stepchildren).
- Rejection by stepchildren.

compared and found wanting by their stepchildren. There is a tension between expectations that they fulfill the mothering myth—that mothering comes naturally, and that women offer the best parenting for children—and the stigma of being a stepmother, with the negative connotations of that role (Ganong & Coleman 2004, p. 134).

Typologies of Stepmothers

In the last few years as interest in stepmother roles has increased, several typologies have been proposed based, in the main, on interviews with stepmothers, stepparents generally, and in two cases stepchildren. Table 5.1 summarizes some of these.

If we compare these typologies, it is possible to group them into six broad categories that describe the nature of the stepmothering roles. Box 5.4 shows these groupings.

Table 5.1 Typologies of stepmothers

Weaver & Coleman 2005	Church 1999	Erera-Weatherly 1996	Crohn 2006
'Mothering but not mother'	Nuclear	Super-good step-mom	My father's wife
Other-focused	Extended	Detached	Peer-like girlfriend
	Biological	Friendship	Type of kin
	No family		

Resident Stepmothers

Only about 10 percent of stepmothers are resident—that is, they live most of the time in a household with their partner and his children, her stepchildren. Resident stepmothers commonly take over the main parenting role of their stepchildren, since men are still more likely than women to be in the workforce full time. The 'mothering mandate'

Box 5.4 Categories of stepmother roles in stepfamilies

- 'Imitation nuclear': a role in which the stepmother makes little or no distinction between her own children and her stepchildren (nuclear, Church; biological, Erera-Weatherley).
- 'Kinship role': families where stepmothers have the role of extended kin (extended, Church; types of kin, Crohn).
- 'Friendship role': families in which stepmothers take the role of a friend or facilitator of relationships in the family (friendship, Erera-Weatherley; older close friend/peer-like friend, Crohn; other-focused, Weaver & Coleman).
- 'Surrogate mothering' role: where stepmothers take an active mothering role although are not seen as kin (mothering but not a mother, Weaver & Coleman; supergood stepmom, Erera-Weatherley; like another mother, Crohn).
- 'Detached mother' role: families where stepmothers have a minimal or no role as a parent (my father's wife, Crohn; detached, Erera-Weatherley; couple, Church; outsider, Weaver & Coleman).
- 'Distressed/withdrawn' role: a role where women have withdrawn or been excluded, or regard only themselves and their biological children as part of their family (uncertain, Erera-Weatherley; no family, Church; biological, Church).

mentioned above also contributes to the likelihood that a resident stepmother will take the main responsibility for child rearing in her household.

A resident stepmother faces several potential tasks. The first is to establish a relationship that works with her stepchildren. If they remain in regular contact with their nonresidential biological mother, they may resent the intrusion of another mothering figure into their lives.

Another is to forge a workable relationship with the children's nonresident mother. Nonresident mothers are more likely than nonresident fathers to have frequent contact with their children. However, nonresident mothers often have issues that have prevented them from having their children live with them, such as physical or mental illness, or drug addiction problems. Somehow an accommodation has to be reached so that both women can take appropriate and workable roles in the lives of the children.

Resident stepmothers may also bring their own children to the household, forming a complex stepfamily. Additional complications then come into play. Stepmothers must find ways of behaving evenly to biological and stepchildren. It is remarkably easy for children in such a household to perceive real or imagined favoritism in the attention of stepmothers.

A further complication occurs when stepmothers have further children within their new relationship. Box 5.5 describes the sample of stepmother families that were studied in England by Ferri and Smith (1998).

In some cases a woman with no children of her own becomes a stepmother by forming a partnership with a man with children. She then comes to a parenting situation with no experience, and takes on children without the benefit of getting to know them as infants. This, combined with potential resentment and reluctance from her stepchildren, makes her role particularly difficult as she takes the position of primary parent in the household.

Box 5.5 Characteristics of resident stepmother households in an English sample

- 44 percent had children who were adolescent.
- 70 percent had subsequent children; of these, 73 percent were under five years old.
- Stepmothers were meeting the needs of adolescents and of preschoolers in these households.
- Often these complicated households form when adolescents troubled and in conflict with their mothers come to live with their fathers, so that stepmothers have to negotiate relationships with already distressed young people.

Nonresident Stepmothers

The majority of stepmothers do not live full time in the household with their stepchildren. They live with the children's father and are part-time stepmothers, moving into the role when their stepchildren visit their father.

Because of the part-time nature of their involvement, nonresident stepmothers have in many ways more troubled and ambiguous roles than do resident stepmothers. They are not in a mothering role in relation to the children, and yet when children visit—and especially if they stay overnight—they become involved in parenting. This is particularly likely if the children are young. In essence they are caregiving without authority,

---

VIGNETTE

The challenges of being a nonresident stepmother

Sally is a 35-year-old woman, a professional with a full-time job, who married Jack two years ago. Jack has three children from his first marriage, and stays in close contact with his children George, 13, Susan, 11, and Gregory aged 7. The children stay with Jack and Sally every other weekend. The children have a close relationship with their own mother, but enjoy staying with their father. They refer to Sally as 'Dad's wife' and although polite, they show little affection for her.

Sally feels obliged to welcome the children as well as she can. She cooks meals she thinks they will like (Jack doesn't cook), she makes sure their beds are comfortable and clean. She gives up her own TV watching so they can watch programs they like. However, she feels invaded—they ignore her most of the time, don't thank her for the meals she prepares so carefully, and she feels as if she is a useful but uninteresting appendage. Even worse, she deeply disapproves of how they speak to their father. She comes from a home where respect toward parents is expected and given. George, Susan, and Gregory are rude and demanding toward their father. They compare his house and her meals to those at their mother's home, finding fault always with Jack and Sally's. Sally has come to dread the weekends when they are with them, and feels resentful toward her husband's children. She also feels guilty for her negative feelings, and unhappy that the children are the source of increasing numbers of disagreements between her and Jack. She doesn't see that they can have children of their own, something she would like, while her negative feelings prevail about Jack's children.

---

since the children regard their biological mother as their parent. We do not know whether fathers in these situations take a stronger role in parenting behaviors; regardless, it is likely that nonresident stepmothers find themselves in difficult situations.

This ambiguity in their role results in nonresident stepmothers being more stressed than resident stepmothers. They have fewer opportunities to establish close relationships with their stepchildren because of their part-time involvement (Ambert 1986). They may, too, feel guilty that they have negative feelings toward their stepchildren when the children come to their home and disrupt their lives and are resentful toward them (Doodson & Morley 2006). They may disagree with their partners about how children should be disciplined, with fathers tending to be lenient toward their children because they are visiting.

In summary, the roles of stepmothers are distinguished by ambiguity and a lack of support in what is often a primary parenting role. They face potentially high levels of competition from nonresident mothers and resentment from their stepchildren.

Stepfathers

Stepfather families are, as we have seen, the most common kind of two-parent stepfamily today. Stepfathers enter the stepfamily household with the task of coping with an existing alliance between biological mothers and their children. As one scholar has put it, 'stepfathers . . . merge their lives with their partners' preexisting family dances' (Marsiglio 2004). They may, too, have their own biological children living outside the household, in which case they are likely to have to balance their relationships with them as they enter a second family.

Stigma

Stepfathers face the stigma faced by stepfamilies in general; in addition they are seen as uninterested and possibly abusive to their stepchildren. In literature, for example, they are portrayed as cruel (David Copperfield), sexually exploitative (Lolita), and in movies, murderous (*Stepfather*, and *The Stepfather II: Make Room for Daddy*). In Chapter 8 we examine the evidence for abuse by stepfathers; here we will discuss their roles.

There have been several empirical studies that have explored stereotypes in a more systematic way. For example, a recent study of stereotypes of stepfamily members carried out in Australia found that stepfathers were seen as less caring than biological fathers (Planitz & Feeney 2009). However, in a particularly sophisticated examination of stepfather stereotypes it was found that there are multiple stereotypes of stepfathers,

---

Box 5.6 Challenges for stepfathers

- Stereotype of abusive stepfather.
- Establishing relationships with new partner and stepchildren.
- Potential resistance and resentment from stepchildren.
- Possible challenge from children's biological father.
- Reorganizing relationships with nonresident children and ex-partner.

some negative and some positive (Claxton-Oldfield, O'Neill et al. 2005). They are shown in Box 5.7.

However, when the students who took part in the study were asked to rate stepfathers in general, they were more likely to see positive than negative stereotypes as typical of stepfathers. So, although stigma about stepfamilies and stepfathers in particular remains, there is some evidence that it might be reducing.

Stepfather Roles

In line with the incomplete institutionalization hypothesis (Cherlin 1978), roles for stepfathers are both ill defined and varied. They have been described by Ganong and Coleman (2004) variously as:

- competitors
- heroes
- intruders
- friends
- abusers
- quasikin
- father replacements
- nonparents
- polite strangers.

It is, then, not surprising that stereotypes are common and that men who become stepfathers are confused about how best to behave. It may explain, too, the finding that stepfathers in comparison with first fathers

---

Box 5.7 Stereotypes of stepfathers

Positive Stereotypes	*Negative Stereotypes*
Supportive	Exploiting
Decent	Obnoxious
Unselfish	Patronizing
Encouraging	Unloving
Concerned	Intolerant
Resourceful	Manipulative
	Careless
	Controlling
	Strange

are twice as likely to be depressed (Ferri & Smith 1998). They face high levels of stress as they negotiate their roles, and their roles are far from clear.

Stepfather Parenting Roles

The role of a stepfather is, as we have suggested above, ambiguous. To what extent should he be involved in parenting and disciplining of stepchildren? Surprisingly few couples discuss the involvement of step-fathers before they start living together. In a recent New Zealand study (Graham 2010), only 39 percent of parents (and 36 percent of stepparents) reported that they had discussed coparenting before cohabiting. Robertson (2008), too, reports that only one quarter of his sample of stepfathers discussed issues like discipline with their partners before moving in with them.

The UK New Stepfamilies Study found that although three-quarters of the stepfathers reported being fully involved in parenting their step-children, 60 percent left discipline to the mothers. A few of the mothers wanted their partners to be more involved in discipline than they were. Interestingly, this study found that stepfathers themselves limited their involvement in at least some areas of parenting, rather than being subject to gatekeeping by the children's mothers. Overall, stepparents are not as involved in parenting as are biological parents, although there is great diversity in levels of involvement with some being highly engaged in parenting and others restricting their energies to the relationship with their partner. Focusing on warmth and support rather than discipline appears to be both desirable and effective, at least in the early stages of the stepfamily.

Stepfather Identity

Men who are fathering children who are not biologically related to them do not always own the label 'stepfather'. For example, in the UK New Stepfamilies Study over half of the men in this community sample said they were not stepfathers. Of these, over 50 percent described themselves as 'normal fathers in normal families', while others avoided the term because of stigmatization.

One aspect of a stepfather identity is that of **claiming** stepchildren as their own. Men may claim their stepchildren with varying degrees of intensity, from weak links to regarding them as their 'own' children. Five factors have been suggested as influencing the degree to which men claim their stepchildren and take on an identity as a stepfather (Marsiglio 2004):

- Identification with the stepchild—perceiving similarities with the child.
- Stepfather's personality—an assertive man is more likely to become closely involved in a stepchild's life than one who feels diffident and possibly threatened by the child's biological father.
- Biological mother's involvement—mothers can be gatekeepers, keeping partners at a distance from children, or they may encourage involvement.
- Stepchild's reactions and behavior—a child, especially an adolescent, may prefer a stepfather to keep his distance, to maintain boundaries between them.
- Biological father's presence and involvement—if biological fathers are largely absent from a child's life it is easier for a stepfather to claim a fatherhood role. It depends, too, on whether there is an atmosphere of competition or of cooperativeness between the two men.

In summary, stepfathers face challenges that are similar to those of stepmothers, but also have specific difficulties in negotiating their place in stepfamily households. Like stepmothers, they face stereotyping and stigma and their roles are unclear. However, whereas stepmothers are likely to find themselves taking on primary parenting roles whether or not they want them, stepfathers can struggle to forge a fathering relationship with stepchildren.

Chapter Summary

In most cases, adults in stepfamilies have experienced at least one relationship transition—the one into the stepfamily, as well as those preceding it. An outstanding feature of stepfamily formation is that the parents have not had the chance to develop their relationship unencumbered by parenting responsibilities. Unlike two adults forming a relationship for the first time, they must constantly take into account the presence of children in their lives.

The challenges vary for each kind of adult. Research suggests, however, that adults in stepfamilies suffer adverse levels of mental health and relationship satisfaction in contrast with parents in first families. This may be because of the pressures and issues they face as they form a stepfamily; it may, too, be the result of some selection into stepfamily formation. While biological parents in stepfamily households have to adapt and balance relationships, stepparents in stepfamilies have the added difficulties of stigma and ambiguity in their roles. We know comparatively little about the well-being of biological parents outside the household.

Key Terms

- Selection effect
- Intergenerational effect
- Gatekeeping
- Claiming
- Motherhood mandate
- Stigma

Discussion Questions

1. What might a new stepmother do to make her role easier in a stepmother household?
2. How would you suggest the best ways for a stepfather to ease his way into his role in a new stepfather household?
3. Compare the roles of mothers and stepfathers in stepfather families and think of ways they might be less polarized.

Exercise

Interview a classmate or someone you know who has a stepmother. Ask that person what he or she would advise a stepmother to do in order to feel comfortable in a new stepfamily household.

Additional Readings and Web Resources

Marsiglio, W. (2004). When stepfathers claim stepchildren: a conceptual analysis. *Journal of Marriage and Family*, 66 (1), 22–39.

Robertson, J. (2008). Stepfathers in families. In J. Pryor (Ed.), *The International Handbook of Stepfamilies: Policy and Practice in Legal, Research, and Clinical Environments* (pp. 125–150). Hoboken, NJ: John Wiley & Sons.

Weaver, S. E. & Coleman, M. (2005). A mothering but not a mother role: a grounded theory study of the nonresidential stepmother role. *Journal of Social and Personal Relationships*, 22 (4), 477–497.

Chapter 6

Adult and Sibling Relationships in Stepfamilies

You don't class your stepbrother as your normal brother . . .

Objectives of this Chapter

- To describe relationships among adults in stepfamilies.
- To describe relationships among siblings in stepfamilies.

Introduction

The relationships among the three main kinds of adults in stepfamilies—biological parents, stepparents, and nonresident parents—are all important for the well-being of children, and of stepfamilies overall. A Family Systems perspective suggests that they are some of the key dyads in the overall family system. In this chapter we will consider three inter-adult relationships: the relationship between biological parents and stepparents, that between biological parents and ex-partners (nonresident parents), and the relationships between stepparents and nonresident parents.

We will also discuss another set of key dyadic relationships—those among siblings in stepfamilies. As with adults, there are three kinds of siblings and three dyads to consider: biological sibling relationships, stepsibling relationships, and relationships between stepsiblings and half siblings.

Adult–Adult Relationships

Figure 6.1 depicts the three main relationships that exist between the parenting or potentially parenting adults in stepfamilies.

The Biological–Stepparent Relationship

When two adults decide to form a partnership that involves children from a previous relationship or relationships, they become a stepfamily.

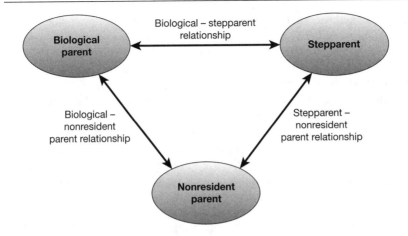

Figure 6.1 Adult relationships in stepfamilies

They may marry, or they may cohabit. One or both will bring children to the new household, and the presence of the children means that, unlike the formation of a first family, they are unlikely to have the opportunity for a relaxed courtship, or time to get to know each other without the presence of children.

Cohabitation

Stepfamily couples are more likely than first family couples to cohabit without making a commitment to each other, to cohabit sooner in their relationship, and to cohabit for longer before marrying. This may be because they feel they know about the pitfalls and challenges of living with another person (unless this is their first relationship, as in the case of a mother who had her child alone). They may, too, be prepared to cohabit without the commitment of marriage since they have experienced the breakdown of earlier relationships and they fear it might happen again. They may see cohabitation as sufficient commitment, having experienced the failure of marriage to guarantee stability. There may, too, be other reasons; for example, they may not be able to afford the costs of a wedding. Whatever the reason, being in a cohabiting relationship (whether first or stepfamily) is linked with instability. When a couple is unstable, so too is the family situation for children.

Relationship Quality in Stepfamily Couples

Forming a second or subsequent partnership is sometimes described as the triumph of hope over experience. It is probable that most repartnering couples believe that they have learned from earlier unsuccessful experiences and that this time it will work. Yet they start with a **weak couple system**, because they have not had the opportunity to build it unimpeded by children. They will, too, have established patterns of interaction in previous relationships that will be brought to the new relationship. It is likely that those patterns established in earlier partnerships have not been successful, so in the stepfamily relationship they will need to change old patterns and adapt to the new relationship. They face a kind of double jeopardy—unsuccessful patterns of relating that need to be changed, and the presence of children and lack of space to work on the new relationship. In contrast, in a first committed relationship the couple learn together how to be a couple, without previous baggage.

It has been found that stepfamily couples are more egalitarian than first-time couples. They are more likely to share housework and income earning, and to avoid traditional gender roles. This is at least in part because mothers who have been single for some time have established a level of independence that they are reluctant to abandon. They have had to make decisions alone, and to be responsible for the well-being of their children and themselves. They are therefore less likely to be comfortable in adopting traditional roles than those who are entering a relationship for the first time.

Perhaps surprisingly, given the circumstances under which they develop their relationships, couples in stepfamilies report high levels of relationship satisfaction, especially in the first two years. They are, though, less romantic and more realistic than those in first-time relationships. Furthermore, relationship quality declines more quickly than it does in first-time relationships (Hetherington & Jodl 1994). *Observations* of their interactions, rather than self-report, suggest that they demonstrate comparatively higher levels of negativity and lower levels of positivity than first-time partners (Bray & Berger 1993; Hetherington & Jodl 1994). And in England high levels of unhappiness in partnerships were reported by men and women in stepfamilies, especially those in stepmother families (Ferri & Smith 1998). In a recent study from Ireland it was found that stepmothers in particular were more unhappy than women in other family types (Hadfield & Nixon 2012). However, the length of time parents have been in the relationship is important, and Mavis Hetherington concluded from her longitudinal study of stepfamilies that 'the quality of marital relations in nondivorced families was found to be far more similar than different in this sample of nondivorced and long-established stepfamilies' (Hetherington, Henderson et al. 1999, pp. 72–73). It is, though, important to note that Hetherington's sample were all married; couples in cohabiting stepfamilies, who are more often included in studies now, may not show similar levels of satisfaction.

Parenting Roles

There is another double challenge for couples in stepfamilies. They are simultaneously working on a new intimate relationship at the same time as they are learning to be coparents. As we have seen earlier, parenting roles can be an exception to egalitarianism.

In stepfamilies biological mothers tend to be the primary parenting figures. They may act as gatekeepers and discourage their partners from taking an active parenting role. Ironically, in stepmother households women also tend to take a primary parenting role, when the children's biological fathers leave the responsibility for day-to-day care of children to them. In either situation, parenting is less egalitarian than are other household roles.

Interparental Conflict in Stepfamilies

Couples in stepfamilies have many things to negotiate, and the complexity of family dynamics mean that there are in principle a large number of potentially contentious issues. They are establishing new arrangements about finances, they are negotiating new family boundaries, and both may have ex-spouses whose presence in their lives provides grounds for conflict. The subject about which step-couples are most likely to disagree is discipline and parenting. Box 6.1 shows some of the areas over which conflict may arise.

One study has compared the amounts of **interhouse conflict** (between ex-spouses and parents in a stepfamily), and **intrahouse conflict** (between biological and stepparents) (Hanson 1999). It was found that intrahouse conflict was no higher in stepfamilies than in first families, and interhouse conflict was lower for stepfamilies than for lone-parent households formed after separation or divorce. However, stepfamilies experienced higher *overall* levels of conflict since they were exposed to both.

Box 6.1 Areas of conflict for couples in stepfamilies

- Discipline and parenting
- Ex-spouses
- Other extended family members
- Finances

Interparental Communication

The study of how adults in stepfamilies communicate is relatively recent and follows from a large body of research that focuses on communication in couples more generally. Interparental communication emerges as one of the strongest predictors of partner satisfaction and of stability in stepfamily households.

An Australian study has compared communication styles of first-time couples and stepfamily couples, and found that stepfamilies were more likely to utilize **avoidance** in communication such as withdrawing, and using fewer negative verbal and nonverbal approaches (Halford, Nicholson et al. 2007). They were also less likely to be conflicted, and to have positive discussion, than those in first families. These findings contradict those of an earlier study in which no differences in avoidant communication were found (Allen, Baucomb et al. 2001). However, the earlier study relied on self-report data from a questionnaire that was completed and posted to the researchers, whereas the Australian study combined self-report with observation of interactions.

Similarly, a Canadian study found that the ways in which stepfamily couples approached disagreements and problems was a strong predictor of stability (Robitaille, Saint-Jacques et al. 2011). In particular, the *intensity* of their responses to difficulties distinguished those who were stable from those who were not. Intensity referred to the number of strategies the couples would try in order to solve a problem. Those in the stable families were also more likely to use **problem-focused strategies**, rather than avoidance of the issues. Problem-focused strategies address the problem in proactive ways by making changes in the environment and the people involved. In contrast, the parents in the unstable group predominantly used avoidance strategies. Avoidance involved approaches such as pretending the problem doesn't exist, and diverting energy to other things rather than the issue being faced.

A third study that examined coparental communication in United States stepfamily couples found that the quality of their communication (for example, perceptions of presence of conflict, mutual support) was related to their satisfaction with the relationship and their mental health (Schrodt & Braithwaite 2011).

In summary, couples in stepfamilies report similar levels of happiness and satisfaction in their relationships to those in first families, although levels of satisfaction appear to drop faster than in first families. The complexity of stepfamily structure means that they have many issues that are potentially subjects of conflict, and at least one study suggests that if interhouse and intrahouse conflict is combined, then they are exposed to higher levels of conflict than first-time families. Communication in particular about coparenting is strongly linked with relationship satisfaction. Their styles of communication suggest that negative strategies they use, such as avoidance, may contribute to the instability of second relationships.

The Parent–Nonresident Parent Relationship

Stepfamily formation brings to a close any lingering hopes on the part of partners and children that reconciliation might take place between biological parents. Children are liable to cling to the hope that their parents will be reunited for a long time after separation and divorce, but the involvement of a new partner for either parent dashes those hopes.

For the nonresident parent, these changes bring a new parenting figure into the lives of his or her children, and an adjustment of the coparenting relationship that existed before the resident parent repartnered. The parent and the nonresident parent need to be able to reconstruct their coparenting relationship in light of these changes, taking into account the involvement of the stepparent.

As we have discussed earlier, the majority (90 percent) of nonresident parents are men, since children are most likely to live with their mothers. Ongoing coparenting between ex-partners is becoming more common as men have increasingly remained in contact with their children in recent years. This means that biological parents have to stay in communication as children move from one house to another, and decisions about schooling, health, and religion are made jointly. Legal changes such as the presumption of equal responsibility in countries such as Australia have added to the likelihood that both parents will remain in parenting roles after divorce, and this continues when one or other repartners.

Coparenting Styles

Two main kinds of coparenting styles have been identified. The first is **parallel parenting,** in which parents have a businesslike relationship and avoid conflict with each other in order to parent satisfactorily. They do not necessarily parent in the same ways.

The second is **cooperative parenting,** where parents work together to coparent their children, with little conflict and shared views of how the children should be parented.

Perhaps surprisingly, the majority of parents manage a cooperative style after they separate. Those parents who are in conflict and use the Courts are those we tend to hear about, but they are a minority. Disagreements about parenting tend to be most common in the first two years after separation; thereafter parents appear to settle into a pattern where they increasingly agree and work together for the sake of their children.

Does Coparenting Change When One Parent Repartners?

It would not be surprising if, when a parent repartners, the contact between a nonresident parent and children reduces and therefore the nature of the coparenting relationship changes. Research findings are somewhat mixed in this regard; it seems that when a resident parent repartners contact with the nonresident parent does not decrease, and in some cases it may increase (Pryor 2008b). When a nonresident parent repartners contact may reduce if he or she has children in the new relationship. Otherwise, some studies suggest that it increases, especially if the new relationship is a marriage. It is not clear, then, whether or how coparenting changes when one or other parent repartners. It almost certainly will depend on factors such as the age of the children, geographical distance, and the quality of the ongoing relationship between parents.

In summary, the relationship between resident and nonresident parents persists because children remain in contact with their nonresident parents, to varying extents. The adults involved, therefore, have to find ways of working together to ensure the successful parenting of their children. The majority manages it well; some, however, find it easiest to parent in parallel, and a small number remain in high conflict. Post-divorce conflict poses particular risks for children's well-being.

The Stepparent–Nonresident Parent Relationship

From a Family Systems perspective, the relationship between stepparent and nonresident parent is a salient aspect of stepfamily well-being. Yet it is one that has had almost no attention. Given the increase in levels of contact between nonresident parents and children over the last few decades, it is likely that this relationship will need to be investigated more closely.

There are several factors that suggest that the relationship between stepparent and nonresident parent might be a competitive one. For example, they have both been in a relationship with the resident biological parent and there may be unresolved issues for one or both of them— perhaps especially if the biological parents have had a warm relationship after separation. They are also both involved in parenting roles with the children in the stepfamily, and there competition for their affection and for the role of parent in their lives may arise. To date there has been little empirical examination of this relationship.

However, the notion of being a 'father ally' on the part of stepfathers has been developed by Marsiglio (Marsiglio & Hinojosa 2007). They suggest that it is possible for stepfamilies to be multifather families in which the stepfather either directly or indirectly fosters the relationship between stepchild and nonresident father. This is a cooperative relationship that is built on the recognition that children are damaged by conflict. Marsiglio identified five aspects of being a father ally, based on interviews with stepfathers. They are:

• Male bonding. This involves the recognition that men and fathers in particular have distinctive experiences and issues around children.

- Avoiding discomfort. Stepfathers develop relationships with non-resident fathers that are limited in closeness, and that are manageable for both.
- Relationship security. Stepfathers who are comfortable and confident in the relationship with their partner will feel more able to establish a cooperative one with the nonresident parent.
- Father's perceived worthiness. To the extent that stepfathers see the nonresident father as a good father, they are more likely to act as father allies.
- Having their own biological children. The experience of being fathers themselves is likely to enable them to empathize with nonresident fathers.

This is a positive approach to a relationship that might at best be neutral, or at times negative. More research is needed into how nonresident and stepparents might cooperate in parenting children in stepfamilies, and into how children's well-being is affected by the quality of this relationship.

Overall, managing relationships among the key adult figures, all of whom are potentially or actually in a parenting role with the children, is vital for the well-being of children and stepfamilies as a whole. The nature of separation and repartnering means that negative emotions such as guilt, competitiveness, and resentment will be very likely to occur. Over time many adults manage at least civil relationships and in some cases positively cooperate in the parenting of children. More research into ways in which these positive dynamics can be fostered is needed.

Sibling Relationships

Very few children are the only child in their family; the majority live with siblings in the same household. Nearly 80 percent of all children in the United States live with at least one brother or sister, and of these, over 12 percent (one in eight) live with either a stepsibling or a half sibling (Kreider & Ellis 2011). The relationships we have with siblings are the longest we have in our lifetimes, yet they are not well understood. Even more than biological sibling relationships in first families, it is important that we understand the variations that occur in stepfamilies.

As stepfamilies are formed, children have to form new relationships with some siblings, and to adapt their relations with others. They may or may not live with their sisters and brothers. Some stepsiblings will live in other households most of the time and live with them only some of the time; they may have half siblings in other households or in their own. Biological siblings may be living in other households. As with other stepfamily relationships, there is great diversity.

There are three kinds of relationships that siblings can have in step-families:

- biological siblings who have the same two biological parents;
- stepsiblings, who share no biological parents;
- half siblings, who share one but not two biological parents.

In our 'typical' stepfamily household described in Chapter 1, the three children are biological siblings. They share the same biological parents. They have stepsiblings (Zeb's children) who live with them some of the time, with whom they share no biological parents. They have a half sibling who does not live with them, but with their nonresident father and his partner. Had their mother, Suzie, and Zeb, had a baby together they would have had another half sibling in their household.

Box 6.2 shows the percentages of children in the United States in stepfamilies with two parents, who live with different kinds of siblings.

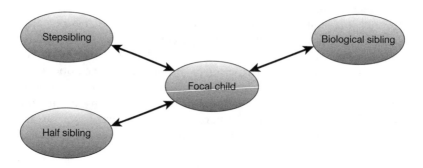

Figure 6.2 Sibling relationships in stepfamilies

Box 6.2 Percentages of children living with different kinds of siblings

- Biological siblings only   48.6 percent
- With stepsiblings   12.2 percent
- With half siblings   34.5 percent
- With stepsiblings and half siblings   4.6 percent

Note that those living with stepsiblings and half siblings may also be living with biological siblings.

(from Kreider & Ellis 2011)

By far the largest percentage of children in stepfamilies live only with their biological siblings, with over a third living with half siblings. It is important to remember, though, that a child may have half siblings and stepsiblings living in other households.

Conceptual Models for Understanding Sibling Relationships

In order to understand the dynamics of sibling relationships, it helps to consider frameworks within which to discuss them. The sibling relationship is one of the dyads that has an impact on other subsystems. These influences are, too, **bidirectional** so that other dyadic systems such as parent–child, and parent–parent relationships impact on, and are impacted by, the sibling relationships. Family Systems Theory is a useful framework for understanding the mutual impact of dyadic subsystems, such as the sibling relationship, on each other.

A comprehensive model has been developed that incorporates many aspects of sibling relationships in stepfamilies, and that depicts the interrelationships of several factors on sibling relationships and the impact of those relationships on outcomes for children (Baham, Weimer et al. 2008). Figure 6.3 shows the model.

This figure emphasizes the factors that are likely to impact on the quality of sibling relationships and, in turn, the impact of these on outcomes for children. It does not mean that, for example, family variables do not have a direct relationship with outcomes for children. Rather, it shows a potential role for sibling relationships in affecting well-being. The figure is intended as a framework for conceptualizing sibling relationships and for guiding future research questions that address the place of sibling relationships in the overall dynamics of stepfamilies.

Biological Sibling Relationships

Biological siblings who together experience the likely breakdown of their biological parents' relationship and the formation of a stepfamily could, in principle, either become closer and more supportive of each other in the face of stress, or they could become more negative and competitive. There is research to support both scenarios. One study of adolescent siblings found that their relationships were as positive as those of siblings in first families (Anderson 1999). However, an English study of young children reported higher negativity in child siblings in stepfamilies (Dunn & Deater-Deckard 1998). These findings suggest that biological siblings may become closer as they get older in stepfamilies, perhaps as family dynamics settle down over time. Overall, findings from several studies suggest that biological sibling relationships in stepfamilies are both more

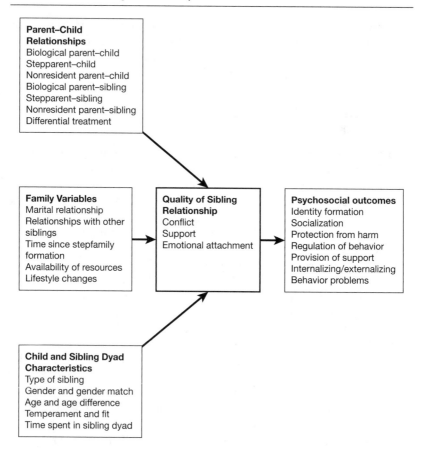

Figure 6.3 A model of the quality of sibling relationships in stepfamilies
Source: Reproduced with permission of John Wiley & Sons.

negative and more positive—in other words, more intense—than those in first families.

Stepsibling Relationships

Stepsiblings do not share genes, and in most cases have separate biological families, including extended family members. They come to a household not through their own volition, but because one of each of their parents has formed a relationship with one of the other's parents. In such a complex stepfamily household, stepsiblings have often to share rooms, household chores, and parents. They may differ greatly in age, or they may be close to the same age. Their challenges, then, are different from and additional to those of full siblings moving into another household.

Overall, research suggests that the relationships between stepsiblings are relatively benign. They are neither very positive nor very negative, and they exhibit comparatively low levels of competitiveness, rivalry and aggression (Anderson 1999). The neutrality of their relationships means that they do not provide each other with a great deal of support, and in adulthood are less likely to stay in contact than do biological siblings (White & Riedmann 1992).

They may, too, experience differential treatment from parents. It has been found that parents tend to treat their biological children differently and usually more positively than they do stepchildren. Relationships are also affected by factors such as the age of the sibling pairs, the age differential, the sex of the pairs, the time they have been together in the stepfamily, and the individual temperaments of the children.

Half-sibling Relationships

In most ways the quality of relationships between half siblings resemble those of full siblings. Although there is often a significant age difference between half brothers and sisters, it seems that they perceive each other simply as siblings, rather than making the distinction implied in the word 'half'. In a study of New Zealand stepfamilies, one adolescent boy said:

> One of the reasons I decided to spend my [last two years of high school] with Dad was 'cause I was sort of missing out on them ... I don't have any strong preferences between Mum and Dad as people, but [my half brother and sister] were one of the major factors.
>
> (Fleming 1999, p. 136)

However, half siblings are less likely to stay in touch as adults than are biological siblings, suggesting that these relationships are not as close as they may seem in childhood (White & Riedmann 1992). Age and gender differences, and the fact that half siblings are related to both parents in a stepfamily whereas other children are not, may explain these findings.

In summary, sibling relationships in stepfamilies vary according to the biological relationship between the siblings. Step- and half-sibling relationships are not as close or as intense as those between biological siblings. There is some evidence too that living with a step- or half sibling is associated with lower well-being (Tillman 2008). These relationships are an important subsystem of the family system, and more research is needed to understand both the predictors and outcomes of the quality of these relationships.

Chapter Summary

Relationships between adults in stepfamilies are not well studied, although the interparental relationship within the stepfamily has received attention as it is seen, along with the stepparent–stepchild relationship, as pivotal to the well-being of the family as a whole. This relationship is found to be comparatively egalitarian, and no more conflicted than those in first families.

Parents and nonresident parents increasingly are having to establish coparenting relationships as nonresident parents stay more involved with their children, and children themselves indicate they want ongoing relationships with both parents. Research suggests that most parents manage cooperative parenting of their children.

We know little about the relationships between nonresident parents and stepparents; one positive approach has been to consider stepfathers as 'father allies' with nonresident fathers, forming a cooperative and supportive cofathering relationship.

Sibling relationships in stepfamilies are comparatively under-studied yet, as with all sibling relationships, they are key aspects of the lives and well-being of children. Those between children who are not full biological siblings are less close and enduring than biological sibling relationships, and are associated with complexity and change in stepfamilies.

Taken together, these two kinds of dyadic relationships are closely associated with the well-being of children and of stepfamilies as a whole. They are vital subsystems that interact with others such as adult–child dyads, and their key roles mean that they deserve further examination.

Key Terms

- Weak couple system
- Egalitarian roles
- Traditional roles
- Inter-house conflict
- Intra-house conflict
- Avoidance
- Intensity of response
- Problem-focused strategies
- Parallel parenting
- Cooperative parenting
- Father allies

Discussion Questions

1. Discuss how parenting figures of the same sex (stepfathers and non-resident fathers or stepmothers and nonresident mothers) might go about forming a parenting alliance that works well for children.
2. How might the resident biological parent foster these kinds of alliances?
3. What factors do you think might account for the finding that half siblings do not stay in touch in adulthood as much as do biological siblings?

Exercise

Interview your parent (or another adult). Ask him or her about the early stages of establishing their partnership or marriage. If they are in their first partnership, ask them to talk about how it would have been if there had been children in their lives. If they are in a second (or more) partnership, ask how the presence of children made a difference.

Additional Readings and Web Resources

Baham, M. E., Weimer, A. A., Braver, S. L., & Fabricious, W. V. (2008). Sibling relationships in blended families. In J. Pryor (Ed.), *The International Handbook of Stepfamilies: Policy and Practice in Legal, Research, and Clinical Environments* (pp. 175–207). Hoboken, NJ: John Wiley & Sons.

Hadfield, K. & Nixon, E. (2012). Comparison of relationship dynamics within stepmother and stepfather families in Ireland. *The Irish Journal of Psychology*, 33 (2–3), 100–106.

Marsiglio, W. & Hinojosa, R. (2007). Managing the multifather family: stepfathers as father allies. *Journal of Marriage and Family*, 69 (August), 845–862.

Tillman, K. H. (2008). "Non-traditional" siblings and academic outcomes of adolescents. *Social Science Research*, 37, 88–108.

Chapter 7

Child–Adult Relationships

If we assume a bond between natural parent and child and some type of positive attraction between the adult partners, then the relationships in the stepfamily that lack raison d'etre are those between stepparent and stepchild . . .

(Crosbie-Burnett 1984)

Objectives of this Chapter

- To examine the relationships among children in stepfamilies, and the adults with whom they have relationships.
- To understand the ways in which these relationships change when stepfamilies are formed.
- To discuss the ways in which children incorporate multiple parenting figures into their lives.

Introduction

In Chapter 6 we focused on the well-being of individual adults in stepfamilies. Recall that a Family Systems framework takes into consideration dyadic relationships—those between two family members—which in turn are subsystems of the family as a whole. In this chapter we will be focusing on dyadic relationships among the adults in stepfamilies and children. The relationships to be discussed are the biological parent–child relationship, the stepparent–stepchild relationship, and the child–nonresident parent relationship. We will examine the changes and adaptations that take place as a result of transitions to stepfamilies, and we will discuss children's relationships with multiple parenting figures. The majority of the research discussed relates to stepfathers rather than stepmothers, since the majority of stepparents are stepfathers, and the main focus of research has been on them.

Biological Parent–Child Relationships

The formation of a stepfamily brings about change in the relationships between biological parents and children that existed before the stepparent became part of the family. Not only does a new adult and potential parenting figure enter the household, but also transitions like that from a lone parent to a stepparent household have an effect on the nature of a parent–child relationship. Most children have spent a period of time— if not all their lives—living with just one parent before the stepfamily was formed. The most common situation after separation and divorce is that children live with their mothers. Girls and their mothers tend to become particularly close. Boys, in contrast, may have vexed relationships with their lone mothers. This may be because they remind mothers of their ex-partners; mothers, too, are less likely to be involved in male activities with their sons, such as football.

A common feature of the relationship between children and lone parents, especially if their parents have divorced, is **parentification**. Children are put, or put themselves, into the position of caring for their parents emotionally and sometimes physically. Daughters in particular are likely to 'parent' their lone parents, both mothers and fathers. And although this is not beneficial for children, they may resent the loss of this parenting role when another adult enters the household.

Surprisingly little attention has been given to the changes that take place in this relationship when stepfamilies form, perhaps because the stepparent–stepchild relationship has been seen as pivotal to the well-being of a stepfamily. Yet it is obvious that when parents repartner, the relationship they have with their children has to adapt. Parental attention becomes divided rather than focused only on children, as parents seek to establish their new intimate relationship, and the close alliance that has existed between parent and child is challenged by this new relationship. Children can resent the intrusion of the person who makes claims on their mothers' attention, and often the adaptation called for by both parents and children is demanding. The changing nature of this relationship between biological parents and children, then, is an important aspect of stepfamily dynamics that needs to be managed.

Perhaps because it is uncommon, there is little research that addresses the situation when lone-resident fathers repartner. Most research examines the repartnership of lone mothers, and suggests that the parenting quality of mothers in the early stages of a new relationship deteriorates. Conflict increases and monitoring and control decrease (Fisher, Leve et al. 2003). Over time, and especially if children are young when the new family is formed, the quality of the relationships tend to improve so that they become similar to parent–child relationships in first families (Hetherington & Jodl 1994). Given the dynamics in lone-parent households before stepfamilies are formed, the relationships between mothers and daughters tend to deteriorate in the first few years, while those between mothers and sons improve.

Whether or not the parents in the stepfamily are married seems to matter for the relationship between biological parents and children. Adolescents have been found to feel closer to their mothers if they are married to their stepparent, perhaps because they perceive a greater commitment on the part of the stepparent to the family (Buchanan & Maccoby 1996). This finding has been confirmed in a more recent study where it was found that adolescent–mother relationships deteriorated if a cohabiting stepfather entered the family, but not if mothers were married to stepfathers (King 2009).

The Views of Children

An in-depth study of the perceptions of children about how the relationships with their mother as a stepfamily was formed, has been carried out by Cartwright and Seymour in New Zealand (Cartwright & Seymour 2002). From interviews with young adults who grew up in stepfamilies, children in stepfamilies, therapists who worked with stepfamilies, and other stepfamily members, they identified several factors that helped or hurt when their parents formed stepfamilies. Box 7.1 shows the findings.

Box 7.1 Factors that helped or hurt children when stepfamilies were formed

Factors that helped:

- Time and attention.
- Continuing to be the parent (putting the kids first).
- Talking about what is happening.
- Taking responsibility for discipline.
- Moving slowly.
- Respecting the child's feeling.

Factors that hurt:

- Loss of attention.
- Not informed and consulted.
- Parents doing something hurtful.
- Parents not being loyal.
- Encouraging the stepparent to discipline children.
- Setting up divided loyalties between biological parents.

It is apparent that good communication, taking time with children, and moving slowly to integrate the family will facilitate adaptation, whereas a lack of communication and attention, and early involvement of the stepfather in discipline, make adaptation more difficult.

In summary, the relationships between mothers and children tend to deteriorate when the mother repartners. However, over time they are restored to their previous levels. The perceptions of children suggest that there are factors that can help or hinder the adaptation of children to stepfamily living.

Stepparent–Stepchild Relationships

The formation of a stepfamily brings children together with an adult who may adopt a parenting role toward them, to whom they are not

---

VIGNETTES
Stepfathers and stepchildren in different situations

Case 1 Carey
Carey was three when his parents separated. He lived with his Mom, and went to his Dad's house occasionally for a day. His Dad sometimes took him to McDonald's, otherwise they stayed home and watched TV. When he was five, his Mom repartnered with Nick. Nick was fun to be around—he kicked balls in the backyard with him, he took him to football matches, and he often read him a story before bedtime. He quickly adapted to Nick as a stepfather and was happy to be treated as if he was Nick's own son.

Case 2 Georgina
When Georgina was 11, her parents separated. She lived with her Mom and stayed with her Dad two nights a week. When she was with him she often cooked, and they watched TV together or went to movies. She had a good relationship too with her Mom, until Mom's new partner Bill moved in. Bill immediately tried to tell her what to do and didn't seem interested in things she liked to do. She felt angry with him and with her Mom, and sorry for her Dad. She felt torn because she knew her Mom wanted her to get on well with Bill, but she preferred her father and felt pressured to like Bill for her Mom's sake. It made her especially cross when Bill tried to stop her going over to her friends' houses.

---

related, and toward whom they may not feel positive. They did not choose this person, their stepparent, to be in their lives; it is therefore the choice of their biological parent to bring him or her into the family. Children, then, may bring ambivalence and negativity to this relationship.

In turn, a stepparent comes into a family in which there is an existing alliance between the parent and child. He or she somehow needs to integrate into these family dynamics and existing relationships, and to form a relationship with a child with whom they have no previous history or biological relationship. Clearly, this is a relationship that has potential challenges; at the same time, many researchers and clinicians view it as pivotal to the well-being of children and of stepfamilies as a whole. Not surprisingly, then, it has been closely examined.

What Factors are Important for the Quality of the Stepparent–Stepchild Relationship?

Several elements are salient for the stepparent–stepchild relationship, and are listed in Box 7.2.

The *age of children* at the time a stepfamily is formed is a key factor that affects the relationship; when children are young, stepparents are more likely to be involved in childcare activities that promote closeness. Young children, too, are more likely than adolescents to be open to a close relationship with a new parenting figure. If the stepfamily forms when children are adolescent, however, the relationship is much less likely to be close. Teenagers are actively seeking autonomy and independence, and are therefore unlikely to welcome parenting efforts by new adults in their lives. Generally, they are most likely to want stepparents to be friends rather than parenting figures.

Gender, too, is relevant to the nature of the stepparent–stepchild relationship. As we have mentioned earlier, girls tend to form close relationships with their lone mothers and to see their stepfathers as an

---

Box 7.2 Factors related to the quality of the relationship between stepparents and stepchildren

- Age of children.
- Gender of children (and stepparents).
- Non-resident children of stepparent.
- Non-resident parents of children.
- Gatekeeping by biological parent.

intrusion into that relationship. Stepfathers and boys, conversely, may share activities, such as sport, that promote close relationships. Stepfathers might also be cautious about forming close relationships with adolescent stepdaughters, particularly as they approach puberty. It is commonly found, then, that boys adapt more easily than do girls to this new relationship.

If stepfathers *have children outside the household* with whom they are in regular contact, they may find it difficult to engage closely with their stepchildren if their biological children are jealous of the attention given to those in the household. This may also have an impact on how much stepfathers attempt to form a close relationship with stepchildren.

The presence of a *nonresident parent* in children's lives may also have an effect on the nature of the child–stepparent relationship. If a nonresident parent is worried that their child may become too close to the resident stepparent, they may discourage the child from having a warm relationship. In turn, the child may feel that a stepparent is trying to replace their nonresident parent and resent attempts by the stepparent to form a friendship. They may also experience loyalty conflicts, worrying that if they become too close to a stepparent they will be disloyal to their nonresident parent. As we saw in the previous chapter, some mothers limit the involvement of stepfathers with their children by *gatekeeping*.

Parenting Styles for Stepfathers

Stepfathers are in an ambivalent situation when they form a stepfamily. The lack of norms for stepparent behavior means that they face dilemmas —should they aim to be social parents, friends, or polite strangers? In Chapter 5 we discussed Marsiglio's concept of '**paternal claiming**' as 'readiness to nurture, provide for, protect and see a stepchild as though the child were his own' (Marsiglio 2004). It implies a willingness to be a fully committed social father. Other stepfathers aim only to support mothers of their stepchildren, and to play an indirect role; some are disengaged from a parenting role.

Many studies have concluded that authoritative parenting (as described in Chapter 3) is optimal in stepfamilies, as it is in first families. However, few have examined the impact of **permissive parenting**, which encompasses the features suggested by children's views of the stepparent role— warm and supportive, but not in a disciplining role. One study that did study permissive parenting styles by stepparents found that in those families where stepparents were warm and supportive but low in control and discipline, not only was the relationship reported as being of high quality but also the levels of family happiness were high (Crosbie-Burnett & Giles-Sims 1994).

How does the Stepparent–Stepchild Relationship Change Over Time?

Research findings are mixed about how the relationship changes. Some findings suggest that as the stepfamily becomes more established, stepparents and their stepchildren become closer over time. Others find that the relationship becomes less close, especially as children enter adolescence. However, this happens in first families as well, as teenagers seek to establish independence from their parents. It seems, though, to happen to a greater extent in stepfamilies.

Young adults who have grown up in stepfamilies have described five trajectories in relation to their developing relationship with their stepfathers. Figure 7.1 shows the trajectories over time (Kinniburgh-White, Cartwright et al. 2010).

Continuous positive regard was characterized by warmth and support from the beginning of the relationship. Stepparents did not discipline the children, leaving that to the mothers.

Deterioration and recovery: in this trajectory relationships between stepchildren and stepfathers were initially warm and positive, but deteriorated for sometimes specific reasons such as the birth of a half sibling. Some young adults blamed adolescence and their striving for autonomy for the deterioration; recovery occurred as they matured.

Gradual improvement occurred in relationships that started with low warmth and sometimes hostility—especially from the stepchild. Over time it became more positive although these relationships never reached the quality of the first two.

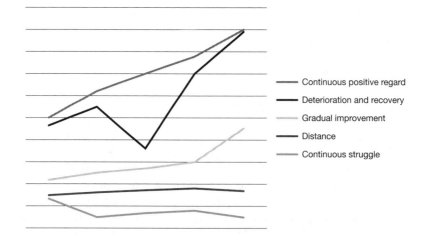

Figure 7.1 Trajectories of relationships with stepfathers

Source: Adapted from Kinniburgh-White, Cartwright et al. 2010.

Distance: this kind of trajectory was characterized by low levels of warmth and by controlling behaviors on the part of the stepfather. Stepchildren never became close to them.

Continuous struggle: this trajectory differed from the distance style by involving conflict, including emotional and physical abuse on the part of the stepfather. In adulthood there was no contact between the stepfather and stepchildren.

There is, then, great diversity in the ways in which relationships between stepchildren and their stepparents develop. There is no one 'right' pathway, and this illustrates well the incomplete institutionalization of stepfamily relationships.

In summary, the stepparent–stepchild relationship is central to a stepfamily, and is related to the well-being of the family as a whole, as well as that of individual members. It has unique challenges, including the fact that it is imposed on children rather than sought by them, and that stepparents face challenges of ambiguity, lack of role clarity, and possible resistance from stepchildren. A parenting style that encompasses high levels of warmth and low levels of monitoring and discipline is optimal, especially in the early stages of stepfamily formation.

Child–Nonresident Parent Relationships

The majority of children in stepfamilies have nonresident biological parents living outside their household. Most of these parents who are not living with their children are fathers; 80–90 percent of nonresident parents are men. Increasingly, they stay in contact with their children. If the stepfamily has come about through divorce or the breakdown of cohabitation of biological parents, children are likely to have lived with that parent and established a close relationship. On the other hand, if their other parent has died, or they did not have him or her in their lives because, for example, they were born to a lone mother who had no contact with their father, their experiences of the transition to stepfamilies will be different.

Children, whether they live with a lone parent or in a stepfamily, spend varying amounts of time with their nonresident parents. Some see them rarely or never, and others spend up to half their time in their nonresident parents' households. Those who never or rarely see the parent with whom they are not living are likely to experience '**ambiguous loss**'— their parent is not dead, but is not readily available to them. They experience the *physical* absence but the *psychological* presence of their parent. This is in contrast to those who have lost a parent through death—in which case, they suffer unambiguous loss—and those who have not before had a father figure in their lives.

Contact is increasingly more than just face-to-face interactions such as visiting, going to the movies, and staying overnight. Children stay in touch with their nonresident parents via texts and e-mail, and it may be that for adolescents this is a more comfortable form of communication than face-to-face as they feel more able to talk about their feelings in these indirect ways. Overall, levels of contact with nonresident parents appear to be rising as children express their desire to see more of that parent and (usually) fathers want more time with their children.

Nonresident mothers are more likely than fathers to keep regular contact with children and to remain involved in their lives. This contact, however, may be complicated by factors related to the reasons why they are not living with their mothers, such as mental illness or drug abuse.

Contact between children and their nonresident parents is not straightforward, given the complexities of multiple households in stepfamilies. Boundaries can be blurred and roles unclear for each adult. Children have described tensions between several aspects of the relationship (Braithwaite & Baxter 2006). On one hand, they wanted their nonresident parents to be involved as parents, but they found the communication required for this to be difficult. They also wanted 'open and intimate' communication with their nonresident parents but found this awkward as well because of lack of understanding of each other and their separate lives.

A distinction needs to be made between *contact* and *closeness* to nonresident parents. Contact is a measure of time spent together, although it can also incorporate phone, text, and e-mail contact. Closeness is a measure of the warmth in the relationship. Although they are often linked, they are not the same. A child can, for example, spend time with their nonresident parent that involves little interaction. They may spend most of the time in front of TV or at movies. In the next chapter we look at the impact of contact, closeness, and the *quality* of the relationship on well-being for children.

What Predicts Contact with Nonresident Parents?

A major factor for both mothers and fathers who are nonresident is *geography*; if they live near a child they are more likely to have frequent face-to-face contact than if they live at a distance.

A second factor is the *relationship between the biological parents*. If they have a cooperative coparenting relationship, then nonresident parents will see more of their children than if it is a conflicted relationship.

The *status of the parents' relationship when the child is born* is also salient. If parents are not living together or are cohabiting when the child is born, the father is less likely to form a strong commitment to the child and may not have spent much time living with him or her. Contact then is likely to be low.

The *age of the child* at the time of separation is also important. If a child is young, then he or she may not have established a relationship when they lived together that endures the rearrangements of separation and repartnering.

What Predicts Closeness to Nonresident Parents?

The factors that predict whether or not children are close to their nonresident parents vary somewhat for fathers and mothers. Some also overlap with predictors of contact, since some contact is necessary for closeness to flourish. Box 7.3 summarizes predictive factors for nonresident fathers and mothers.

Box 7.3 Factors associated with closeness to nonresident parents

Predictive factors for closeness to nonresident fathers:

- Gender (boys closer).
- Race (Black closer than White).
- Frequency of contact.
- Age/time in stepfamily (closer to nonresident parent if older).

Predictive factors for closeness to nonresident mothers:

- Race (Black closer than White).
- Non-resident mothers' education.
- Time in stepfamily.
- Frequency of contact.

Does the Relationship between Children and Nonresident Parents Change when Either Parent Repartners?

When a single parent who is the main caretaker of children repartners, we might expect that a child's relationship with their nonresident parent will change. Children may find it difficult to accommodate two parenting figures of the same sex into their lives, and so become either more distanced from their nonresident parents in order to accommodate the relationship with stepparents in the household; or they may reject stepparents and move closer to nonresident parents. Likewise, a nonresident parent may try to intensify the relationship with their child in the face of a perceived threat that they may lose the affection of the child to the stepparent; or they may draw back from the relationship in the belief that it is better for the child.

In turn, if nonresident parents repartner, they may become absorbed by the new family into which they have entered, and lose interest in their children living in the household headed by their ex-partner. Their children, too, may believe that their nonresident parent is not so available to them now that he or she has repartnered and has another family.

Much of the research that has addressed these questions has been cross-sectional, comparing relationships between situations where, for example, a nonresident parent is repartnered and where he or she is not. The difficulty with this is that cross-sectional data cannot examine changes in contact. It may be that nonresident parents repartner *because* they have less contact with children, rather than contact reducing as a result of their repartnering. Longitudinal studies can better identify whether or not contact levels change as a result of repartnering.

Two longitudinal studies have examined changes in contact for children and young people at different ages. Juby and colleagues found that for 0–11-year-olds, if a resident mother repartnered, then contact with nonresident fathers reduced (Juby, Billette et al. 2007). This has also been found in cross-sectional studies (Seltzer & Bianchi 1988; Stewart 2010). If the resident parent has more children, the contact seems to reduce even more.

If a nonresident father repartners, however, contact is not likely to reduce unless he repartners shortly after separation (Juby, Billette et al. 2007). It may be that if there is an interval between partnerships for nonresident fathers, they are likely to have established patterns of contact that stay stable.

Several cross-sectional studies have reported that if a nonresident father has biological children in his new relationship, contact with children from his previous family reduces (Manning, Stewart et al. 2003; Cooksey & Craig 1998). This suggests that some fathers may swap families, investing in the families with which they live, rather than those they are no longer living with.

In contrast to these findings, in a study of young adults Aquilino examined the trajectory of relationships between nonresident fathers and young adults (Aquilino 2006). He found that if either parent repartnered during the young person's adolescence, contact *increased*. Furthermore, the birth of a subsequent biological child did not reduce the contact fathers had with their nonresident children. It is important to note that Aquilino's study involved young adults (18–24 years).

In summary, Aquilino's findings, and the general lack of consensus about the impact of repartnering, particularly of nonresident parents, suggest that a great deal more research, and particularly longitudinal research, needs to be done in this area. The age difference between the samples in the two longitudinal studies suggests the importance of this variable being taken into account in future research.

Relationships with Multiple Parenting Figures

The reality for children in stepfamily households is that they have potential or actual relationships with several parenting figures. This raises the question of how they manage and maintain relationships among their nonresident and resident parents and their stepparents, and whether they are able to 'add' parents to their lives, or whether they substitute one for another. For example, it may be that a resident stepfather replaces a nonresident father in the affections of a child; conversely, that same child may refuse to accept the stepfather as a parent and stay steadfastly loyal to their nonresident father.

This question can be approached by considering comparisons among the relationships that children have with the adults in their lives when they live in stepfamilies. White and Gilbreth have proposed three scenarios for the ways in which children handle multiple relationships (White & Gilbreth 2001):

- **Accumulation** suggests that children can add parents to their lives and benefit from both relationships with parents of the same sex.
- **Substitution** suggests that children substitute one parenting figure for another. For example, a stepfather may replace a nonresident father in their lives.
- **Loss** suggests that children do not benefit from relationships with either nonresident parents or stepparents.

Comparison of Closeness

Investigations of stepfather families have generally found that children feel closest to mothers, followed by stepfathers and nonresident fathers (Berg 2003; King 2006; White & Gilbreth 2001). Another study, however, found that children felt closer to their nonresident fathers than to stepfathers (Pryor 2004). They also felt more secure and expressed higher warmth toward their nonresident parent than to their stepparent. This was a group of younger children, however, most of whom had regular contact with their nonresident fathers.

The comparisons look somewhat parallel in stepmother families. In these, children report being closest to their fathers, followed by their stepmothers and then their nonresident mothers (Berg 2003; King 2007). If, though, they had regular contact with their nonresident mothers, then levels of closeness became similar for stepmothers and nonresident mothers. Thus, in both kinds of stepfamilies the *resident biological parent* is the one to whom children feel closest, followed by the stepparent and then the nonresident parent. Ranking of closeness does not tell us, though, whether parenting figures are accumulated, substituted, or lost.

Relationships among Relationships

Another way of considering these relationships is to look at the correlations among them. Table 7.1 shows the significant interrelationships found in two studies.

These positive and significant correlations suggest that children can *accumulate* several parenting figures in their lives. If they are close to a nonresident parent, for example, then they are likely also to be close to their resident mother and (in one study) their stepfather. They do not appear to substitute one parent of the same sex for another.

Closeness to Parenting Figures

A third way of addressing this question is to consider how many children feel close to both parents of the same sex. Valerie King has examined this in two studies, one of stepfather families and one of stepmother families (King 2006, 2007). Table 7.2 shows her findings.

It is evident from these findings that young people in stepmother families maintained close relationships to nonresident mothers at higher rates than young people in stepfather families did with their nonresident fathers, were less likely to feel close to neither, and were more likely to be close to both stepparents and nonresident parents. This may reflect the fact that nonresident mothers tend to stay in closer contact with their children than do nonresident fathers. These findings provide mixed evidence for each of White and Gilbreth's scenarios. In stepfather families, one quarter of young people accumulated parents, and another quarter were close to neither parent of the same sex (loss). Over one third supported the

Table 7.1 Correlations among scores for the quality of relationships with mothers, stepfathers, and nonresident parents

Relationships compared	White & Gilbreth 2001	Pryor 2004
Resident mother–stepfather	.49	.236 (happy with relationship) .2 (closeness)
Resident mother–nonresident father	.25	.23 (warmth) .29 (security)
Stepfather–nonresident father	Ns	.22 (closeness)

Table 7.2 Percentage of adolescents who felt close to both, one, or neither parent of the same sex

	Stepfather families percent	Stepmother families percent
Close to both parents of the same sex (accumulation)	25	38
Close to neither parent (loss)	24	12
Close only to stepparent (substitution)	35	29
Close only to nonresident parent	16	21

substitution scenario by apparently replacing nonresident parents with stepparents. In stepmother families, however accumulation was the most likely outcome with nearly 40 percent reporting being close to both parenting figures of the same sex. However, the substitution scenario was also supported by nearly 30 percent of them. Loss was relatively uncommon in stepmother families.

There are also race differences in closeness to nonresident mothers, with Black adolescents feeling closer to them than White adolescents, and less close to stepmothers and resident fathers. This may reflect the finding that Black men find being custodial parents more challenging than do White men (Hamer & Marchioro 2002).

In summary, there is considerable support for the ability of children to accumulate parenting figures in their lives. Positive relationships with nonresident parents are either positively correlated with positive relationships with stepparents or show no relationship. No negative associations between these two relationships have been found. A majority of children in stepmother families report being close to both nonresident mothers and stepmothers, although in stepfather families most children report being close to stepfathers only. A major factor in explaining closeness is the amount of contact children have with their nonresident parent; where this is high and regular, differences between levels of closeness tend to disappear.

In the next chapter we will examine the evidence for the possible benefits of closeness to parenting figures by considering the outcomes for young people that are linked with those relationships.

Chapter Summary

When stepfamilies form, children gain one potential parenting figure and lose another from the household. The relationships that existed with their biological parents change and need to be adapted, and the new relationship with a stepparent needs to be established.

Parent–child relationships are vulnerable at the time of stepfamily formation, with children needing reassurance and time with their parent, who is managing the changes with children as well as the building of the new relationship with a partner.

The establishment of the relationships between stepchildren and stepparents can be fraught as stepparents seek a way to get on with children who may resent their presence. These relationships show a diversity of trajectories, with no one pattern being dominant.

The relationships between nonresident parents and their children also undergo adjustment under these new circumstances. Although some research suggests that contact reduces when parents repartner, findings are mixed. The repartnering of a resident parent appears to have the greatest impact on contact. Children, however, are able to maintain multiple relationships with parenting figures; they are likely to accumulate parents rather than substitute one for another.

Key Terms

- Parentification
- Ambiguous loss
- Paternal claiming
- Permissive parenting
- Contact versus closeness versus quality of relationships
- Accumulation
- Substitution
- Loss

Discussion Questions

1. What might help children to adapt to having a stepparent in the early phases of stepfamily development?
2. How do you suggest stepparents approach the relationships with stepchildren?
3. Can you think of ways in which having relationships with multiple parenting figures might benefit children? How might they make things difficult for them?

Exercise

Talk to someone whose parents have divorced and ask them about their relationship with their nonresident parent. What helps it? What makes it difficult? What advice would that person give to parents who have separated or divorced?

Additional Readings and Web Resources

Cartwright, C. & Seymour, F. (2002). Young adults' perceptions of parents' responses in stepfamilies: What hurts? What helps? *Journal of Divorce and Remarriage*, 37 (3/4), 123–141.

Kinniburgh-White, R., Cartwright, C., & Seymour, F. (2010). Young adults' narratives or relational development with stepfathers. *Journal of Social and Personal Relationships*, 27 (7), 890–907.

White, L. & Gilbreth, J. G. (2001). When children have two fathers: effects of relationships with stepfathers and non-custodial fathers on adolescent outcomes. *Journal of Marriage and Family*, 63, 155–167.

Chapter 8

Children in Stepfamilies

> *If the stylized facts about the relationship between outcomes for*
> *children and family structure reflect the influences of variables other*
> *than family structure, then policies that affect family structure may*
> *have little or no effect on outcomes for children.*
>
> *(Ginther & Pollack 2004, p. 693)*

Objectives of this Chapter

- To describe the prevalence and living arrangements of children in stepfamilies.
- To describe outcomes and well-being for children in stepfamilies.
- To discuss explanatory factors for outcomes.
- To examine the evidence for child abuse in stepfamilies.

Introduction

In Chapter 1 we discussed the difficulties facing demographers when they assess the prevalence of stepfamilies. These difficulties are equally daunting when the numbers of children living in stepfamilies is addressed. The most recent source of data on children's living arrangements in the United States is the Survey of Income and Program Participation (SIPP), the latest survey being in 2009 (Kreider & Ellis 2011). For the purposes of the SIPP, the definition of a blended family is as follows: '*Blended families* are formed when remarriages occur or when children living in a household share only one or no biological parents. The presence of a stepparent, stepsibling, or half sibling designates a family as blended' (Kreider, p. 1).

Prevalence of Children Living in Stepfamily Households

In practice, most research addresses stepfamilies where two parents are present in the household. The definition used by Kreider widens the scope to include, for example, children who live with one parent and a step or half sibling (or both, or more). In Box 8.1. the prevalence of children in stepfamily households is shown.

Clearly, it is not unusual for children in the United States to live in a stepfamily household. There are two things to note in particular from Box 8.1:

1. Nearly 18 percent of children in two-parent households live in stepfamilies. However, they are not all necessarily stepchildren—many are the biological children of the parents in the stepfamily. Nonetheless, they live in and with the dynamics of a stepfamily. Black children are particularly likely to do so—one in five, or 20 percent of Black children live in stepfamily households.
2. Nearly 12 million children live in some kind of blended family as defined by Kreider. Over half of these do *not* live with a stepparent.

There are racial differences in these figures. For example, approximately 15 percent of Black children but only about 7 percent of Asian children are stepchildren. If we count only those children who live with two parents, 28 percent of black children and 6 percent of Asian children live in stepfamilies.

Stepfamily Households

A somewhat different picture emerges when we look at the composition of stepfamily households that children live in. If we use the broad definition of a stepfamily adopted by Kreider that includes those who live with a stepparent, and/or a stepsibling, and/or a half sibling, then

---

Box 8.1 Prevalence of children in the United States living in stepfamily households

- Of all children living in two-parent households, 10.4 percent or 5.3 million live with a biological parent and a stepparent. These children are stepchildren.
- Of all children living in two-parent households, 17.6 percent live in blended families. This figure includes children who are half siblings and are not stepchildren in the family.
- Of all the children living in the United States, nearly 16 percent (4 in every 25) live in a blended family as defined by the US census (Kreider).

> **VIGNETTE**
>
> **John lives in a blended family; Mary lives in a stepfamily but is not a stepchild**
>
> *John lives with his mother. His father lives in another state and visits him twice a year. Also living with John is Lizzy, who has the same mother but whose father lives in Canada. Although there is no father figure living in the household, by Kreider's definition this is a stepfamily household.*
>
> *Mary lives with her Mom and Dad. She also has an older half brother, Dave, who has the same mother as her but a different father. Mary is not a stepchild, but she lives in a stepfamily.*

the diversity of stepfamily households becomes even more apparent. Table 8.1 shows the kinds of stepfamily households in which children in the US lived in 2009.

There are some notable aspects of this table. First, less than half of children living in a stepfamily (defined as the presence of a stepparent, stepsibling or half sibling) live with a stepparent. This means that the majority of children living in stepfamilies so defined are living with a single parent and, in the main, half siblings, i.e. siblings with a different father or fathers.

Second, nearly one in four live with a stepparent but no stepsiblings. This represents a 'simple' stepfamily where in most cases the children of the mother live with her and her partner who is not their biological parent.

Third, there are racial differences. These are highlighted in Box 8.2.

In summary, the proportions of children who live in stepfamily households vary depending on how stepfamily households are defined. Black

Table 8.1 Living arrangements of children in stepfamilies, 2009 (SIPP data, adapted from Kreider & Ellis 2011)

Kind of step household	Total	Asian	Hispanic	Black	White
Stepparent only	23.2	30.1	19.2	21.7	25.5
Stepsiblings only	2.4	7.5	2.9	3.9	1.9
Half siblings only	48.1	44.6	52.5	56.0	43.3
Stepparent + stepsibling	5.8	2.7	3.2	4.3	7.9
Stepparent + half sibling	16.5	10.2	19.7	12.7	16.7
Stepparent, half sibling, stepsibling	2.2	0	2.3	0.8	2.5
Percentage living with stepparent	47.8	43.0	44.5	39.4	50.4

Box 8.2 Racial differences in living arrangements for children in stepfamilies

- Asian children are the most likely to be living in a 'simple' stepfamily household (stepparent only).
- Comparatively high numbers of Hispanic children live in 'complex' family structures (stepparent and half sibling).
- Black children are the most likely to live with half siblings only.
- White children are the least likely to live only with stepsiblings and the most likely to live with a stepparent.

children are most likely to live in a stepfamily; Asian children are least likely, and when they do are most likely to be living in a simple stepfamily. If a stepfamily household is defined as one in which a stepparent or a stepsibling or a half sibling lives, then more than half of children in stepfamilies do not live with a stepparent.

The Well-being of Children in Stepfamilies

Given the diversity of the families of children in stepfamilies, determining the likely impact of stepfamily living is complicated. The majority of studies that examine outcomes and well-being for children in stepfamilies compare them in one of two ways:

- with lone-parent households;
- with two-parent households.

Lone-parent Households versus Stepfamily Households

An obvious comparison in considering outcomes for children in stepfamilies is with those children living in lone-parent households, since in both they are likely to have experienced the separation and possible divorce of their parents.

A detailed analysis of research up to the year 2000 that compared outcomes for children in stepfamilies and those in lone-parent families was made by Pryor and Rodgers (2001). Overall, few differences were found in outcomes for the two groups. One that stood out was the age of leaving home and forming partnerships; English adolescents living in stepfamilies were markedly more likely than others to leave home early and to enter partnerships at young ages (Kiernan 1992).

We might expect that moving from a single-parent household to a two-parent stepfamily household would confer advantages for young people in terms of resources and numbers of parenting figures. Some recent findings indicate that children in stepfamilies do better in outcomes such as health and behavior, suggesting that these resources are beneficial; however, they do less well in emotional well-being, suggesting that the transition to a stepfamily is a stressful process for them (Sweeney 2010).

Stepfamilies versus Two-parent First Families

The second comparison is with children in two-biological-parent households, since both kinds of family include two adults. Studies that have compared well-being between these show that on average, children in stepfamilies are at greater risk than those raised in two-biological-parent homes for low educational attainment, high levels of delinquency and externalizing behaviors, emotional and internalizing problems—including suicidal thoughts—and peer problems (Barrett & Turner 2005; Hofferth 2006).

These findings are summarized by Amato, who undertook a meta-analysis of studies that had compared children in stepfamilies, one-parent families, and first families, and combined the findings (Amato 1994). Table 8.2 summarizes his findings.

Table 8.2 Comparisons of outcomes for children in stepfamilies with those in first families and lone-parent families (adapted from Paul R. Amato, 1994)

Measure	Stepfamily vs. two-parent family	Stepfamily vs. lone-parent family
Academic achievement		
Conduct problems	✔✔✔	
Psychological adjustment	✔✔✔	✔✔
Self-esteem	✔✔✔	
Social relations	✔✔	
All outcomes	✔✔✔	

Cohabiting versus Married Stepfamilies

A third comparison can be made between children living in cohabiting and in married stepfamilies. Findings are mixed. One study found no differences between young people from these two kinds of families on measures of depression and suicidal ideation (Sweeney 2007). On the other hand, differences in the incidence of smoking and drinking have been found, with adolescents in cohabiting stepfamilies more likely to do so than young people in married stepfamilies, single-parent households, and two-biological-parent households (Brown & Rinelli 2010).

In summary, the risks for children growing up in stepfamilies appear to be similar to those in single-parent families and higher than those in two-biological-parent households. Cohabitation seems to confer an extra measure of risk, perhaps because of the relative instability of this kind of household.

Are Children in Black Stepfamilies as Disadvantaged as those in White Stepfamilies?

There is some evidence that suggests that Black children in stepfamilies are not as adversely affected by stepfamily living as are White children. Early research suggested that stepfamily living was positively associated with teen pregnancy and birth for White adolescent girls, but negatively for Black teenagers (McLanahan & Sandefur 1994). One study reported that living in a stepfamily increased the likelihood of nonmarital birth by 51 percent for White adolescents, but reduced it by 8 percent for Black adolescents (Wu & Martinson 1993). Moore found that early sexual activity was less likely for Black girls living in a stepfamily than in any other family structure (Moore 1999). A recent study suggests, however, that living in a stepfamily reduces educational achievement (GPAs) for Black children in comparison with those living in two-biological-parent families (Heard 2007). No differences in depression, self-esteem or conflict management skills between Black young people living in stepfamilies and first families have been found in another recent study (Adler-Baeder, Russell et al. 2010).

More research is needed into the different dynamics for Black (and other racial groups) children in stepfamilies. It is likely that differences that exist are explained by cultural and demographic factors. Recall from Chapter 3 that Black women are less likely to marry, to divorce, to go from a cohabitation to a marriage, and to cohabit or remarry after the dissolution of a partnership (Bramlett & Mosher 2002). And because over 70 percent of Black children are born outside marriage, they are more likely than White children to experience the move to a stepfamily as their first family transition. Overall, household structure is less stable in Black families. However, cultural and kinship differences may mean that there is greater kin and community for children than there is in White communities. Furthermore, Black stepfathers may bring monitoring and supervision into the household that has a greater positive impact for children in the context of neighborhoods that have high levels of social stress.

Box 8.3 Spotlight on racial differences

According to Heard (2007):

> the fact that family structure has more enduring consequences for White children suggests that their families have not yet adapted to the sudden demographic changes that have characterized American families during the latter half of the 20th Century. The normative family structure for this group, around which family support and cultural norms are organized, is still the two-parent nuclear family. As a result, White children may have an especially difficult time adapting to a nontraditional family, whereas for minorities, these consequences are attenuated by the social resources available from kin and cultural group … family responses to structural forces are embedded in cultural practices and traditions. Racial and ethnic differences in the forces acting on these families, and in the cultural traditions on which they base their responses, help to condition the impact of family structure on child well-being.

Explanatory Factors and Determinants of Outcomes

Although the majority of research shows differences in well-being for children living in stepfamilies when compared with those living with two biological parents, it is important to note that the majority of children in stepfamilies thrive, and that the differences discussed above are risks, not inevitabilities. The differences between groups of children in stepfamilies, single-parent families, and biological parent families are small. In his meta-analysis of differences Amato has shown that although means on outcomes differ, 43 percent of children in stepfamilies do *better* than the average child in a biological family, and 43 percent of children living with biological parents do *worse* than the average child in a stepfamily (Amato 1994).

It is important, then, to consider factors other than family structure that might explain outcomes for children. Box 8.4 shows the kinds of explanatory factors that are important in understanding why risks are comparatively high for children in stepfamilies.

Selection factors include characteristics of adults who separate and enter stepfamilies, such as young age at birth of children, low socio-economic and education levels, poor mental health, and drug and alcohol

Box 8.4 Factors explaining outcomes for children in
stepfamilies

- Selection factors—factors that predate stepfamily formation and are
  characteristics of adults in stepfamilies.
- Socioeconomic factors—education and household income.
- Factors within the family, e.g. parenting, parental investment, time
  spent with children, family cohesion, parent–child and sibling relation-
  ships.
- Instability and previous transitions.
- Exposure to stress, e.g. conflict, violence, trauma, chronic stress.

abuse (Amato 2000; Nicolson, Fergusson et al. 1999). Selection can
work in two ways. First, the personalities of parents may be at least
partly genetically determined and therefore likely to be passed on to
their children. The impact can be twofold—affecting characteristics of
children, and affecting the ways in which parents interact with them.
Second, personality characteristics may impact adversely on the ability
of adults to maintain relationships with partners, contributing to family
instability. Men who become stepfathers may also have characteristics
that are not conducive to effective parenting and family stability.

Socioeconomic factors. Stepfamily households tend to have lower
household income levels, and parents to have lower levels of education
than those in first married families. This is especially true of cohabiting
stepfamilies.

Family factors include whole-family variables such as family cohesion
and negativity; parenting variables such as parenting style, and parental
investment in children in terms of time and support. The characteristics
of dyadic relationships such as parent–child and sibling relationships
may also be predictive of well-being. Some of these family factors may
be compromised in stepfamilies.

Instability and previous transitions. Not only do families and households change neighborhoods when stepfamilies are established, children
have also usually experienced previous family structure transitions.
Children born to lone mothers may have the fewest transitions—just
one into a stepfamily. Others may have many, as their parents move in
and out of relationships. The impact of transitions is discussed in more
detail later in the chapter.

Exposure to stress. The experience of family conflict and violence, of
lifetime trauma and chronic stress, may contribute more to risk of poor

outcomes for children in stepfamilies than the fact of being in that family structure. It has been found that young people in stepfamilies are more likely than those in first families to report high levels of lifetime traumas (violence, discrimination), and recent life events such as going on welfare (Barrett & Turner 2005).

Overall, these factors provide significant levels of explanation for the links between living in a stepfamily and poor outcomes. In other words, it is not living in a stepfamily per se that accounts for the risk of adverse outcomes, but factors that are often associated with stepfamily living.

In summary, children in stepfamilies face higher risks for a variety of adverse outcomes in comparison with those who grow up in two-biological-parent families. However, the majority of children thrive, and much of the link between stepfamily structure and poor outcomes is accounted for by factors that are often, but not always, associated with stepfamilies.

Contact with Nonresident Parents and Well-being

As contact between children and nonresident parents increases, attention has been given to whether or not this matters for children's well-being beyond the fact that most children and parents enjoy time together. Amato and Gilbreth undertook a meta-analysis of studies that had examined this question (Amato & Gilbreth 1999). They considered three aspects of the relationship:

- levels of contact;
- closeness of the relationship;
- the quality of the parenting by the nonresident parent.

They found that contact by itself had little impact on outcomes for children. Closeness of the relationship had some effect, but the most salient aspect is the *quality* of parenting. To the extent that a nonresident parent is involved in the life of his or her child, and supports and monitors them, the child's well-being is enhanced. This kind of parenting is **authoritative parenting**. Of course, it is difficult to be an involved, effective parent if you see your child rarely, but the main point to note is that contact by itself is not the most important factor.

Closeness to Parents and Well-being

In Chapter 7 we examined the dynamics that exist among children and the several adults with whom they have relationships in stepfamilies, including their resident parents, their nonresident parents, and their stepparents. These findings were considered in the frameworks of accumulation, substitution, and loss. Here we consider the impact of these relationships on the well-being of children and adolescents. Recall that children appear to be able to accumulate parenting figures, rather than substituting one for another—for example, rejecting a nonresident parent in favor of a stepparent. We will discuss outcomes within a framework suggested by Valerie King (2006).

King has suggested five possible hypotheses for understanding how children's relationships with two parenting figures of the same sex— for example, a nonresident father and a stepfather, might have an impact:

- The **additive** hypothesis predicts that children will benefit from relationships with both parents of the same sex, and that a close relationship with both is better than with just one or the other.
- The **redundancy** hypothesis suggests that children need positive ties to only one parenting figure in order to thrive. The addition of a second of the same sex will confer no further advantage and may in fact be deleterious if the child is put into a position where there is a loyalty conflict.
- The **primacy of biology** hypothesis predicts that the tie with their biological nonresident parent will be of most benefit to them in comparison with a stepparent of the same sex.
- The **primacy of residence** hypothesis suggests that the parent who lives with the child will be most salient for their well-being. This means that the relationship with the stepparent will be more important than the relationship with the nonresident parent.
- The **irrelevance** hypothesis predicts that neither parent of the same sex is beneficial for the child as neither will be sufficiently invested in the child to promote well-being.

Outcomes of Being Close to One or More Parents

In stepfather families, feeling close to stepfathers is as beneficial for behavioral outcomes as is feeling close to both fathers, and feeling close only to a nonresident father confers fewer benefits than being close only to a stepfather (King 2006). This suggests support for the primacy of residence. It appears, too, that boys benefit more than girls do from closeness to stepfathers and nonresident fathers.

In stepmother families two studies have found that closeness to resident fathers is important, for externalizing and internalizing behaviors (King 2007) and for self-esteem (Berg 2003). Closeness to nonresident mothers is also associated with behavior outcomes, whereas ties to stepmothers are not. Stepmothers were not relevant for behavioral outcomes, but were found to be predictive of high self-esteem. These findings confer partial support for primacy of biology since closeness to stepmothers is not associated with behavior. However, they do appear to benefit in terms of psychological well-being by being linked with self-esteem.

The outcomes of feeling close to parenting figures provide partial support for primacy of residence in stepfather families, and for primacy of biology in stepmother families. The mixed findings suggest that what might be important are the specific outcomes that are being considered. Different parenting figures may be salient for different outcomes for children and young people.

The Impact of Multiple Transitions on Children's Well-being

When a family transition occurs, the disruption to children is considerable. The composition of their household changes; adult members either leave if the breakdown is of a two-parent household, or join if the transition is from a single-parent household to a two-parent one. Siblings may move out of the same house, they may move houses and neighborhoods with the accompanying disruption to their peer groups and schools. Transitions, therefore, can be disruptive and difficult for children and teenagers.

A body of research has demonstrated a link between multiple transitions and poor outcomes on children. These include school performance, behavioral difficulties, and emotional adjustment (Goodnight, D'Onofrio et al. 2013; Martinez & Forgatch 2002), and cognitive ability and achievement (Fomby & Cherlin 2007). These effects are elevated beyond those associated with experiencing one transition such as parental separation or divorce.

As we discussed earlier, there may be at least two ways in which transitions affect children and adolescents. Selection effects mean that characteristics of parents may influence both the likelihood of transitions, and the well-being of children. Environmental effects mean that factors such as poverty resulting from transitions, and reduction in parenting quality that is associated with changes, may result in young people being adversely affected. Evidence has been found for both processes (Fomby & Cherlin 2007; Goodnight, D'Onofrio et al. 2013; Martinez & Forgatch 2002).

Some research suggests that there are racial differences in the impact of experiencing multiple transitions, at least between White and Black children (Fomby & Cherlin 2007; Heard 2007). Fomby & Cherlin found that there were no associations between the number of transitions and several outcomes (cognitive development, externalizing behavior, and delinquency) for children in Black families. They suggest that the impact of stress on Black children may be reduced by social support networks

---

VIGNETTE
Carly's experience of transitions

When Carly was ten, she had a close group of friends at school and she liked her teachers. She and her friends did things together after school, belonged to the same sports clubs and church groups. She learned piano from a teacher in the same street, and was making good progress. When she was 11, all this changed. Her parents divorced and she went to live with her Mom in a small house on the other side of town. This meant she had to change schools, and although they tried to stay in touch, she lost contact with her friends at her old school. Gradually she made some new friends at her new school, although she found it hard to break into groups that were well established by the time she came along. Her Mom couldn't afford piano lessons any more.

When she was 13, her Mom found a new partner. Carly was faced with deciding whether to move again with her Mom and partner to another part of town, or to go and live with her Dad. She and her Mom started arguing a lot, so she went to her Dad's house and started another school. She found it even harder to make friends, and missed her Mom. Her Dad's girlfriend wasn't very friendly and she felt like a visitor in the house when she was there. She went back to her Mom's house and started to enjoy a friendship with her new stepdad. However, he and her Mom separated after a year, and Carly didn't see him any more.

---

outside the household. The stress within the family is also, as we have noted, often in the context of a more stressful social context than that experienced by White children so that comparatively, family stress does not have a significant impact on their well-being.

Do Different Kinds of Transitions have Different Impacts on Children?

There has been little research that has investigated whether or not different kinds of transitions affect children differently. The main difference is whether an adult joins the household (as in the formation of a stepfamily from a single-parent household), or leaves the household (when a two-parent family dissolves). Two studies have concluded that moving into a two-parent household from a single-parent household has a greater negative impact than the other way around, especially if the two-parent household is a cohabiting stepfamily (Brown 2006; Fomby & Cherlin 2007).

In summary, multiple transitions increase the risk for children for poor outcomes, partly because of selection effects whereby characteristics of parents have impacts on both the likelihood of transitions and on children's behavior, and partly through the environmental effects associated with transitions such as reduced household income and poor parenting.

Child Abuse in Stepfamilies

One of the most contentious issues regarding stepfamilies is the question of abuse. Both mythology and common belief suggest that stepparents are likely to abuse or even kill their stepchildren. In this section we will consider the evidence for high levels of abuse and violence, and the frameworks suggested for explaining the findings.

Abuse of Children: The Evidence

Evidence suggests that children living in stepfamilies are at greater risk of physical and sexual abuse than those in first families (Adler-Baeder 2006; Daly & Wilson 1996; Giles-Sims & Finkelhor 1984). There are, however, some studies that do not find that children are overrepresented in abuse statistics (e.g. Gelles & Harrop 1991; Malkin & Lamb 1994). It is safe to say that the evidence is mixed, and that there are methodological issues that confuse any attempt at an overall conclusion. Box 8.5 shows some of these.

Under-estimation of numbers of stepchildren: some estimates of the rates of abuse include only children who live with stepparents, yet many are exposed to nonresident stepparents who may also potentially abuse them. If the numbers of stepparents used in estimates included these, then the rates go down.

Box 8.5 Issues in studying abuse in stepfamilies

- Underestimation of the number of children living in stepfamilies.
- Failure to report the relationship between the perpetrator and the victim.
- Small and nonrepresentative sample sizes in many studies.
- Socioeconomic representation.

A related issue is the number of stepchildren used in estimates. As we saw in Chapter 1, the numbers of stepchildren are probably underreported because of the ways in which data are collected. If higher estimates of stepchildren are used, the risk becomes lower.

Failure to report the relationship between perpetrator and victim: many studies base their findings on the household composition of the children, rather than the relationship between the victim and the abuser (Adler-Baeder 2006). It is possible that cases of abuse by household include those perpetrated by the biological parent or some other adult in the household. For example, a recent Brazilian study finds comparatively high levels of physical abuse of children living with a stepfather; however, the elevated risk was due to abuse by biological mothers in those families (Alexandre, Nadanovsky et al. 2010).

Small sample sizes: many of the studies that report overrepresentation of stepfamily households in abuse statistics use small nonrepresentative samples, such as women in refuges.

Socioeconomic comparisons: a high proportion of children living in stepfamilies are living in low socioeconomic households, households in which in general levels of abuse are likely to be higher than in higher socioeconomic families. It would, then, be more accurate to compare stepfamilies with first families in similar socioeconomic groups than with first families in general.

Adler-Baeder (2006) concludes: 'It should be clear that there is no conclusive answer to the over-representation question for stepchildren among physical abuse victims' (p. 78). She notes the diversity of conditions in stepfamilies and the surprising lack of rigorous research into abuse of children.

Theoretical Explanations

There are several explanatory frameworks for the possibility that there is a higher level of child abuse in stepfamily households. Five have been suggested by Giles-Sims and Finkelhor (1984):

- Social-Evolutionary Theory. As we have seen in Chapter 2, an evolutionary perspective suggests that nonbiological parents in stepfamily households will seek to concentrate their resources in their biological offspring, and are more likely to physically abuse or kill stepchildren because they do not carry their genes. Similarly, an incest taboo is unlikely to be in place for a stepparent in relation to stepchildren, so sexual abuse is more likely. Giles-Sims et al. discuss the problems with these explanations, including the likelihood that by abusing stepchildren stepparents are likely to *increase* the resources needed to look after them rather than freeing them up for their biological children, unless they kill their stepchildren (which is comparatively uncommon).

- Normative Theory. This theory also refers to the incest taboo, but to its social disapproval rather than its biological basis. However, there is no evidence that weaker incest taboos exist for stepparents than for biological parents.

- Stress Theory. Stress is known to be associated with child abuse, and stepfamilies experience comparatively high levels of stress. Stresses arise from complex family relationships and uncertainty about roles such as parenting by the stepparent. Furthermore, given the likelihood that stepfamilies experience low socioeconomic status, including low income and education, and large families, the link between stress and abuse is an obvious one.

- Selection effects. This framework suggests that the same factors that are associated with being in a stepfamily are also linked with the likelihood of abuse. These include personality factors, lack of ability to manage conflict, and being more violence-prone.

- Resource Theory. This focuses on authority held by the stepparent. As we have seen, the roles of stepparents, particularly in regard to parenting stepchildren, are ambiguous and they are likely to be challenged by children. This lack of parenting authority, it is suggested, can lead to frustration and violence on the part of a stepparent.

These theories were proposed nearly 30 years ago, and to date none of them has been identified as having the strongest explanatory power. Much attention is given to Social-Evolutionary Theory, yet it remains almost impossible to prove empirically. In a recent report on partner violence in Canadian stepfamilies, Brownridge found that no one theoretical framework explained the finding that women in stepfamilies were at twice the risk of partner violence of those in first families (Brownridge 2004). Evolutionary factors had the smallest explanatory power of four frameworks that were tested. Instead, he concluded that explanations for partner violence are multifactorial. We can assume that if children are at greater risk of abuse, the explanations for the higher levels will be similarly complex.

The Brazilian study raises some key questions. Why might it be that biological mothers are more likely to abuse their own children when living with partners who are not their children's biological parents? Stepfamily households are typically more stressful to be in than first families; it may be, too, that in focusing on a new relationship a mother's divided attention leads her to hurt her children in frustration. Research examining this finding is needed.

Chapter Summary

In this chapter we have discussed the outcomes for the many millions of children who live in stepfamily households, noting that if we count biological children who are half siblings of stepchildren, the numbers are around 12 million. In considering outcomes there are three common comparisons made: between children in stepfamily households and in two-biological-parent households; between those in stepfamilies and those in lone-parent households; and between those in cohabiting and those in married stepfamily households. Overall, children in stepfamilies are at higher risk than those living with two biological parents and at similar levels of risk as those in lone-parent households.

Much of the impact on children can, however, be explained by factors other than family structure. Selection effects, socioeconomic status, stress, instability and family dynamics associated with stepfamilies explain most of the variance in outcomes.

Multiple transitions can expose children to even greater levels of risk than living in stepfamily households, largely because of the accumulation of factors associated with transitions, and with genetically related (selection) effects.

The evidence for abuse of children being higher in stepfamilies is mixed. There are methodological issues that make it difficult to come to definitive conclusions. Inasmuch as it is higher, explanations are multifactorial, with stress possibly playing a major role.

Key Terms

- Outcomes
- Selection effects
- Environmental effects
- Additive hypothesis
- Redundancy hypothesis
- Primacy of biology hypothesis
- Primacy of residence hypothesis
- Irrelevance hypothesis
- Multiple transitions

Discussion Questions

1. What do you think is the most valid comparison to make with children's well-being in stepfamilies—children living with two biological parents, or with lone parents?
2. Discuss what changes children's experience during transitions, and how these might have an impact on their well-being.

3. How might genetic factors have an impact on children's well-being in stepfamilies?
4. Discuss the finding that biological mothers are more likely to abuse their children in stepfamilies. Why might this be, given what you know so far about stepfamilies?

Exercise

Interview someone of your age who lived in a stepfamily. Ask them what they consider the most important factors that either helped or hindered their well-being.

Additional Readings and Web Resources

Adler-Baeder, F. (2006). What do we know about the physical abuse of stepchildren? A review of the literature. *Journal of Divorce and Remarriage*, 44 (3/4), 67–81.

Fomby, P. & Cherlin, A. J. (2007). Family instability and child wellbeing. *American Sociological Review*, 72 (2), 181–204.

Giles-Sims, J. & Finkelhor, D. (1984). Child abuse in stepfamilies. *Family Relations*, 33, 407–413.

Goodnight, J. A., D'Onofrio, B. M., Cherlin, A. J., Emery, R. E., Van Hulle, C. A., & Lahey, B. B. (2013). Effects of multiple maternal relationship transitions on offspring antisocial behavior in childhood and adolescence: a cousin-comparison analysis. *Journal of Abnormal Child Psychology*, 41, 185–198.

Martinez, C. R. & Forgatch, M. (2002). Adjusting to change: linking family structure transitions with parenting and boys' adjustment. *Journal of Family Psychology*, 16 (2), 107–117.

Sweeney, M. M. (2010). Remarriage and stepfamilies: strategic sites for family scholarship in the 21st century. *Journal of Marriage and Family*, 72 (3), 667–684.

Chapter 9

Intergenerational Relationships in Stepfamilies

For many Americans, multigenerational bonds are becoming more important than nuclear family ties for wellbeing and support over the course of their lives.

(Bengston 2001)

Objectives of this Chapter

* To examine the importance of grandparents in the lives of children.
* To describe the nature of step-grandparenthood in stepfamilies.

Introduction

As life expectancy has increased in the twentieth and twenty-first centuries, so too has the likelihood that children and young adults will have grandparents (and great-grandparents) involved in their lives. At the beginning of the twentieth century, fewer than half of teenagers had two or more grandparents alive; by 2000 it has been estimated that all grandparents will be alive for a third of children up to age ten, and at least one grandparent will be alive for three-quarters of 30-year-olds (Block 2002). Another way of looking at this is that 95 percent of 20-year-olds will have at least one grandparent alive today. The shape of the population in terms of age is changing from a pyramid—where the oldest form the smallest group on top—to a beanpole, where nearly equal numbers of people are in each age group. There are many more years of shared lives for grandparents and grandchildren than there were a century ago.

The grandparent–grandchild relationship can be the most important for children, aside from those they have with parents. Grandparents become particularly salient when family transitions occur. In the first part of this chapter we will discuss aspects of grandparent–grandchild relationships that are relevant to all children, whether or not they are step-grandchildren. We will then consider relationships specific to children in stepfamilies.

The Importance of the Grandparental Relationship

Grandparents have been described variously as oral historians and family archivists; as establishing and upholding family identity; as providers of emotional support for grandchildren; as transmitters of family values and beliefs (including cultural and religious beliefs); and as providing links with past generations. Grandparents are also more freely able to be playmates, to read to grandchildren, and to take the role of 'friends', than parents can because they do not have day-to-day responsibility for them unless they are in **quasi-parenting roles**—situations where they are helping to raise their grandchildren or doing it single-handed, when parents are unable to do so.

We tend to forget that a relationship with grandchildren is closely linked to the well-being of grandparents as well as grandchildren. Grandchildren provide a sense of continuity, of genetic transmission, and a path to the future.

Conceptual Frameworks for Considering Grandparenting

Bengston (2001) uses the term 'intergenerational solidarity' to characterize relationships between generations. Box 9.1 shows the dimensions of this construct.

All of these aspects of intergenerational solidarity are impacted by separation and divorce, and by stepfamily formation. Associational, functional, and structural solidarity are all affected when parents separate. Frequency of contact may reduce, especially for paternal grandparents; families may move further away from grandparents, and the ability to provide material and emotional support reduces with both these changes.

VIGNETTE

A grandmother's perspective on having a grandchild (from *Eye of My Heart*, edited by Barbara Graham)

The day my first grandchild was born I looked at him and knew that I would never die . . . a little boy carrying my DNA, looking up at me with huge dark eyes. My lifelong dread of death fell from my shoulders like a worn-out cloak. My DNA was safe with this little boy and he would care for it when I was gone. To hell with infinity. My lifetime and his seemed like all the time anyone could ask for.

**Box 9.1 Components of intergenerational solidarity
(Bengston 2001)**

Affectual solidarity:	closeness and affection
Associational solidarity:	frequency of contact
Consensual solidarity:	agreement in values and beliefs
Functional solidarity:	giving and receiving of material and emotional support
Normative solidarity:	expectations about obligations to family members
Structural solidarity:	'opportunity structure' for interaction (geography)

When a stepfamily is formed, affective, consensual, and normative solidarities are at stake. Obligations, values, and beliefs need to be established with the new family and new step-grandparents; closeness and affection build only over time.

The theoretical frameworks in Chapter 2 also underpin this relationship in ways that are shown in Box 9.2.

It is clear from these perspectives, and from the components of the intergenerational solidarity framework, that the grandchild–grandparent relationship is likely to be central to the lives and well-being of children.

Box 9.2 Theoretical frameworks and intergenerational relationships

- Family Systems Theory: the grandparent–grandchild relationship is a key part of the overall family system.
- Family Social Capital: the social capital available to children is increased by the involvement of grandparents in their lives.
- Evolutionary Theory: biological grandparents are more likely to be involved with their grandchildren than are step-grandparents as they have a biological investment in their well-being.
- Life Course Theory: the lives of grandparents and their grandchildren are interlinked over time.

The Nature of the Grandchild–Grandparent Relationship

The nature of the relationship between children and their grandparents is affected by several factors:

- Whether they are resident or nonresident. When grandparents live with their grandchildren, they often adopt quasi-parenting roles.
- Whether they are maternal or paternal grandparents. Children tend to be closer to maternal than paternal grandparents (and especially to maternal grandmothers).
- Whether they are same sex or opposite sex grandparents in relation to the child. Children are likely to be closer to same sex grandparents.
- Race and socioeconomic status. In African-American and Hispanic families, grandparents tend to be more involved with grandchildren.

Is the Grandparental Relationship Related to the Well-being of Children?

The impact of grandparental involvement with grandchildren can be both direct and indirect. **Direct influences** act through the interactions between grandparents and grandchildren. These are characterized, in the main, by support, friendship, and unconditional love that can happen in ways that are more difficult to achieve for parents. **Indirect influences** are via the support that grandparents give to the middle generation— their adult children. These are likely to work by enabling parents of their grandchildren to have the support and resources they need to be effective parents, especially when families are in stressful circumstances.

The quality of grandchild–grandparent relationships are linked to the well-being of children. For young children the involvement and support of grandparents, and in particular maternal grandparents, has been found to reduce levels of externalizing and internalizing behavior (Barnett, Scaramella et al. 2010; Lussier, Deater-Deckard et al. 2002). For adolescents, positive emotional involvement with grandparents is linked with future pro-social behavior (Yorgason, Padilla-Walker et al. 2011). Closeness to grandparents moderates the link between stress and psychopathology—young people are less likely to report conduct and emotional problems, and more likely to show pro-social behavior if they are close to a grandparent (Attar-Schwartz, Tan et al. 2009; Flouri, Buchanan et al. 2010).

It is also found that extended family support, including that of grandparents, is associated with psychosocial aspects of educational outcomes, especially for Black young people (Pallock & Lamborn 2006). Factors such as work orientation, teacher bonding, and school values are strongly linked with extended family support, although grade point average is not—suggesting that there are other factors impacting on actual achievement.

Young adult grandchildren also benefit from support and closeness to grandparents, especially those who have grown up in single-parent families. Specifically, depression has been found to be less likely if young adults have a cohesive relationship with their grandparents (Ruiz & Silverstein 2007). It is common for single parents to live with their own parents at least for a time when their children are young. Grandparents can offer extra support and monitoring for grandchildren with whom they are living. However, the involvement of coresident grandparents is not always positive; one study found that 16-year-olds living in a house with mothers and grandmothers were more likely to drop out of school than those living with just their mother (McLanahan & Sandefur 1994). It is possible that the involvement of a grandparent sometimes interferes with the parent–child relationship, making it more difficult for parents to be effective.

Grandparents and Divorce

Separation and divorce are accompanied by the reorganization of families and relationships. When parents separate, newly separated women often move to live with their parents at least for a time. Grandparents in these situations have day-to-day contact with their grandchildren. The roles of grandparents at these times of transition have been characterized as 'watchdogs', and 'volunteer firefighters' who become important resources for grandchildren as family structures change (Ganong & Coleman 2004). Their roles may change from being friends and indulgent playmates to those of caregivers and quasi-parents. They may, too, provide financial support for their children and grandchildren.

In contrast to maternal grandparents, paternal grandparents may have reduced contact with their grandchildren after separation. The relationships between them and the children's mothers are important for facilitating or blocking contact. It has been found that when divorce occurs, levels of contact, feelings of closeness, and involvement become stronger for maternal grandparents and weaker for paternal grandparents. And as an illustration of the bidirectional nature of an adult–child relationship, in situations where grandparents lose contact with grandchildren after an event such as divorce, they are more liable to depression than those who do not lose contact (Drew & Silverstein 2007).

Grandparents play vital roles as confidants, and sources of support and stability for children when their parents separate. They are the people most likely to be confided in by children about their worries at the time of parental separation (Dunn & Deater-Deckard 2001) and they are those who children talk to most in the weeks after parents separate.

Although it is common for children to have closer contact with maternal than paternal grandparents after separation, paternal grandparents can and do play a vital role in supporting their sons. They may, for example, act as catalysts for nonresident fathers' ongoing relationships with their children by encouraging contact and helping with parenting skills. One study found that paternal grandparents were likely to compensate when their sons lacked parenting skills, to support their sons through the transition of separation, and to affirm the membership of grandchildren in the paternal family (Doyle 2010).

Grandparents are, then, sources of support and stability for grandchildren and parents when separation occurs. As with other kinds of families, their impact can be direct via helping and providing parenting resources, and indirect by supporting the middle generation and brokering fragile relationships.

Becoming a Step-grandparent

Given the high rate of repartnering by separated or single parents, it is not surprising that a considerable number of older adults find themselves in the somewhat ambiguous position of being step-grandparents. This may happen even if they have not had children themselves.

Using data from 1994, Szinovacz (1998) found that 20–25 percent of grandparents will be step-grandparents, and that 55 percent of Black couple families included step-grandparents. Of White and Hispanic couple families, 40 percent included step-grandparents. Those data are now 20 years old, so it is very likely that today many more grandparents are also step-grandparents.

Ganong (2008) have described three ways in which step-grandparent relationships are created.

1. **Later-life step-grandparenthood**: this pathway occurs when an individual forms a partnership with someone who already has grandchildren.

2. **Long-term step-grandparenthood**: remarriage or repartnering starts before step-grandchildren are born—the step-grandchild is usually the child of a stepchild whom the step-grandparent has helped to raise.

3. **Inherited step-grandparenthood**: this occurs when a person's adult child forms a partnership with someone who already has children.

In the case of *later-life* step-grandparenthood, step-grandparents may not be regarded as family members; they may be referred to as 'Dad's

VIGNETTE
Later-life step-grandparenthood

Rebecca had not married early in adulthood, but in her mid fifties she married George. George and his wife Clarissa had divorced and had three adult children. One of these, Fergus, had a daughter named Molly. Molly was 13 when George and Rebecca married. Molly then had five grandparents including Rebecca, who became a step-grandparent. She called her Rebecca and never referred to her as a grandparent. Instead she referred to her as Grandpa's new wife.

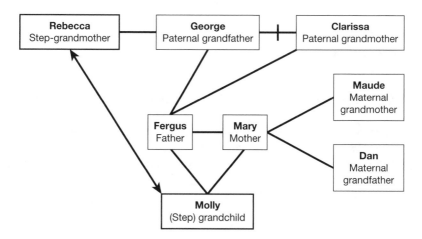

Figure 9.1 Later-life step-grandparenthood

VIGNETTE
Long-term step-grandparenthood

Jules married Sandy when her children Betty and Jim were aged two and four years. He was fully involved in their lives as a stepfather, as they grew through adolescence to adulthood. When Betty was 25 she partnered with Greg and they had a baby, Sally. Sally had six grandparents: Greg's parents, Betty's father John and his new partner Mary, and Sandy and Jules. Jules was her step-grandfather and Mary was her step-grandmother.

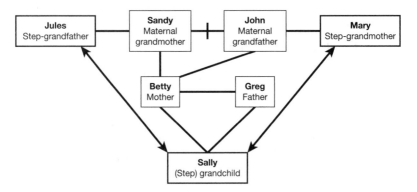

Figure 9.2 Long-term step-grandparenthood

VIGNETTE

Inherited step-grandparenthood

Mavis and Chuck have a son, Bill, who didn't marry until he was in his mid thirties. When he did, it was to Charlene who had a son from her previous relationship—Tim. Bill became his stepfather, and Mavis and Chuck became his step-grandparents. He already had four other grandparents—their father's parents, and Charlene's mother and father.

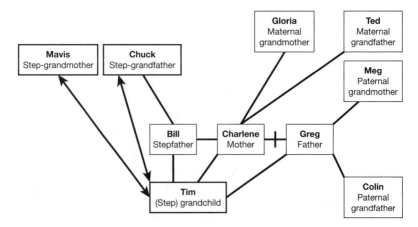

Figure 9.3 Inherited step-grandparenthood

new wife', or 'Mom's husband'. They will not have had the opportunity to form close bonds with the grandchildren's parents as they were growing up, and they come to the family when both parents are adults. There is often no incentive or opportunity to become close, and in fact they may even be seen as a threat. They may jeopardize the inheritance of children and grandchildren by being entitled to marital property; they may also present a concern about responsibility for their care should their partner die leaving adult children and grandchildren responsible for someone regarded at best as a friend.

The nature of a *long-term* step-grandparenthood relationship may be determined largely by the quality of the relationship between the adult stepchild (who is the parent of the grandchild) and his or her stepparent—now the step-grandparent. If the stepparent–stepchild relationship has been close, then it is likely that step-grandparents will have relationships similar to those of biological grandparents. Even when the stepchild–stepparent relationship has not been particularly close, there is some evidence that step-grandparents can function in a grandparenting role, if the middle generation (parents of the grandchild) accept the value of the step-grandparent–grandchild relationship (Clawson & Ganong 2002). It is easier, too, for grandchildren to enjoy relationships with a variety of grandparenting figures without loyalty conflicts since they are a generation removed (unless these are set up by, for example, biological grandparents who are jealous of the step-relationship). Most children have multiple grandparents in their lives; it is possibly easier for step-grandparents to have warm relationships with children than it is for stepparents.

Inherited step-grandparenthood is perhaps the most common way of becoming a step-grandparent, and for the child the relationship is created at the same time as they acquire a stepparent. There are several factors that have an impact on the establishment and the quality of the relationship. One is whether or not the stepparent lives with the child. If they live in the same household, then the child is more likely to have contact with the step-grandparents and to have the opportunity to build a relationship. Given that children commonly reside with their mothers after divorce and when stepfamilies are formed, they are most likely to form close relationships with their stepfathers' parents.

Another factor is the age of the grandchild. Younger children are more likely than those who are older to form a close relationship with step-grandparents since they find it easier to accept and adapt to a stepfamily household and the grandparents that come with it.

A third factor is whether or not the grandparent has genetic grand-children. If they do, then they may have difficulty treating their biological and their step-grandchildren equally.

Paths to Step-grandparenthood

We have seen that grandparenthood is not only an involuntary status in the sense that adults cannot *choose* to become grandparents (and nor do they have much influence over its timing); it is also increasingly likely that the nature of grandparenthood changes as family transitions occur. Four developmental stages have been suggested for the transition to step-parenthood that apply in particular to inherited step-grandparenthood (Henry, Ceglian et al. 1993).

1. *Accepting losses.* When separation and divorce occurs, grandparents as well as other family members experience several losses. One is the hope for an intact 'normal' family. The idea of a life-long happy marriage has to be relinquished when their child divorces his or her partner. They may, too, mourn the loss of a relationship with their child's partner, the other parent of their grandchildren, if they become estranged. Paternal grandparents in particular are at risk of reduced contact with their grandchildren. One Maori grandmother said: 'I always stay on good terms with my son's partners; they are raising my mokopuna (grandchildren)'.

2. *Accepting their child's single status.* The family life of their adult children will change as their child becomes open to new friends and new relationships. The boundaries of the family in which the grandparent has been involved become less defined and more permeable, and roles become ambiguous as the former partner either steps away from day-to-day care or becomes the main caregiver. As we have seen, contact with grandchildren is likely to increase if children live with the grandparents' child (usually their mother), or decrease if their child is a nonresident parent.

3. *Accepting the adult child's entrance into a new relationship.* The establishment of a new partnership by a grandparent's adult child brings further changes to family dynamics, including ongoing ambiguity about how relationships should function and, indeed, who is a family member. This is the point at which many adults become step-grandparents to the children brought into the family by the new partner. The relationships the children have with their biological grandparents are also likely to need particular nurturing and strengthening as this transition takes place.

4. *Establishing new relationships in the stepfamily context.* Grandparents have no choice about the establishment of a stepfamily by their adult children. They enter the family by default and may have little idea of how stepfamilies best function. Along with other family members they face the establishment of new relationships and redefinition of existing ones, while not being 'insiders' in the new family. Furthermore, if they have been in a caregiving role with the

children while their adult child is single, they may resent the new stepparent's involvement with the children.

As with step-relationships generally, step-grandparents develop warm relationships optimally with step-grandchildren by moving slowly and not expecting instant love. There is still much to learn about the establishment and development of these relationships. How, for example, do grandparents balance the relationships with biological and step-grandchildren? It is a particularly uninstitutionalized relationship. However, it may be one that is comparatively easy to form given the roles of grandparents more generally, as friends and playmates.

Contact between Children and Grandparents and Step-grandparents

An English study compared contact with grandparents and step-grandparents in children in stepfather and stepmother families (Lussier, Deater-Deckard, et al. 2002). Table 9.1 shows the findings.

There are four main patterns in these findings.

1. Children have more contact with grandmothers than with grandfathers.
2. Most contact is with resident biological parents' parents.
3. Next most contact is with resident stepparents' parents (step-grandparents).
4. In stepmother families there is more contact with step-maternal grandparents than with maternal grandparents.

The salience of the middle generation (children of grandparents and parents of grandchildren) is evident in a study that examined the impact

Table 9.1 Percentage of children who had contact with several types of grandparents (from Lussier et al. 2002)

Type of grandparent	Stepfather families percent	Stepmother families percent
Maternal grandmother	90	50
Maternal grandfather	76	47
Paternal grandmother	59	100
Paternal grandfather	44	73
Step-maternal grandmother	27	87
Step-maternal grandfather	19	67
Step-paternal grandmother	67	0
Step-paternal grandfather	58	13

of the step-grandparent–grandchild relationship on shared family identity —the sense that the step-grandparent or grandparent is an important part of the child's family (Soliz 2007). From the perspective of the young people, the extent to which their parents encouraged contact with step-grandparents was a strong predictor of how strongly they felt that their grandparent was a part of their family identity.

In a study of stepparents in England, Allan and colleagues noted the difference between biological and social grandparents that was apparent— the 'solidarity of nature' (Allan, Crow et al. 2011). Relationships were closer between grandparents and their biological grandchildren. This provides some support for the Evolutionary perspective on relationships. They conclude:

> This was more than just a question of the time in which the relationships had been active. It was a matter of kinship and of belonging. Being a natural grandparent meant a level of connection, interest and emotional attachment that could not easily be forged with other children who were not part of one's 'blood'.
>
> (p. 152)

There is almost no research that addresses the links between step-grandparent relationships and well-being in children. In one English study closeness to step-paternal grandparents was linked to lower levels of externalizing behavior in children in stepfather families, but few other significant links were found (Lussier, Deater-Deckard et al. 2002). More work is needed in this area.

The small amount of research that has addressed closeness and contact with step-grandparents suggests that overall children and young people are not as close to or supported by step-grandparents as they are by biological parents. However, the quality of the relationship, as we have seen, depends on many factors, including age and gender, whether or not the step-grandparents are maternal or paternal, and whether the stepfamily is a stepmother or stepfather family. The two most important elements appear to be the facilitation or otherwise by the middle generation parent, and whether this parent is a (step)mother or a (step)father.

Chapter Summary

Intergenerational relationships in all families are increasingly common as life expectancy increases and the population 'pyramid' changes to a 'beanpole'. Grandparents are a vital source of support for children, and especially so at times of separation and divorce of their parents and at other points of transition.

When stepfamilies form, it is common for members of the older generation to attain the status of step-grandparenthood. There are three main pathways to step-grandparenthood: later-life step-grandparenthood, long-term step-grandparenthood, and inherited step-grandparenthood. The establishment and maintenance of these relationships depends a great deal on the facilitation or otherwise by the middle generation in families. It depends, too, on the willingness of grandparents to accept their child's new partner and his or her children.

Grandparents themselves are vulnerable to the loss of connections to grandchildren that sometimes happen when parents separate. And if a grandparent has only step-grandchildren, we might speculate that these step-relationships are salient for the well-being of the older generation. The impact on them of the relationships they have with grandchildren and step-grandchildren is an area for future investigation.

Grandparents and step-grandparents are becoming increasingly common and important in stepfamilies. Their links with grandchildren are vital parts of the family system as a whole. We need to know more about how to facilitate intergenerational relationships and to optimize the contribution elders can make to the stability and success of stepfamilies.

Key Terms

- Quasi-parenting roles
- Direct influences
- Indirect influences
- Intergenerational solidarity
- Later-life step-grandparenthood
- Inherited step-grandparenthood
- Long-term step-grandparenthood

Discussion Questions

1. How might a grandparent best go about establishing a relationship with their adult child's stepchildren?
2. Discuss the conditions in which children might most easily accommodate multiple grandparenting figures into their lives.
3. Think about the outcome for children of losing a relationship with a step-grandparent, if the grandparents or their parents separate. How might they keep that relationship? Would it be good for them to do so?

Exercise

Find a grandparent, and preferably one who is a step-grandparent, and ask him or her about their experiences grandparenting children. If they have both grandchildren and step-grandchildren, explore with them the possible differences in the relationships and, if differences exist, ask them why they think they are there.

Additional Readings and Web Resources

Bengston, V. L. (2001). Beyond the nuclear family: the increasing importance of multigenerational bonds. *Journal of Marriage and Family*, 63 (1), 1–16.

Ganong, L. (2008). Intergenerational relationships in stepfamilies. In J. Pryor (Ed.), *The International Handbook of Stepfamilies: Policy and Practice in Legal, Research and Clinical Environments* (pp. 394–422). Hoboken, NJ: John Wiley & Sons.

Henry, C. S., Ceglian, C. P., & Ostrander, D. L. (1993). The transition to stepgrandparenthood. *Journal of Divorce & Remarriage*, 19, 25–44.

http://susanadamspsychotherapist.com/grandparentsandstepfamilies.html

www.ehow.com/how_2320342_be-stepgrandparent.html

Chapter 10

Gay and Lesbian Stepfamilies

In western societies homosexual couples... are increasingly deciding on parenthood and family life—and are attributed by some as 'postmodern family pioneers'.

(Zvab 2007)

Objectives of this Chapter

- To describe the demographics of stepfamilies headed by same-sex parents.
- To describe the well-being of adults and children in same-sex stepfamilies.

Introduction

Until now we have discussed stepfamilies headed by either one parent, or by two parents in heterosexual relationships. Increasingly, stepfamilies exist today that are headed by same-sex parents. They are either two men—a gay stepfamily—or two women—a lesbian stepfamily. It is important to note that the term 'gay and lesbian stepfamily' does not imply that all members of the family are gay or lesbian. Indeed, as we will see, the chances of a child having a same-sex orientation are no higher than if they are raised by heterosexual parents. For simplicity, however, we will use that term in reference to the parents in the family.

In this chapter we will discuss the demographics of gay and lesbian individuals, couples, and families. We will examine attitudes to same-sex marriage and families, challenges to well-being, and the evidence for the well-being of children in same-sex stepfamilies.

Formation and Definition

The majority of same-sex stepfamilies are formed when one parent brings children to the household who were born in a formerly heterosexual union. Because children usually remain with their mother, they are most likely to enter a lesbian-headed stepfamily, although in some cases fathers who move to a same-sex union have the children living with them. It is more common, however, for gay stepfamilies to have children as visiting members of the household rather than to have them living with them.

Other ways in which gay and lesbian stepfamilies are formed are by adoption, or through artificial reproductive technologies such as sperm donation or surrogacy. Scholars are divided about whether or not these households should be considered stepfamilies. Although they conform to the definition of one parent not being biologically related to the child or children, they resemble more closely first families who have adopted children at birth. They include biological parents, and *social* parents, in contrast to those formed after a heterosexual union, where parents are biological and *step*parents.

Research reports are sometimes vague about the genesis of the gay/lesbian stepfamilies they are studying. There is, too, a relative paucity of research on same-sex stepfamilies, especially those headed by two men. In this chapter we will review what is known to date. The discussion

---

VIGNETTE

A family with same-sex parents formed via sperm donation

Clara and June became partners when they were both in their twenties and working in professional positions. When they decided to have a child, they utilized a fertility clinic for sperm donation, with Clara being the biological mother of the baby. Although June was not biologically related to their son, she was from his birth his social mother.

VIGNETTE

A family with same-sex parents formed via separation and repartnering

When Simon and Jenny separated, Simon went into a relationship with Nick and they set up house together. Simon and Jenny's daughter, Candice, chose to live with her father and his new partner. They constituted a stepfamily in the sense that Nick was her stepparent, and she had a nonresident parent (Jenny) as well.

will be restricted to those stepfamilies formed after a heterosexual union, and which contain a child or children from that union since, as discussed above, families formed as a result of artificial reproduction techniques have more in common with adoptive first families.

Demographics of Gay and Lesbian Stepfamilies

The prevalence of gay and lesbian stepfamilies depends not only on how a stepfamily is defined, but also on how being gay or lesbian is defined. Being homosexual can be defined variously as having at least one same-sex partner after the age of 18; a mixture of same-sex and opposite-sex partners but more of the first; exclusively same-sex partners; and self-identification as gay, lesbian or bisexual (Black, Gates et al. 2000). The first definition yields higher prevalence than the last (3.6 percent versus 1.1 percent for women, 4.7 percent versus 2.5 percent for men). Given the variation in definition, the following section is based on a consensus of information from various sources and conveys patterns, if not accurate numbers.

Table 10.1 shows three aspects of prevalence that underpin lesbian and gay stepfamilies, with international comparisons.

New Zealand and the United States have comparatively high percentages of individuals who identify as gay, lesbian, or bisexual. Similar percentages of total couples are reported in all the countries covered apart from England, which has low rates; Canada reports comparatively low levels of same-sex couples who have dependent children in their households.

Table 10.1 Percentages of populations who are LGBT, in same-sex relationships, and parenting children (table compiled from several sources)

Country	Percent of population reporting being LGBT*	Same-sex couples as a percent of all couples	Percent of same-sex couples with children
USA	3.5	0.6–0.8	16.4
Canada	1.1	0.8	9.4
UK	1.5	0.4	15.8
Australia	1.2	0.7	5 percent gay, 15 lesbian (about 12 percent total)
New Zealand	4.0	0.7	8 percent males 26 percent females (about 12 percent total)

* LGBT = lesbian, gay, bisexual or transsexual.

Characteristics of Gay and Lesbian Couples

Table 10.2 shows some characteristics of same-sex couples across countries. With the exception of the United States, same-sex couples are comparatively younger than heterosexual couples. This is likely to be because of attitude change; younger adults will more readily both acknowledge their sexual orientation and feel able to form partnerships.

Same-sex couples, in comparison with heterosexual couples, are more highly educated, more likely to be in professional roles, and to have higher incomes than heterosexual couples. They are less likely to report having a religious affiliation, and are more likely to live in metropolitan areas.

In the United States and New Zealand, indigenous groups are more likely than others to be in same-sex relationships. In the United States, Black and Asian same-sex couples are comparatively less prevalent.

In summary:

- Same-sex couples are comparatively young.
- Same-sex couples are likely to be highly educated and employed.
- Most are likely to live in metropolitan areas.
- They are less likely to have a religious affiliation.

Attitudes to Same-sex Stepfamilies

There has been a remarkable change in attitudes to and acceptance of homosexuality in the last few decades. From a situation where homosexual acts were illegal and marriage between two people of the same sex was certainly not allowed, we are now in a time when same-sex marriage is legal in The Netherlands (the first to allow homosexual marriage), several other European countries, Canada, Mexico City, New Zealand, England, and some states of the United States. Other countries are in the process of legalizing same-sex marriage. Change in legislation is so rapid that it is recommended checking the Internet to see which other countries have legalized same-sex marriage (e.g. http://en.wikipedia.org/wiki/Same-sex_marriage).

In the United States attitudes to homosexuality and to same-sex partnerships have become more liberal. Research from the Pew Research Center shows that in 2011 a majority of people thought that homosexuality should be accepted by society. Table 10.3 shows recent findings from the Pew Research Center.

Support for accepting homosexuality is particularly high in women, Hispanics and Blacks, young people and college graduates, and those who do not acknowledge a religious affiliation.

Table 10.2 Characteristics of gay and lesbian couples across countries (data gathered from several sources)

Country	Age	Education	Income and occupation	Ethnic/cultural differences	Geographical differences
United States	Comparatively older than unmarried heterosexual couples (average age 48) mostly in 45–54-year age group	More likely to have higher degree or qualification	Comparatively higher income and more likely to be in professional occupations	Lower likelihood in African-American and Asian population; higher in American Indian, Hawaiian/Pacific Island communities	High prevalence in DC, California, Maine, Massachussets, New Mexico; low prevalence in Iowa, Nebraska, South Dakota, Wyoming
Canada	Most likely to be in younger age group (15–34 years)	Data unavailable	Data unavailable	Data unavailable	High prevalence in Vancouver, Toronto, and Montreal
UK*	Mostly in 25–44-year age group	More likely to have higher qualification	Comparatively high income, occupation level	Most likely to be White, have no religious affiliation	Most prevalent in London and south-west England
Australia	Comparatively younger than other couples (peak age 35–44 years)	More likely to have higher educational qualifications	More likely to have higher income and professional occupation	More likely to be born in New Zealand or North America than Australia; less likely to have religious affiliation	
New Zealand	Comparatively young —most in 35–39-year age group	More likely to have high educational qualifications	Higher income and level of occupation	Maori more likely to be in same-sex relationship than other groups	Cities; high levels of geographical mobility

* Data for individuals for the UK.

Table 10.3 Attitudes to homosexuality and same-sex marriage. From 'Most Say Homosexuality Should be Accepted by Society', May 13, 2011, the Pew Research Center for the People and the Press, a project of the Pew Research Center

Statement	Percent agreeing (March 2011)
Homosexuality should be:	
Accepted by society	58
Discouraged by society	33
Don't know	8
Gay and lesbians marrying legally:	
Favor	45
Oppose	46
Don't know	9

Changing Attitudes on Same-Sex Marriage

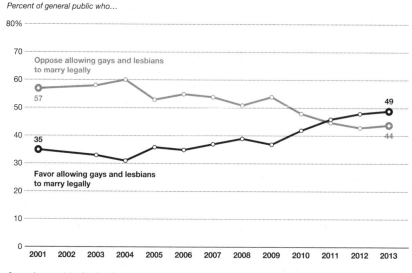

Percent of general public who...

Oppose allowing gays and lesbians to marry legally

Favor allowing gays and lesbians to marry legally

Source: Aggregated data from Pew Research Center polls conducted in each year. 2013 figures are based on one poll.
Pew Research Center • Updated March 2013

Figure 10.1 Pew Research Center, 'Changing Attitudes on Gay Marriage', © 2012, http://features.pewforum.org/same-sex-marriage-attitudes/index.php

Acceptance of same-sex partnership has also increased, with just under a half of the United States public in favor in a 2012 survey. Figure 10.1 shows that support for same-sex marriage is now higher than is opposition.

There is also a reduction in disapproval of children being raised by same-sex parents. Table 10.4 shows recent change.

Table 10.4 Changes in attitudes to same-sex parents raising children. From 'Most Say Homosexuality Should Be Accepted By Society', May 13, 2011, the Pew Research Center for the People & the Press, a project of the Pew Research Center

More gay and lesbian couples raising children . . .	Feb 2007 %	Jan 2010 %	Oct 2010 %	Mar 2011 %
Good thing for society	11	13	12	14
Bad thing for society	50	42	43	35
Does not make much difference	34	40	41	48
Don't know	5	4	4	3
	100	100	100	100

Source: Pew Research Center 2011 Political Typology, 2007–2010 trend from Pew Social and Demographic Trends. Figures may not add to 100 percent because of rounding.

Stigma

Nonetheless, gay and lesbian stepfamilies still face stigma. **Heterosexism**— the belief that only heterosexual unions are acceptable and natural—and **homophobia**—the fear and dislike of homosexuality—still exist both socially and at an individual level. It has been suggested that gay and lesbian stepfamilies experience *triple stigma* since they belong to three minority groups (Berger 2000):

- gay people;
- gay parents;
- stepfamilies.

They are vulnerable, therefore, to experiencing stigma from three sources —homophobia from society in general, stigma from the gay community for being parents, and stigma from being stepfamilies.

Adolescents and young adults who grew up in families headed by same-sex parents also experience stigma (Robitaille & Saint-Jacques 2009). All the young people interviewed in this Canadian study had experienced stigma as a result of having gay or lesbian parents; the stigma was related to their parents' sexuality, not to the fact that they lived in stepfamilies. Box 10.1 summarizes the findings.

A particular aspect of gay and lesbian orientation is the lack of family support and understanding of difference. The majority of gay and lesbian individuals are born to heterosexual parents, who often do not understand the stigma their children face. Green contrasts this with other minority groups in which parents and children share their experiences of difference, and parents are able to provide strategies for coping, such as kinscripts in Black communities, discussed in Chapter 3 (Green 2004). This poses a dilemma for gay and lesbian individuals and couples; either they stay

> **Box 10.1 Experiences of stigma in young people living in gay or lesbian stepfamilies**
>
> • Stigma was directed at them as individuals.
> • Indirect stigma operated via homophobic views expressed by others.
> • They felt abnormal in comparison with their peers.
> • Peers assumed they too would be gay.
> • They experienced dilemmas about whether or not to disclose their family structure, which led to feelings of isolation.

closeted from their parents and distance themselves in case their sexual orientation is discovered—and therefore suffer the stresses of secrecy; or, they come out to their family and risk lack of acceptance and even rejection.

How do Children and Young People View Same-sex-headed Families?

Two New Zealand studies have examined children's views of what constitutes a family, and have included same-sex parent families (Anyan & Pryor 2002; Rigg & Pryor 2007). Only 48 percent of young children considered this configuration as a real family; however, 80 percent of adolescents did. These studies were carried out a few years ago; if they were repeated they may well show higher levels of endorsement, given the changes in attitudes shown in the Pew data, and the high proportion of the New Zealand population identifying as gay or lesbian (Table 10.1).

In summary, members of gay and lesbian stepfamilies face considerable challenges in terms of being accepted as 'real' families. Stigma and prejudice still exists, although there is a steady change toward acceptance of homosexuality generally, and of same-sex marriage.

Legal Structures: Domestic Partnerships, Civil Union, and Marriage

Legally, gay, and lesbian stepfamilies are especially disadvantaged since they cannot yet marry in many parts of the world. Marriage confers rights in relation to property, tax, home ownership, medical benefits, and custody and contact rights in relation to separation and divorce. These rights are not available to same-sex couples in the same way they are to heterosexual stepfamilies and first families. This situation is, though, changing rapidly. In March 2013 nine states of the United States had legalized same-sex marriage (Connecticut, Iowa, Maine, Maryland, Massachusetts, New Hampshire, New York, Vermont, Washington, as well as District of Columbia and two Native American groups). However, the Defense of Marriage Act (DOMA) prohibits the Federal Government from recognizing same-sex marriages.

In some states same-sex couples can enter **domestic partnerships**. These are low-level legal agreements that confer only some of the legal rights of marriage, although they vary among states. California, District of Columbia, Nevada, Oregon, Washington, Wisconsin, and Maine allow domestic partnerships.

The right to enter a **civil union** exists in several states (Vermont, the first to enact civil unions; Delaware, Connecticut, New Jersey, Hawaii, Illinois, and Rhode Island). Similarity to marriage varies from state to state. In most cases, however, there are significant differences and these apply to domestic partnerships as well as civil unions.

1. Civil unions are not portable across states—in states where they do not exist they are not recognized.
2. Federal benefits are not available to those in domestic partnerships or civil unions.
3. Couples in these kinds of unions in some states and countries are not allowed to adopt children.
4. There is variable international recognition of domestic partnerships and civil unions.
5. Rights and benefits vary from state to state.

In summary, same-sex partners in the United States are able, in most states, to have legal agreements that fall short of marriage. However, in several states marriage is allowed although it is not recognized at a federal level.

Relationships and Roles in Gay and Lesbian Stepfamilies

The Adult Relationship

Research findings are consistent in showing that most same-sex couples, and especially women, hold an ideology of egalitarian roles in their relationships. They are therefore more likely to share child-care and provision for the family equally than are heterosexual couples.

Comparisons of relationship well-being with heterosexual couples tend to involve couples without children, which limits their relevance to stepfamilies. However, studies that compare relationship quality including conflict indicate that there are few or no differences among gay, lesbian, and heterosexual couples (Kurdek 2006). In one study, gay and lesbian couples reported less support from families than heterosexual couples; however, lesbian couples reported higher relationship positivity and heterosexual couples reported higher levels of negativity (Kurdek 2001). It is difficult to generalize, however, given the challenges of recruiting community samples of gay and lesbian couples.

Relationship quality and couple cohesion has been compared across three kinds of gay families: cohabiting partnerships, repartnerships, and gay stepfamilies (van Eedenfield-Moore, Pasley et al. 2012). It was found that gay stepfamilies reported the highest levels of relationship quality. The authors suggest that gay stepfamilies offer the opportunity to men who were in previous heterosexual relationships to reconcile their sexuality with their ideals about family life.

Same-sex couples also experience **relational ambiguity** as they seek to establish their relationships (Green & Mitchell 2002). Gay communities are accepting of a wide variety of relationships, including nonmonogamous relationships and relationships of short duration. Those that form stepfamilies need to find different modes of commitment and stability because of the presence of children. As civil unions and marriage become increasingly available same-sex couples may move closer to the model of heterosexual commitment (Solomon, Rothblum et al. 2004).

In summary, same-sex couples appear to be more similar than different from heterosexual couples in levels of satisfaction and well-being despite stigma, lack of norms, and low levels of social and family support (Green 2004). Limitations to the verifiability of these conclusions include the difficulty in recruiting sufficiently large samples for comparison, and ambiguity about appropriate comparison groups.

Coming Out

A significant question for parents in gay and lesbian stepfamilies is whether and when to come out in terms of their homosexuality. The issues are somewhat different for biological and stepparents. Biological parents have usually been in heterosexual relationships in which their children were born. When they form a same-sex stepfamily, they have simultaneously to adapt to a gay or lesbian identity, *and* to living in a stepfamily. They face the task of merging a socially sanctioned role of motherhood, with a socially rejected one of being gay or lesbian. Most report that internally this is not difficult—they are comfortable with those dual identities. Externally, though, their concern is to manage the process with the best interests of their children in mind (Lynch & Murray 2000).

Their partners, the children's stepparents, are likely to have developed their identity as a lesbian or gay person, and may be well integrated into the gay and lesbian community. They face a change, and sometimes a loss, of status in that community when they enter a stepfamily. They simultaneously take on the role of a stepparent, taking on a parenting identity they did not have before forming the relationship with their partner with children.

Together, the couple makes the dual transitions to becoming a couple and becoming a family at the same time, transitions which they have in common with heterosexual couples forming a stepfamily. They have, though, the third issue of coming out as gay or lesbian. They face the dilemma of whether and when to come out to their children, to their ex-partners, and to wider family and community. Of paramount concern is the well-being of their children (Lynch & Murray 2000). As one gay father said, 'My first obligation was to my kid and my gay lifestyle sort of had to fit around it' (Lynch & Murray 2000).

The possibility of their children facing discrimination, teasing and bullying if their peers know their parents are the same sex is a factor that is commonly taken into account by parents. And as we have seen earlier in this chapter, they can experience stigma when it is known that their parents are gay or lesbian. Factors that are related to coming out include:

1. Age of children: young children cope best with the information that their parents are gay or lesbian; adolescents have more difficulty because of the developmental stage they are at. They are discovering and exploring their own sexuality, and they are acutely sensitive to the opinions of their peers.
2. Concern about homophobia in relation to the well-being of their children. One parent is quoted by Lynch as saying: 'You always have to think—will the neighbors guess; if they do, will they reject my children? Have I warned my children enough about homophobia; what strategies have I given them to cope and is it enough?' (Lynch 2004, p. 105)
3. Fear of rejection by their children: when a couple decide not to come out to their children, they use strategies such as sleeping in separate rooms and not expressing affection in front of children. This restraint on their ability to behave naturally puts a stress on their relationship.
4. Custody issues (fear of losing custody of children to ex-partners if their sexual orientation is known). Coming out to ex-partners brings with it the risk that lesbian mothers, in particular, will lose custody of their children. Courts have been loathe to acknowledge the right of lesbian women to parent because of the 'risk' to their children.

Court officials now seem to be less stigmatizing about custody for gay and lesbian parents, although they remain legally vulnerable.

In general it is best for both parents and children to be 'out' despite the risk of stigma and rejection. Secrets in families and the inability to express affection is linked with depression and other negative outcomes.

Once parents are out, the family has to work out what it means to be a gay or lesbian stepfamily, and to develop coping mechanisms especially for their children. When this is successful, children appear to grow up with robust coping mechanisms and a respect for diversity in families.

Coming out to families of origin also has its risks and challenges. Experiences range from complete acceptance by parents and grandparents, to outright rejection. Often there is a process of acceptance over time, and that acceptance can be superficial—pictures of the family are not on the grandparents' walls, gay or lesbian partners are not invited to family functions, and the couple feel constrained from showing affection to each other in front of their parents. One grandmother who appeared to accept her grandson's coming out was heard at family occasions to talk of 'Ben's tragedy'. However, superficial acceptance may be the best that can be achieved given the context in which older generations grew up.

Coping Mechanisms and Resilience

Two strategies have been identified that are used by gay and lesbian families to confer resilience to the family (Oswald 2002).

Intentionality: gay and lesbian families engage in this strategy by choosing family members and friends who are supportive, with whom to spend time. They manage the disclosure of their identities carefully, and they use rituals and ceremonies (in the absence of the availability of marriage) that affirm and strengthen family relationships.

Redefinition: the main aspect of this strategy is to name relationships and individuals in ways that affirm the family as a unit. This means going beyond legal and biological relationships and definitions. An example is of a stepparent changing his or her name to match that of the biological parent and child. Redefinition also includes political action aimed at changing perceptions of homosexuality.

Well-being in Gay and Lesbian Stepfamilies

Concern is frequently expressed about the potentially negative outcomes for children raised by gay or lesbian parents. Fears are held about their psychological well-being, the parenting they receive (in relation to the perceived inability of lesbians and gay men to parent effectively), and their sexual identity and orientation. As a result, considerable effort has gone into understanding the impact of being raised by same-sex parents. To date, there is little research on children raised by gay men; stepfamilies headed by two men are sufficiently rare that it is difficult to find adequate numbers to study. Similarly, there is little or no research that examines same-sex families of color or gay and lesbian families in low socio-economic circumstances, or bisexual and transgender families. The summaries in this section, then, are based mainly on research with White lesbian stepfamilies.

Given the emotionally charged nature of the subject, it is especially important that studies are carried out both carefully and ethically. Those discussed in this chapter have been undertaken by well-recognized academic researchers. Furthermore, given the small numbers and the difficulty of recruiting representative samples for research with gay and lesbian stepfamilies, it is important to look for patterns in findings rather than relying on any one individual study.

Lesbian Mothers

The psychological well-being of lesbian mothers has been found to be similar to, or in some cases better than, heterosexual mothers. They are no more anxious or depressed, for example. Their parenting styles and quality are also the same as heterosexual mothers, and some studies find that they are less likely to smack their children (Golombok, Perry et al. 2003). Lesbian mothers are comparatively more flexible, nontraditional, and relaxed in their parenting (Patterson 2000). It has also been suggested that children whose mothers have left a heterosexual relationship and entered a lesbian one see more of their fathers than those whose mothers have entered a subsequent heterosexual relationship. This implies that lesbian mothers may retain better quality relationships with their ex-partners than do heterosexual women.

Outcomes for Children in Gay and Lesbian Stepfamilies

Research that addresses outcomes for children in gay and lesbian households is constrained by problems of recruitment and sample size. Very few children are raised by gay parents, and the numbers raised by lesbian parents are sufficiently few that it is difficult to obtain representative samples. Consequently, the majority of research has been done with convenience samples and includes, in the main, White middle-class parents. Nonetheless, there is a considerable body of studies that have reached similar conclusions. Table 10.5 summarizes the major studies that have examined the well-being of children raised by lesbian parents.

Table 10.5 Findings on psychosocial well-being for children and young people raised by same-sex parents, in comparison with those raised by heterosexual parents

Age group of children	Study details	Outcomes
7–12-year-olds	Golombok et al. 2003, study of community sample. Longitudinal study of children in hetero-, lone-parent and same-sex parent households (several references to this work available). Bos & Sandfort 2010	No differences in self-esteem, anxiety, peer relationships, behavior problems, etc. More imaginative play in children. One study had psychiatrist do blind assessments, found no differences. One study found that children in same-sex households more likely to be teased about parents' sexual orientation.
Adolescents	Wainwright, Russell et al. 2004 US adolescents. Rivers, Poleat et al. 2008 Adolescents in England	No differences in psychosocial behavior and adjustment, or in sexual behavior or relationships. Similar levels of social support *except* support from school.
Adults 18 +	Golombok & Badger 2010 Goldberg 2007	Mothers showed higher emotional warmth, young adults had less anxiety about distancing. Lower levels of depression, anxiety, hostility in young adults. Higher self-esteem and perceived scholastic competence.

Recently, a new cohort has been established, in the New Family Structures Study (NFSS), that includes nearly 3,000 young adults. Of these, 175 reported that their mother had had a same-sex relationship and 73 that their father had. It was concluded in the first report that there were significant and in most cases adverse differences between those whose mothers had had same-sex relationships, and those who had lived in intact households with biological parents (Regnerus 2012). The findings, however, need to be considered with the following major caveats.

First, most of those in the lesbian mother group had experienced transitions from previously heterosexual families to single-parent households and then to same-sex parent households. They had therefore gone through family transitions similar to those in single-parent or stepparent households. As commentators have pointed out, the differences found are as likely to be attributable to those experiences as to living with same-sex parents (e.g. Amato 2012).

Second, many had not, in fact, lived in same-sex parent households. The criterion for being in the lesbian group, for example, was that their mother had had a same-sex romantic relationship.

Third, many had experienced multiple transitions through households. As we have discussed earlier in the book, multiple transitions heighten the risk for adverse outcomes for children and young adults.

Fourth, it is not established in this study (or in many others) that the fact that parents are of the same sex is a risk factor for children. Those raised by same-sex parents, for example, are likely to be exposed to stigma. Furthermore, those in lesbian-headed families were in a diversity of family situations that included cohabitation and stepfamilies. As one commentator says, 'Confounding the same-sex relationship with a variety of family forms (and changes in family forms) is a limitation of the Regnerus study' (Osborne 2012, p. 783).

Overall, it is not viable to conclude from the findings of this study that being raised by parents of the same sex confers disadvantages for children. The findings are confounded by many other factors, including multiple transitions, ethnicity, and socioeconomic factors. The effect sizes shown are very similar to those between children raised in single-parent or stepparent households—where the same confounding factors are often in place, such as poverty and experience of transitions.

In summary, young people raised by same-sex parents in stepfamilies have not been shown to be at risk for adverse psychological outcomes, at least as a result of living with parents of the same sex. In some studies, in fact, they show elevated levels of adjustment. Disadvantages they face are external; they are likely to be teased about their parents' sexual orientation, and are less likely to seek support from their school environments—perhaps from a fear of being teased. As Amato (2012, p. 772) points out:

> If growing up with gay or lesbian parents were catastrophic for children, even studies based on small convenience samples would have shown this by now. Correspondingly, these studies demonstrate that children with gay and lesbian parents can be well adjusted, at least under optimal conditions.

Sexual Development and Outcomes

The fear that a child raised by same-sex parents will him- or herself have a same-sex orientation is common, despite all the evidence that shows that most homosexual individuals are raised in heterosexual households, and that those raised by same-sex parents are no more likely to be gay or lesbian. Table 10.6 shows the outcomes of recent studies that have investigated sex and gender outcomes.

Table 10.6 Sexual development and behavior in children and young people raised in same-sex parent households, compared with those raised by heterosexual parents

Age group of children	Relevant studies	Outcomes
Pre-schoolers	Fulcher, Sutfin et al. 2008	Gender transgressions, occupational aspirations, gender development related to parents' attitudes and behavior (e.g. division of labor), not to sexual orientation.
8–12-year-olds	Bos & Sandfort 2010	Less parental pressure to conform to gender stereotypes. Less likely to experience own gender as superior. More likely to be uncertain about future heterosexual involvement.
12-18-year-olds	Wainright et al. 2004	Romantic relationships and sexual adjustment no different from heterosexual peers.
Adults	Tasker & Golombok 1997 Goldberg 2007 Regnerus 2012	Daughters more likely to have a homoerotic relationship or attraction. More open-minded and tolerant of diversity. No more likely to be in same-sex romantic relationship. Less likely to identify as entirely heterosexual (along with young adults raised in single-parent and stepfamilies).

In summary, children raised in gay and lesbian households are no more likely to have a same-sex orientation than those raised in heterosexual homes. However, they may be more open about the possibility of homosexual attraction and experience, which is perhaps not surprising since they are not in a context where homosexuality is unacceptable. Overall, they are more likely to be heterosexual than homosexual and they are more likely to have open minds about diversity in families.

Chapter Summary

Although the numbers of gay and lesbian stepfamilies are small, they are increasing and are likely to become more common in the future. They arise mainly when a heterosexual partnership dissolves and one parent enters a same-sex relationship, bringing a gay or lesbian stepparent into the lives of his or her children.

Many of the challenges faced by gay and lesbian stepfamilies are similar to those faced by all stepfamilies, including the imperative to form partnerships *and* a stepfamily simultaneously. For gay and lesbian families, there are the added challenges of social identity change for both parents, and for children in accepting their biological parents' identity change from heterosexual to homosexual.

Gay and lesbian stepfamilies are further limited by a lack of social and legal sanctions for their families. Although they can form domestic partnerships and civil unions, and in a few instances can marry, in the majority of situations they lack the legal backing of marriage. Changes in legislation are ongoing and should be checked on the Internet. Gay and lesbian family members also face stigma from society in several ways, although it is apparent that opposition to same-sex marriage is decreasing. The 'deinstitutionalization' of gay and lesbian stepfamilies is more intense than that of heterosexual stepfamilies.

Both children and adults in gay and lesbian stepfamilies appear to function well—as well as those in heterosexual families and in some cases better. Adult relationships are reported to be of high quality, parenting quality is high, and outcomes for children are not compromised. However, most research has had to rely on convenience and small samples and more is needed on larger samples in order to understand better the dynamics of gay and lesbian stepfamilies, in order to support their resilience and well-being.

Key Terms

- Homophobia
- Heterosexism
- Sexual orientation
- Domestic partnerships
- Civil union
- Intentionality
- Redefinition
- Relational ambiguity

Discussion Questions

1. How might families formed via artificial reproductive techniques differ from those arising from separation and divorce?
2. How do egalitarian roles on the part of parents impact on their children?
3. If stigma is the only adverse aspect of being raised by parents of the same sex, how might this be addressed?

4. Why do you think children raised by same-sex parents tend to have positive attitudes to diversity?

Exercise

Find some websites that address the issue of same-sex marriage. What arguments are made on both sides of the debate? How informed are they by research?

Additional Readings and Web Resources

Amato, P. R. (2012). The well-being of children with gay and lesbian parents. *Social Science Research*, 41, 771–774.

Berger, L. M. (2000). Gay stepfamilies: a triple-stigmatized group. *Families in Society*, 81 (5), 504–516.

Biblarz, T. J. & Savci, E. (2010). Lesbian, gay, bisexual and transgender families. *Journal of Marriage and Family*, 72 (June), 480–497.

Oswald, R. F. (2002). Resilience within the family networks of lesbians and gay men: intentionality and redefinition. *Journal of Marriage and Family*, 64 (2), 374–383.

Regnerus, M. (2012). How different are the adult children of parents who have same-sex relationships? Findings from the New Family Structures Study. *Social Science Research*, 41, 752–770.

Robitaille, C. & Saint-Jacques, M. C. (2009). Social stigma and the situation of young people in lesbian and gay stepfamilies. *Journal of Homosexuality*, 56, 421–442.

http://en.wikipedia.org/wiki/Same-sex_marriage

Chapter 11

The Stepfamily as a Unit
Challenges and Well-being

The crux of the need to measure family wellbeing is that the family is an interdependent caring unit that impacts on the wellbeing of its members across the age range, from cradle to grave.
(Wollney, Apps et al. 2010)

Objectives of this Chapter

- To discuss stepfamilies as whole family units.
- To address the definition of family well-being.
- To examine well-being in the stepfamily group.

Introduction

In this chapter we will approach the stepfamily as a unit—as a whole, rather than as individuals or dyads. In practice, the study of a whole family unit is much more complicated than the examination of dyadic (two-person) or individual factors. Perhaps for that reason empirical research that undertakes rigorous investigation is rare. However, there exist conceptual frameworks and some work within those, that can inform our understanding of the complicated group that is a stepfamily. The fact that stepfamilies are often multihousehold families adds to the complexities of the task. As in all families, the ways in which the family group—however defined and structured—functions has a far-reaching impact on the well-being of individuals in that group.

It should be apparent by now that the stepfamily as a 'unit' is a far more complicated phenomenon than a first family. Just who constitutes the family is often contested, and the establishment and maintenance of nurturing relationships within the stepfamily is far from straightforward. Nonetheless, the formation and identification of 'the family' is as important for the well-being of stepfamily members as it is for other family structures. In Chapter 2 we discussed boundary ambiguity; recall that *physical* boundary ambiguity refers to disagreement among family members about who actually lives in the house, and this can occur when a child spends more or less equal amounts of time in a mother's and father's home. *Psychological* ambiguity refers to disagreement about whether or not an individual is a member of the family.

In considering the family as a unit, we need to identify variables that might be examined. Box 11.1 shows a list of variables that are often measured in whole-family approaches.

In this chapter we will consider some of these variables, and how they relate to family well-being. In addition, we will examine well-being in stepfamilies and how it might be enhanced and sustained.

Challenges for Stepfamilies

By now it will be very obvious that stepfamilies face challenges that arise from their histories and their complexity. In Chapter 12 we will summarize again those aspects of stepfamilies that characterize their differences from first families.

Patricia Papernow, a stepfamily therapist, has identified five major challenges for stepfamilies as they become established, from a clinician's perspective (Papernow 2008). They are:

- *Insider–outsider roles*—the biological parent is stuck as an 'insider', and the stepparent is often stuck as an 'outsider'.
- *Children bring losses and loyalty binds*—children have lost their day-to-day relationship with one parent, and can fear the loss of the other relationship as a new partner moves into the life of their resident parent.
- *Parenting tasks can polarize adults in a stepfamily*—biological parents are close to their children and have established parenting styles, while stepparents have to forge parenting styles.

Box 11.1 Whole-family variables

- Cohesion
- Communication
- Family identity
- Family belonging
- Commitment
- Shared activities
- Mutual support

- *A new family culture has to be established*—each adult, and children too, comes to the new family with patterns of rituals and behavior that have to be adapted to the new family form.
- Ex-spouses have to be incorporated into the life of the new family.

In a qualitative study of stepfamilies in which 90 interviews were carried out with parents, stepparents, and stepchildren, Golish identified seven key challenges that were apparent from the interviews (Golish 2003). They were:

- 'Feeling caught'—usually children with loyalty binds between their biological parents.
- Regulating boundaries with noncustodial families.
- Ambiguity about parenting roles (particularly for stepparents caught between roles of friendship and parenting).
- 'Traumatic bonding'—the bond formed between mothers and, in particular, their daughters in the period between divorce and repartnership. This made the position of the stepparent in the family difficult to establish.
- Vying for resources—space, territory, money.
- Discrepancies in conflict-management styles.
- Building solidarity as a family unit—'the feeling that everybody's working toward the same goals'.

Box 11.2 compares the challenges from two perspectives. The five identified by Papernow are also listed by families in the Golish study; two others are added—vying for resources and conflict management.

Box 11.2 Comparison of challenges for stepfamilies from clinical and family member perspectives

Golish Challenges	*Papernow Challenges*
Feeling caught	Losses and loyalty binds
Regulating boundaries	Ex-spouses incorporated
Ambiguity about parenting	Parenting tasks
Traumatic bonding	Insider–outsider
Building solidarity	New family culture
Vying for resources	
Conflict management	

In summary, stepfamilies as a group face difficulties and tasks that differ from those encountered by first families as they form. Some of them are directly related to individuals and dyads; all of them ultimately affect the family as a whole and may have to be addressed by the family as a group.

Developmental Trajectories of Stepfamilies

The diversity of stepfamilies means that they develop a sense of being a family at different rates and in different ways. A study that interviewed stepfamily members focused on describing trajectories of development, rather than prescribing them from a conceptual framework (Baxter, Braithwaite et al. 1999). Parents, stepparents, and young adults who grew up in stepfamilies, were asked about **turning points** in the paths taken by their families toward a sense of 'feeling like a family', or family identity. A turning point is described as 'a transformative event that alters a relationship in some important way, either positively or negatively' (Baxter, Braithwaite et al. 1999). Turning points were identified as either positive or negative in the experience of the interviewees, and the ratio of positive to negative turning points was calculated. Participants indicated the extent to which they 'felt like a family' as a percentage, ranging from 0 to 100 percent.

Five trajectories were identified, and the turning points that characterized the pathways were noted. Box 11.3 shows the five trajectories.

The *Accelerated* trajectory was described by 31 percent of the families interviewed. This was a pattern of relatively fast progress to 100 percent 'feeling like a family'. The ratio of positive to negative turning points for them was 3.6 to 1.

The *Prolonged* group—27.5 percent of the sample—moved more slowly than the accelerated group, and started from a lower level of feeling like a family than they did. This group had a ratio of 3.1 to 1 ratio of positive to negative turning points.

The *Stagnating* group (14 percent) reported a ratio of 2 to 1 positive to negative turning points. They started and remained at a low level of feeling like a family.

The *Declining* cluster comprised 6 percent of the cases, and started at the highest level of feeling like a family of all the groups, declining thereafter to a low level. They had a negative ratio of positive to negative turning points.

The *Turbulent* group comprised 21.6 percent of the sample. Their trajectory resembled a roller coaster. Their ratio was 1.7 positive to 1 negative turning points.

'Feeling like family' was described by participants as including support, openness, comfort, caring, and sharing. Those in the five trajectories

Box 11.3 Types of trajectories for stepfamily development

Trajectory	Most Prevalent Turning Points
Accelerated	Changes in household composition
	Holidays and special celebrations
	Quality time
Prolonged	Changes in household composition
	Conflict and disagreement
	Holidays and special celebrations
	Quality time
Stagnating	Changes in household composition
	Conflict and disagreement
Declining	Changes in household composition
	Conflict and disagreement
	Holidays and special celebrations
	Family crisis
Turbulent	Changes in household composition
	Conflict and disagreement
	Holidays and special celebrations
	Quality time

reported different levels of feeling like family; the accelerated group were highest, followed by the prolonged and turbulent groups. The declining and the stagnating groups were lowest in feelings of family identity.

In summary, stepfamilies move at different paces and on different trajectories toward achieving a sense of family identity. Some may never feel completely like a family, while others move rapidly toward a sense of being a cohesive family group.

Family Well-being

The concept of well-being is fundamental to studies of all families, yet like the term 'family' itself, it is remarkably difficult to define. Definitions vary according to the purpose of the definition, and the perspectives of those trying to define it. Two approaches are commonly taken. First, because individual well-being is comparatively easy to conceptualize and measure, family well-being often relies on indicators of well-being in individual family members. This, however, misses the important point that whole-family functioning differs from that of individual members, and the sum of the individual well-being is not the same as family well-being as a whole.

A second way of approaching family well-being depends on identifying measurable factors such as income and housing, and inferring well-being from their presence or absence. Although these external resources are vital for the optimal functioning of families, they do not by themselves define well-being.

Although definition is difficult, it is safe to conclude that 'family well-being is overwhelmingly thought of as a multi dimensional concept encompassing different domains, and as an amalgamation of different types of wellbeing—physical, social, economic and psychological' (Wollney, Apps et al. 2010).

In this chapter the concept of well-being is considered using a Family Systems perspective, which emphasizes the interdependence of personal relationships and interactions within families (see Chapter 2). Objective measures of well-being such as environment, living conditions, financial resources and social networks are obviously crucial for well-being, but will not be discussed here. They are represented in the model as 'resources'.

Figure 11.1 shows a framework for thinking about well-being in all families, but especially in stepfamilies. We consider its components below.

Family Social Capital

In this model, Family Social Capital—defined as 'the stock of good will created through shared norms and a sense of common membership upon

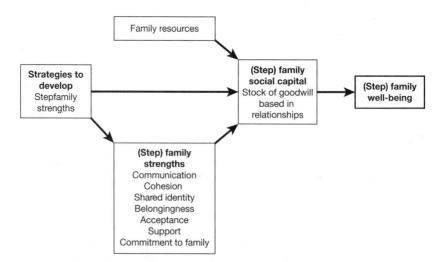

Figure 11.1 A model of well-being in families

which individuals may draw in their efforts to achieve collective or personal objectives' (Furstenberg & Kaplan 2004)—facilitates **family well-being** by enabling family members to utilize their strengths and resources optimally. It is entirely feasible that families have access to ample resources, and have strengths as both individuals and a group, but both resources and strengths may not be brought into play in order to enhance the well-being of either the group or of the individuals in it. Family Social Capital, then, is the store and utilization of strengths available to families.

Family Strengths

Several ways of thinking about family strengths have been offered by scholars, all of which refer to group variables such as those shown in Box 11.1. They include communication, cohesion, shared family identity, belongingness and acceptance, mutual support, and commitment to the family.

How do Stepfamilies Compare with First Families on these Strengths?

The few studies that have compared cohesion and similar constructs between stepfamilies and first families report mixed findings. Some find lower levels of cohesion in stepfamilies (Barber & Lyons 1994; Barrett & Turner 2005); others find no differences (Smith 1991). Two factors appear to be important. First, the *length of time* a stepfamily has been in place has an impact on cohesion. Early in its formation cohesion is reported to be lower than in first families. However, as children become older, cohesion is both reported and observed to be no different from that in first families (Bray & Berger 1993). In adolescence, however, family cohesion reduces in both kinds of family but reduces more in stepfamilies.

The second factor is *how cohesion is measured*. If adolescent accounts are considered, then findings are likely to show that stepfamilies have lower levels of cohesion. However, one study used reports of cohesion from three members of stepfamily households (two parents and an adolescent). If adolescent accounts were included, then differences were significant. If, though, adults' accounts only were used, there were no differences (Smith 1991). Teenagers in stepfamilies appear to feel less closeness in their families than their counterparts in first families, although it may depend too on how old they were when the stepfamily was formed.

It is perhaps noticeable that the references cited here are, with one exception, at least 18 years old. This suggests that more recent research is desirable in this area.

Impact of Family Strengths on Outcomes for Children in Stepfamilies

Studies that have examined the impact of family strengths such as cohesion on the well-being of children and adolescents have all found that whole-family variables such as cohesion, support, and family time are linked with well-being (Sweeting, West et al. 1998; Barrett & Turner 2005). For example, children's assessments of stepfamily cohesion predict high levels of prosocial behavior and low levels of behavior problems (Pryor 2004). In turn, a sense of belongingness appears to be associated with the quality of relationships young people have with parents and stepparents in stepfamilies (Leake 2007; Pryor 2004).

Strategies for Developing Family Strengths

An effective way of identifying strategies that are associated with strength in families is to examine those used by families who see themselves as strong. (Another way is to decide as a researcher what is an indicator of strength, and some researchers do this.) Tamara Golish (2003) divided stepfamilies into two groups—those in which all members saw the family as strong, and the rest where at least one family member did not. She then investigated the ways in which the two groups differed according to the communication strategies they used. Box 11.4 shows a list of activities based on her findings.

The strategies marked with an asterisk are of particular relevance to stepfamilies, and pose specific challenges for them. The *creation of shared meaning* can be thought of as an outcome of the others. For example,

---

Box 11.4 Some strategies used by stepfamilies in building family strengths

- Spending time together/shared activities.
- Creating shared meaning/common ground.*
- Blending old and new family rituals and developing new ones unique to the family.*
- Communicating a sense of inclusion.*
- Confronting problems, redefining conflict as positive.
- Establishing boundaries and clear rules.*
- Supportive communication.
- Humor.
- Openness.

communicating a sense of inclusion, family rituals, gradual construction of the definition of the family, and establishing boundaries are all pathways to shared understandings of what the stepfamily stands for and values.

Creating shared meaning involves *fostering a sense of inclusion* in those who are considered to be members of the family. This calls for ongoing discussion among members of the new stepfamily about who belongs. This is a complicated process for members of stepfamilies since children are often members of more than one family, and come and go from households. In turn, this is linked to who is 'in' and who is 'out' of the family, and to boundary ambiguity as discussed in Chapter 2. Inclusion might stretch to family members who do not live regularly in the stepfamily household, such as stepgrandparents and stepsiblings.

Establishment of rules and boundaries involves the relationship with ex-spouses, and with children with nonresident parents. Permeable boundaries that allow communication and clarity about roles and openness seem to be most effective in developing strong stepfamilies.

The process of *co-constructing a 'natural definition'* of the stepfamily is one that is best taken slowly. Agreement to disagree can be adaptive in this regard, and the gradual emergence and agreement about who is 'family' may take years. In some cases agreement may not happen at all. Flexibility, the agreement to disagree, and the gradual emergence of family boundaries is likely to be optimal for the long-term well-being of the stepfamily.

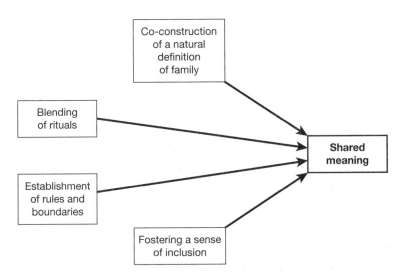

Figure 11.2 Relationships among communication strategies in strong stepfamilies

The Blending of Family Rituals

Family rituals are patterns of behavior that take place in all families and serve to develop and sustain shared beliefs and understandings. A typical example of a family ritual is the pattern of behavior that accompanies Christmas or other religious observances. At another level, reading to a child every night becomes a ritual that holds meaning for both parent and child, and tends to follow a similar pattern each time. Pages are turned in the same way, and the same words are read. A child quickly notices if a parent tries to skip passages, and the activity takes on meaning for both people.

Three functional aspects of rituals have been identified (Pryor 2006):

- to develop, convey, and at times modify meaning;
- to link family members in a shared understanding of their family identity; and
- to provide opportunities for reflection on past, present and future, and to convey stability and continuity.

In first families, couples establish their own unique rituals before children are born and their children are inculcated into the microculture that is distinctive to that family. Ways of celebrating birthdays and Christmas are developed and as the family grows so does a shared history upon which they can draw. As Serpell puts it: 'Each family co-constructs its own unique intimate culture, blending the specifics of its constituent personalities, its particular ecological niche, and its own history of shared events' (Serpell, Sonnenschein et al. 2002).

Implicit Rituals

Although many rituals are explicit and intentional—for example, the celebration of a religious observance—some are emergent and implicit. The latter grow from routines of behavior that have the potential to foster communication and to become imbued with meaning by the participants. As an example, shopping together on a Friday night may start as a functional activity with the purpose of stocking the refrigerator. Over time, however, it may become important as a time when family members talk together, make decisions about food, and develop a shared sense of what *this* family likes. It becomes important for its meaning as well as for its functionality.

Rituals in Stepfamilies

As a stepfamily is formed, two sets of routines and rituals are brought to the new household and family members need to bring these together in ways that hold meaning for everyone. Successful rituals that develop in stepfamilies embody aspects of both old and new families. And children who spend time in two households need to be able to hold and maintain separate sets of rituals. As explicit rituals such as Christmas are negotiated and new forms of celebration developed, so too do implicit rituals at both dyadic and whole-family levels. For instance, a stepparent may drive a stepchild to sports practice every week—a routine activity with the function of conveying the child to the practice field. Driving provides a chance for communication, and extension of the activity to, for example, include a hamburger stop on the way home can put in place a routine that starts to become imbued with meaning for them both and thus becomes a ritual.

Both implicit and explicit rituals hold the potential to help stepfamilies to form a new identity, to develop cohesion and communication, and to develop a sense of inclusion, to negotiate roles and define and reinforce membership. The establishment of flexible boundaries can be an important part of the role of rituals.

It is notable that of the trajectories of stepfamily development described earlier in the chapter, those reporting the highest levels of family identity were those who also reported high levels of quality time spent together. Holidays and special celebrations, reflecting the involvement of rituals, were also turning points for the three groups highest in feeling like a family.

In summary, well-being in stepfamilies is fostered through open communication and the development of shared meanings of what it means

---

VIGNETTE
Development of a ritual in a stepfamily

Soon after Jodi's new stepfather Bill joined the family, he suggested that she and he do the dishes on Sunday nights by themselves. Jodi thought this was weird, and did it only because she knew her mother wanted her to. At first they didn't talk; she dried the dishes in silence. After a few weeks he started asking her about school. She found herself telling him about her friends, and about some things she couldn't easily tell her mother. As the time passed she began to look forward to Sunday nights, and she and Bill talked freely about her life, and about his before he joined the family. The routine of doing dishes together became an important ritual for them both, and helped them to become close as friends and family members.

to be a family. The complexities of stepfamilies provide unique challenges beyond those of first families. 'Strong' stepfamilies are typified by the co-construction of a definition of the family, the development of rituals, the establishment of permeable boundaries between households, and the fostering of a sense of inclusion or belonging for individuals in the family.

Chapter Summary

When the family is taken as the unit of interest, we find that whole-family variables such as cohesion, identity, and belonging come to the fore. There is no doubt that they are much more than a sum of individual characteristics or factors. For stepfamilies, the development of optimal whole-family well-being presents challenges that are not apparent for first families. These challenges arise from the histories that individual members bring to the family, from the likelihood that stepfamilies are multihousehold families, and from the complexity of relationships that exist both within and outside the main household.

The definition of well-being is contested and difficult to specify. It encompasses measures of both external and internal, objective and subjective, aspects of families. Most definitions include its multidimensional character, and the optimal functioning of families as a whole and as separate individuals.

Family strengths include internal dynamics of cohesion, support, communication, and time spent together. This chapter has discussed ways in which family strengths can be developed and sustained. These include communication, and the use of rituals.

Finally, there is a dearth of research that approaches stepfamilies from a perspective of whole-family well-being. It is a promising area of investigation given that the family as a group is the site of strength and stability for its members.

Key Terms

- Family well-being
- Family identity
- Cohesion
- Commitment
- 'Feeling like a family'
- Creation of shared meaning
- Implicit rituals
- Explicit rituals
- Turning points

Discussion Questions

1. Why is it difficult to study empirically whole-family variables such as cohesion? What methods, e.g. multiple informants, might be useful?
2. How do the findings here fit the Family Systems Framework discussed in Chapter 2?
3. Think of a ritual in your family that has developed gradually and might be described as 'an implicit ritual'. Discuss how it came to take on meaning for the participants.

Exercise

Interview a person who is a member of a stepfamily and ask them to identify the factors that make their families strong, and the challenges faced by the family in developing its sense of identity. See if their experiences are similar to those discussed in this chapter.

Additional Readings and Web Resources

Baxter, L. A., Braithwaite, D. O., & Nicholson, J. H. (1999). Turning points in the development of blended families. *Journal of Social and Personal Relationships*, 16 (3), 291–313.

Golish, T. D. (2003). Stepfamily communication strengths: understanding the ties that bind. *Human Communication Research*, 29 (1), 41–80.

Papernow, P. (2008). A clinician's view of 'stepfamily architecture'. In J. Pryor (Ed.), *The International Handbook of Stepfamilies: Policy and Practice in Legal, Research, and Clinical Environments* (pp. 423–454). Hoboken, NJ: John Wiley & Sons.

Chapter 12

Interventions for Stepfamilies

Stepfamilies don't blend; they curdle.

(Stepmother)

Objectives of this Chapter

- To address issues of intervention and therapy.
- To discuss evaluation of interventions.
- To consider models of therapy for stepfamilies.

Introduction

The earliest writing about stepfamilies was done mainly by clinicians, who were aware from their clinical work that the stepfamilies in their offices were facing difficulties somewhat different from those of couples in first families. Much of what we know about stepfamilies arises from this early work, and today it is complemented by an increasingly large body of research-based writing.

In this chapter we will discuss some of the kinds of intervention that exist, issues of evaluation, and we will focus on a few major models of intervention that have been evaluated. We will also describe therapeutic models for stepfamilies.

So far in this book we have discussed and examined many aspects of stepfamilies that distinguish them from first families. A summary list of these is in Box 12.1.

These distinguishing features need to be kept in mind as we examine factors relevant to intervention and therapy.

The Stepfamily Cycle

Patricia Papernow, a stepfamily clinician, has described three phases of stepfamily development that are useful as frameworks in considering intervention and therapy (Papernow 2008).

Box 12.1 Characteristics of stepfamilies that distinguish them from first families

- Adult partners have been in relationships before, and so come to the family with previously established patterns of relating.
- They usually do not have a 'honeymoon' period in which to establish their relationship because children are present.
- The parent–child relationship is disrupted as both adapt to changes in family configuration.
- The stepparent–stepchild relationship has to be established in a situation where they are likely to be relative strangers, and one or both may be reluctant participants.
- All family members may need to incorporate the existence of at least one nonresident parent into their lives.
- Children may have to incorporate step- and half siblings into their family constellations.
- The family as a whole has to learn to function as a family unit, but with dynamics that necessarily differ from those in first families.

1. **Early stages:**
   Fantasy: the invisible burden. These are fantasies that the new family will solve previous problems, will be harmonious, children will love and be loved, and all will be well.
   Immersion: the reality of stepfamily living starts to exert its influence on family members (jealousies, loyalty binds, blame and confusion).
   Awareness: adults in particular become aware of the issues and can articulate them to themselves and to others—if successful, this stage is characterized by curiosity and compassion.
2. **Middle stages:**
   Mobilization: differences begin to be discussed openly and change discussed. This stage is difficult if there are communication difficulties.
   Action: beginnings of resolving differences and finding solutions to problems.
3. **Later stages:**
   Contact: in this phase real intimacy in relationships becomes established. There is agreement on how a relationship might be—for example, a stepparent may be accepted as an 'intimate outsider', which works for both stepparents and stepchildren.

Resolution: in this final phase a sense of togetherness and family identity is reached that serves as a foundation for facing future challenges as a family.

Papernow has also pointed out the importance of **middle ground** for couples and families. Middle ground encompasses areas of agreement where joint action is easy and does not need discussion because of shared understandings. In first families middle ground is established before children are born; in stepfamilies middle ground exists between parents and children but is thin between the parents in the family. Children in first families enter this established middle ground of shared under-standings, rituals, and values. There is a mini-culture in place by the time they are born, and are easily integrated into it. Stepfamilies do not have this advantage; instead, most understandings are up for negotiation and discussion, especially in the early stages.

The dimension of time is clearly important. Middle ground is not present in the early stages of stepfamily formation and development. Furthermore, the stepfamily cycle can vary in the length of time it takes to reach resolution. As we saw in Chapter 4, trajectories and endpoints vary. Some families move relatively quickly toward a sense of family identity and belonging; others may never achieve it.

Interventions and Therapy

Therapists and counselors have worked with stepfamilies for many decades. However, it is comparatively recently that interventions have been either designed or examined systematically. Evaluation of interven-tions is even less common. There are two issues to be considered in regard to interventions.

1. **Education versus therapy:** Interventions can have at least two purposes. One is to provide *information and support* for stepfamily members, especially before formation or in the early stages as families are learning how to function as a stepfamily. A second is *therapy*, in which problems that have arisen for family members are addressed. Of course, these can overlap—it is very likely, for example, that therapeutic interventions will include components of education. Often stepfamilies do not seek help either before or in the early stages of being a family, because there is a paucity of support available and they do not know where to seek help, or because they are reluctant to acknowledge problems until they become significant. It is widely accepted that there is a need for early education for stepfamilies in order to avoid the need for therapy for serious problems.

2. **Couple focus versus parenting focus:** Over time there have been differing views about where the focus of interventions should be. Most

---

VIGNETTE

Two scenarios for stepfamily interventions

Joy and Glenn were both excited and hopeful when they joined their families together as a stepfamily. From the start they encouraged their children to love each other, to think of themselves as part of an 'ordinary' family, and to form close relationships with their stepparents. They were dismayed when the children refused to accept the new household as a happy family, and became quarrelsome and unhappy. In turn, their relationship started to come under strain as they disagreed about how to handle the conflict. The family stress became so bad that one of the children left the home and went to live with her father, while one of Glenn's sons developed behavior problems at school. Finally, after 18 months of struggling, Joy and Glenn sought the help of a family therapist. It took many months to repair the damage that had been done because of their lack of understanding about stepfamily relationships.

In contrast, Fred and Georgina were aware from the start that setting up their new household would hold its challenges. They were able to find a course being run at their local church, which was designed for people intending to form stepfamilies or in the early phases of stepfamily living. The course gave them both information and skills that helped them to move slowly toward family unity, and to listen to how their children were feeling.

---

family therapists advise attention to the marital/partner dyad and some stepfamily therapists have agreed. However, the stepparent–stepchild relationship is also pivotal to the well-being of the family and that, combined with the challenges to the parent–child relationship, suggests that a parenting focus may be more appropriate. It is generally accepted that in first marriages the inter-parental relationship is the basis of family well-being. In stepfamilies, however, it may be the case that the stepparent–stepchild relationship is pivotal to both family functioning and the quality of the inter-parental relationship.

Partnership Interventions

Several findings from research suggest that the couple relationship in stepfamilies is fragile. First, they show lower levels of commitment to the relationship than do first-marriage couples. Second, they tend to have relatively inefficient communication skills. Third, they come to the relationship with differing expectations about how a family should function. Lastly, they often have difficulty in reaching consensus about how children should be parented.

One approach to the support of the adult partnership is to consider the factors that predict strong relationships in stepfamilies. Utilizing an *eco-systemic* framework, similar to Family Social Capital and Family Systems theories, the following predictors have been identified (Falke & Larson 2007).

Background and contextual factors:

- first-marriage influences (stepchildren, stepfamily complexity, economic demands of first family);
- multiple partner transitions (personality traits, relationship styles, emotional health);
- current contexts (social support, financial viability).

Individual traits and behaviors:

- attitudes toward partner's ex-partner;
- attachment to ex-partner.

Couple interactional processes:

- couple consensus (e.g. family rules);
- role ambiguity and strain.

These factors provide a layered framework within which partnership interventions might be designed.

An example of a major intervention, which focuses on the quality of the marriage or couple relationship, has been initiated by the US Government through the Healthy Marriage Initiative (HMI see www.acf.hhs.gov/programs/ofa/resource/the-healthy-marriage-initiative-hmi). As part of the HMI, a program called 'SmartSteps' has been developed for stepfamily couples (see http://ncsu.edu/ffci/publications/2008/v13-n3-2008-winter/higginbotham-adler.php).

Parenting Interventions

Two major interventions have focused on the parenting relationship, and parenting skills. One is the Oregon model, based on **Social Interaction Learning Theory** (SIL), (Forgatch, DeGarmo et al. 2005). It is based on the assumption that parenting skills are a vital interface between the context in which families live and the well-being of children. SIL identifies four core relational skills:

- communication;
- effective problem solving;
- positive and supportive social exchange;
- conflict resolution skills.

The second is a series of interventions carried out in Australia (Nicholson, Sanders et al. 2008). They are based on **Behavioral Family Interventions** (BFI) that encourage appropriate positive and negative reinforcement of children's behavior by parents. Both of these are discussed in more detail later in the chapter.

Evaluation of Interventions

Although many interventions have been developed for stepfamilies, the majority are either not evaluated, or the evaluation methods are inadequate. Box 12.2 shows some of the issues that need to be considered in evaluations.

Sample size and control groups: rigorous evaluation should include large sample sizes, and **control groups**. A control group is one that does not receive the intervention that is being evaluated. Usually, control groups receive no information, or are on waiting lists to be part of the intervention under examination. They may, depending on what is being evaluated, receive the intervention in a different format if one aspect of the evaluation is assessing the presentation format. For example, one group may have the intervention delivered by professionals, such as psychologists or counselors, while the control group obtains the information on line.

Box 12.2 Issues for evaluating intervention studies

- Sample sizes
- Control groups
- Randomized allocation to treatment and control
- Recruitment issues
- Presentation mode
- Follow-up
- Outcome measures (self-report versus observation; multiple informants)
- Ongoing intervention

Random assignment: if couples are not randomly assigned to intervention conditions (e.g. control versus intervention, self-administered versus therapist administered), then outcomes may reflect differences in the groups rather than the impact of the intervention. **Random assignment** means that as couples enter a program they are directed to control or intervention groups without consideration of their characteristics.

Issues of recruitment and retention: it is difficult to recruit stepfamilies for interventions because they are often reluctant to identify as stepfamilies and because they do not like to acknowledge problems, especially in the early phases of stepfamily life when intervention would be most effective. Retention is also problematic for many reasons, including difficulties in attending with child-care responsibilities, and the risk that the couple will dissolve their relationship. Many studies report a significant drop-out of participants throughout the course, making it difficult to evaluate the true impact of the intervention.

Presentation mode: this includes questions such as whether interventions are offered to groups, to couples, or to individuals. The benefits of families working as a group on the intervention have been found to be strong, as aspects of being a stepfamily become normalized and members of the group learn from each other's experiences. They offer mutual support for the issues they share.

Another aspect of presentation mode is the benefit or otherwise of combining couples from first families with those from stepfamilies. Many of the family issues for first families are similar to those in stepfamilies. However, there are issues specific to stepfamilies and these may need to be addressed separately if first family and stepfamily couples are combined.

The benefits of self-directed intervention programs are primarily in the saving of resources. However, this mode of delivery also enables flexibility so that family members can take part when it suits their schedules. One study has found that self-directed delivery was as successful as therapist delivery, although participants preferred the involvement with a therapist (Nicolson, Sanders et al. 2008).

Follow-up of the groups receiving the intervention, and the control groups, is also important in order to examine the long-term impact of the intervention. It is sometimes found on follow-up that members of the control group have also changed in the direction that is desired, suggesting that time, rather than the specific intervention, brings about the effect.

Outcome measures: these vary widely, with some being as minimal as measures of satisfaction with the course and others being multiple and mixing self-report with observation. The more rigorous the outcome measures, the more likely the evaluations will be thorough.

Ongoing interventions as families change: interventions early in the development of a stepfamily have been shown to be successful. However, the challenges for families change as children grow older and as the family establishes itself more firmly. The provision of *follow-up interventions* as needed would help families to remain resilient and successful.

In a recent review of intervention studies, Whitton and her colleagues noted that sample sizes are usually small, and that measures and methods used to evaluate outcomes were problematic (Whitton, Nicholson et al. 2008). The authors identified only two that were rigorously evaluated: the Australian study that focused on children's behavior problems and used parenting interventions, and the Oregon-based study that also focused on management of parenting.

In summary, rigorous evaluations that give a true picture of the efficacy of interventions are both difficult and, therefore, rare. At best, we can glean an overall picture of the success or otherwise of different kinds of interventions.

Outcomes of Interventions

In this section the three major interventions for stepfamilies identified earlier in the chapter are discussed. All have been evaluated, with varying degrees of rigor. Two address parenting issues and one addresses the parental relationship.

Couple Relationship Interventions

The main example of this kind of intervention is the SmartSteps Couple Relationship Education program. Although others have been developed, most have focused on White middle-class (re)married couples. This program was aimed at low-income White and Latino couples, both remarried and cohabiting.

The program has eight core content areas:

- utilizing basic marital skills;
- developing understanding and a positive view of stepfamilies;
- utilizing effective stepparenting practices;
- navigating relationships with former partners;
- negotiating stepfamily roles and rules;
- utilizing financial management skills;
- utilizing effective parenting practices;
- building supportive connections within and outside the family.

Unfortunately, evaluations of these programs have not been rigorous. They are largely (although not completely) based on qualitative data, and follow-up times are short. Small increases in levels of commitment, agreement on finances, parenting, and ex-partners were found one month after the 12-week course finished (Higginbotham & Skogrand 2010). However, in a later meta-analysis of the impact of couple relationship education programs, it has been found that this kind of intervention has at best modest impact on the quality of couple relationships in stepfamilies (Lucier-Greer & Adler-Baeder 2012).

Overall, interventions based on couple relationships have not yet been shown to be effective. This is in part because they have not been thoroughly evaluated over time. Other issues, too, may be important— for example, the use of relevant outcome measures. It is too early to suggest that this is not an effective focus for interventions, and in first families it is comparatively more successful.

Parenting-based Interventions

Behavioral Family Interventions (BFI)

In Australia two evaluation studies have been carried out on interventions that focus on parenting skills and are based on **Behavioral Family Interventions** (see Nicolson, Sanders et al. 2008). The bases for both were:

- education on the causes of problems for children in stepfamilies;
- positive parenting skills;
- coparenting skills;
- problem solving and communication; and
- family activities promoting family cohesion.

Both of these interventions included random allocation to treatment groups and multiple measures of outcomes including self-report and observations.

The first intervention was a treatment intervention involving a group of children who had been diagnosed with behavioral problems. The program ran for ten weeks and involved eight modules. Assessments were carried out pre- and post-intervention, and six months after completion of the course. The researchers found that there were significant reductions in children's behavior problems and in interparental conflict about parenting. Those in the control group also showed reduction in behavior problems, although not as marked as in the intervention groups. This suggests that, at least in part, time was a factor in reducing children's problems.

The second intervention was based on the findings of the first, and included a module on the parental relationship. It was focused in particular on prevention of problems and included families in the early stages of stepfamily formation. Assessments were carried out two years after the intervention, as well as pre- and post-intervention and 12 months later.

Children's behavior problems were not affected by this intervention; however, their emotional well-being increased (higher self-esteem and lower levels of depression). Because this study did not have a control group, it is not possible to know whether or not this was a function of time. Parenting coerciveness reduced and parenting efficacy increased, and parenting conflict about parenting decreased. Again, it is not possible to know whether this would have happened over time. Evaluating the impact of a parenting intervention was, in this case, confounded by the inclusion of the parental relationship module.

Parent Management Training (PMTO)

This intervention is based on the assumption that good parenting skills can ameliorate the impact of adverse environmental effects. It identifies five core parenting skills:

- skill encouragement;
- discipline methods;
- monitoring children;
- problem solving; and
- positive involvement with children.

The program is called Marriage and Parenting in Stepfamilies (MAPS). Participants were randomly assigned to intervention groups (intervention and control). Multiple assessments were done at baseline, and 6, 12 and 24 months after the course (Forgatch, Degarmo et al. 2005). The evaluation over time showed that the intervention changed parenting practices one year later. Of greatest interest is that through changes in parenting it had an impact on child outcomes both one year and two years after the intervention (Bullard, Wachlarowicz et al. 2010).

Of particular interest are the findings that this intervention, aimed primarily at improving parenting practices, also had an indirect impact on marital relationship processes and marital satisfaction. Figure 12.1 shows the links among the subsystems.

These findings provide strong evidence in support of a Family Systems framework for understanding stepfamily dynamics. An intervention that was aimed primarily at the parent–child dyads had a positive impact on the parent–parent dyad, by improving parenting practices.

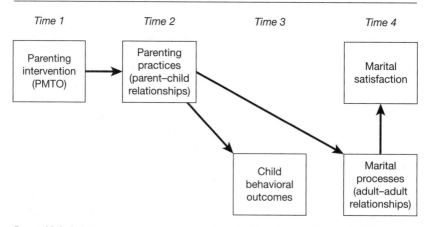

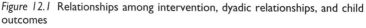

Figure 12.1 Relationships among intervention, dyadic relationships, and child outcomes

Source: Adapted from Bullard et al. 2010.

This program of intervention is perhaps the most rigorously evaluated of all. It includes control groups, multiple assessments, and a long timeline for follow-up. Its findings suggest that, when well done, interventions can have positive impacts on several aspects of stepfamily functioning.

In summary, educational interventions are rarely well evaluated. Part of the reason for this lies in the difficulties in recruitment and retention of stepfamily members, and the resources needed for rigorous outcome measures and follow-up. One stands out as being measurably successful, and it illustrates vividly the interlinking of subsystems in stepfamilies.

It is important to note that just because a program is not evaluated or is not well evaluated, it is not necessarily ineffective. We can't know, however, whether or not it is until it is evaluated thoroughly in the ways suggested here.

Therapeutic Interventions

Early educational intervention can be instrumental, when successful, in preventing stepfamilies from entering therapy. However, given the paucity of effective intervention and education services, many stepfamilies find themselves with problems that require therapeutic intervention.

Stepfamilies may present with problems they see as being those of an 'ordinary' family, and will approach therapists who may not have the knowledge and skills to work with the unique challenges faced by step-family members. One therapist has likened approaching therapy with models based on first-family dynamics to using a map of Boston to navigate in New York City. In this section two major therapeutic models will be described. They are representative of recent innovations in therapeutic approaches, and both are grounded in research and clinical experience.

Papernow's Model for Therapeutic Intervention

Earlier in the chapter we noted five challenges for stepfamilies delineated by Patricia Papernow (2008). Her therapeutic model has three levels.

1. *Psycho-education*: the 'what' of therapy, in which information about stepfamily dynamics is conveyed. It is important first to assess the gaps in the knowledge and understanding that stepfamily members have. Given the hopes and beliefs that clients can hold, this needs to be done in the context of an empathetic connection between therapist and client as knowledge that conflicts with beliefs may be unwelcome.
2. *Interpersonal skills*: the 'how' of therapy. The therapist question is how stepfamily members communicate about their issues. Communication skills in stepfamilies tend to be comparatively ineffective, and skills might need to be taught. Commonly, the subsystems in the family are overwhelmed by the issues they face, so Papernow suggests offering one or two skills at a time for people to incorporate.
3. *Intrapsychic dynamics*: the 'why' of therapy. Papernow proposes the 'bruise' theory of feelings: 'If you bump your arm in a place where the flesh is healthy, it hurts. However, if you already have a bruise there, it hurts much more. If the bruise is deep, even a slight touch will elicit a very strong response.' The therapist's task is therefore to elicit previous experiences in clients that lead to acute responses to stepfamily challenges. Papernow suggests, too, that it is not wise to start at the intrapsychic level as working at the other two levels may be therapeutic without needing to delve into possibly distressing intrapsychic issues.

Browning's Ten-step Therapeutic Model

Browning's clinical approach to stepfamilies is explicit in its focus on the family as a collective of subsystems, in accordance with Family Systems Theory (Browning & Artelt 2012).The ten steps are organized into three parts: diagnostic phase, clinical intervention, and stepfamily integration. They are as follows:

1. Diagnostic steps:
   - recognize the structure of the stepfamily;
   - determine the membership of the first session;

- clarify the distinct subsystems in the stepfamily as a guide for the direction of clinical treatment.

2. Primary clinical interventions:
   - introduce research findings that normalize the experience of the stepfamily;
   - assess and assist in the recognition of empathy and build on it within the family;
   - identify unhelpful beliefs and labeling in the family, and challenge them;
   - support the parent–child subsystem;
   - teach the family about its own systemic functioning.

3. Stepfamily integration:
   - assist coparenting, including nonresident parents;
   - encourage and assist communication between stepfamily members and move toward integration of the subsystems into a well-functioning stepfamily.

These two approaches have somewhat different ways of organizing their models of therapy. One works through the levels of intervention (what, how, and why), while the other works through the steps and processes of a carefully constructed model of therapy that has a start and a finish. Both are based on earlier work by therapists in the late twentieth century, and they do not contradict each other in aims and underlying principles. They have several features in common:

- psycho-education and normalizing of stepfamily life;
- dispelling unhelpful beliefs about stepfamily dynamics;
- focusing on subsystems;
- building empathy with family members;
- encouraging slow movement toward cohesion, and flexibility in defining membership and roles.

In summary, there are many models of family therapy, and in this section we have focused on two that are recent, developed specifically for stepfamilies, and are based in research and clinical work. It is vital that therapists understand the unique issues for stepfamilies, alongside those for first families.

Chapter Summary

There are several characteristics of stepfamilies that mean that interventions based on the dynamics of first families are not appropriate by themselves. Interventions for stepfamilies fall into two broad categories: those that offer education, and those that offer therapy. The first type is most likely to be helpful if stepfamilies take part early in their development. They tend to focus on two aspects of families—the parental relationship, or the parent–child relationship, although in practice many combine both aspects.

Very few have been evaluated, yet evaluation is essential if we are to know whether or not they work. Rigorous evaluation includes use of control groups, random assignment to intervention or control conditions, recruitment and retention of participants, and effective outcome measures. Evaluation should also take place over time after the end of the intervention, in order to examine whether or not effects are lasting.

To date, evaluations of interventions have rarely been undertaken in thorough ways. The few that have find mixed results, although one program has demonstrated over time that a focus on parenting skills leads to improvements in the quality of the interparental relationship, exemplifying the power of a Family Systems perspective on stepfamily dynamics.

Therapy is appropriate when problems have become entrenched in stepfamilies. There are several therapeutic models; two are described here that are representative of modern approaches based on theory and clinical experience.

Key Terms

- Stepfamily cycle
- Middle ground
- Ecosystemic theory
- Social Interaction Learning Theory
- Behavioral Family Interventions
- Control groups
- Random assignment
- Recruitment and retention
- Presentation mode
- Follow-up

Discussion Questions

1. Can you think of ways in which stepfamilies could be encouraged to attend educational programs? What might need to be provided for them?
2. Discuss the ethics of assigning families to control groups in intervention evaluations.

3. How ethical is it to provide interventions that have not been evaluated?
4. How might a therapist utilize a systemic framework in deciding which members of families to work with?

Exercise

Carry out a mini survey of family therapists in your area, either by reading the information they provide, or by interviewing one or more of them. What is their approach to stepfamilies? Do they consider them as similar to or the same as first families? If not, can you identify what specific approaches they take to stepfamilies?

Additional Readings and Web Resources

Adler-Baeder, F., Robertson, A., & Schramm, D. G. (2010). Conceptual framework for marriage education programs for stepfamily couples with considerations for socioeconomic context. *Marriage & Family Review*, 46, 300–322.

Browning, S. & Artelt, E. (2012). *Stepfamily Therapy: A Ten-Step Clinical Approach*. Washington, DC, APA Books.

Faber, A. & Mazlish, E. (1999). *How to Talk so Kids will Listen and Listen so Kids will Talk*. New York: Avon Books.

Lucier-Greer, M. & Adler-Baeder, F. (2012). Does couple and relationship education work for individuals in stepfamilies? A meta-analytic study. *Family Relations*, 61 (5), 756–769.

Papernow, P. L. (2013). *Surviving and Thriving in Stepfamily Relationships: What Works and What Doesn't*. New York, Routledge.

Chapter 13

Legal and Policy Issues for Stepfamilies

Validating stepfamilies as an authentic institutionalized family form is a worthy policy goal.

(Malia 2005)

Objectives of this Chapter

- To offer an overview of the legal situation for stepfamilies.
- To identify major issues for stepfamilies in the twenty-first century.

Introduction

We have referred frequently to stepfamilies as incompletely institutionalized. At the time that Cherlin coined this phrase stepfamilies were generally regarded as married, and deinstitutionalization referred to ambiguous roles within married stepfamily households. Over three decades later, we recognize the astonishing diversity of all families and especially of stepfamilies. Over half of stepfamilies are cohabiting rather than married, many are headed by same-sex parents, and most stepfamilies have members living in several households. Stepfamilies vary across race and culture, and intergenerational step ties are increasingly salient. Incomplete institutionalization, then, applies to a far wider constellation of factors than to relationships and roles within one household of remarried parents and the lack of legal institutionalization persists.

In this chapter we will discuss legal issues affecting stepfamilies, and in particular the relationship between stepparents and stepchildren. Specifically, we will address legal ambiguity for stepparents. Policy issues and questions that arise from the present legal environments will also be addressed.

Stepfamilies and the Law

A major way in which families are 'institutionalized' is through the law. In most countries, the law is reluctant to sanction stepfamilies and fails to support the stepparent–stepchild relationship with full legal endorsement. Stepparents and stepchildren have been described aptly as 'legal strangers'. This is largely because legal systems uphold the primacy of biological (or adoptive) relationships. Lawmakers tend to be conservative, seeing biological relationships as proper, and social parents such as stepparents as deserving fewer rights and claims (Edwards, Gillies et al. 1999). This position lingers, despite the lived reality of stepparents where, in many instances a stepparent is taking a major role in raising the children of another (biological) parent who is not living with the children.

The primacy of biological relationships is reinforced by the rise in involvement of nonresident parents in children's lives after divorce. Children themselves want to maintain a relationship with nonresident parents. In the study of children's views of families in New Zealand (Rigg & Pryor 2007), 99 percent of children included a nonresident parent as a family member. Moreover, we know that a positive relationship with a nonresident parent is measurably good for children (see Chapter 8).

Furthermore, children's rights to know their biological parents are upheld by the United Nations Convention on the Rights of the Child (UNCROC). Article 9.3 states:

> parties shall respect the right of the child who is separated from one or both parents to maintain personal relationships and direct contact with both parents on a regular basis, except if it is contrary to the child's best interests.
>
> To date, the United States, South Sudan, and Somalia are three countries that have not ratified the Convention although Somalia has indicated its intention to do so.

Yet children also value their relationships with their stepparents, and include them as family members when asked to identify family members (Rigg & Pryor 2007). And although this relationship is at times difficult to establish and maintain, it is pivotal to the well-being of both children and stepfamilies as a whole. There is, then, a tension between children's need for biological families and their need for social families, a tension exacerbated by the ambiguities of the legal system.

Reasons for Formalizing Stepparent–Stepchild Relationships

There are several reasons why strengthening the legal relationship between stepparents and stepchildren might be desirable. They are summarized in Box 13.1.

Box 13.1 Issues for legitimizing stepparent–stepchild relationships

- Day-to-day decision making.
- Inheritance.
- Financial support for stepchildren.
- Continuation of the relationship if parents separate.
- Symbolic meaning (emotional legitimacy).

Day-to-day Decision Making

Stepparents have no rights in regard to making decisions for or about stepchildren in areas such as school records, permitting school trips, or medical decisions. This significantly restricts many aspects of their parenting.

Inheritance

Stepchildren cannot inherit from their stepparents unless stipulated in the stepparents' wills. Furthermore, if a stepparent dies intestate (with no will) stepchildren have no claim on the estate of their stepparent.

Financial Support for Stepchildren

In some countries, but not all, stepparents are obliged to support their stepchildren financially. However, this is uneven and in many US states there is no obligation.

Continuation of the Relationship if Parents Separate

This is perhaps the most significant aspect of being legal strangers. In most cases, the relationship is liable to dissolve if the parents separate and under most conditions stepparents cannot apply for custody of stepchildren (but see later in the chapter). In many instances, a long and close relationship exists between children and their stepparents, but this is legally fragile and liable to be terminated if the parental relationship ends.

Symbolic Meaning/Emotional Legitimacy

For children, it is likely that a legal relationship with a stepparent confers a sense of commitment and permanency. A stepparent's marriage to their biological parent is related to well-being; so too might a legal relationship signal commitment and security to a child.

Dangers of Legitimizing the Stepparent–Stepchild Relationship

The main concern about having a legal means to legitimize this relationship is the considerable variation in its stability and levels of commitment. A stepparent may be one of several partners a mother has had, who enter and leave the household with some frequency. Conversely, a stepparent may have raised the stepchild from infancy or early childhood, and be regarded by that child as his or her 'real' father. It is difficult, therefore, to enact law that covers these divergent contingencies.

In summary, there has been considerable reluctance on the part of lawmakers to confer a legal status on the relationship between stepparents and stepchildren. This position does not reflect the day-to-day lives of most stepfamilies in the twenty-first century. There are, though, significant difficulties in finding a way to create laws that work for all stepfamily situations.

The Legal Situation in the United States

At present, two United States laws undermine the ability of stepparents and stepchildren to become legal friends. The first is the doctrine of **Parental Rights**. This gives to biological parents who are fit, fundamental rights to make all decisions regarding their children. In practice, this means that if a parent and a stepparent separate, or the biological parent in the stepfamily dies, the nonresident biological parent has rights in regard to the children, no matter what the circumstances. Children who have rarely seen their nonresident biological parent and who have a close bond with their stepparent are, therefore, subject to the wishes and probably the custody of their nonresident biological parent. Because they and their stepparent are legal strangers, their relationship holds no status in law in comparison with the rights of their biological parent.

The second tenet is that of **Parenthood as an Exclusive Status**. The effect of this is that children cannot have more than two legal parents. It therefore makes it impossible to recognize multiple parenting figures that may in practice exist in children's lives.

Taken together, these two aspects of law in the United States mean that stepparents have virtually no legal status in regard to stepchildren. Because they are not biological parents, they cannot be recognized as having legal parenting rights even if they are taking day-to-day care of the children. The major exception to this is the situation where they adopt their stepchild.

Adoption by Stepparents

Adoption is the most unambiguous way through which stepparents can become legal parents of their stepchildren. It is, however, a clumsy instrument since it is possible only with the agreement of the nonresident biological parent, or in situations where that parent is unfit or has disappeared. Because of the tenet of Parenthood as an Exclusive Status that decrees that children can have only two legal parents, the nonresident biological parent loses legal parenting status when a stepparent adopts a stepchild. In fact, until recently and still in some countries, *both* biological parents lose legal parenting status and the resident biological parent must apply to adopt his or her own child.

There are several drawbacks to adoption. They include the loss to the child of the extended family relationships held formerly with the nonresident biological parents' families. When biological parents lose parenting status, extended family members related to that parent also lose any rights they may have to access to the child.

Another disadvantage is the relative instability of stepfamilies. This may be seen as a factor to take into consideration in thinking about conferring legal parenthood on someone who may not remain in the lives of children.

France has a system called **simple adoption.** Simple adoption creates a legal relationship between a stepparent and a stepchild while leaving the relationships with biological parents intact. This means that grandparents from the nonresident parents' families, for example, can continue to have relationships with their grandchildren. Simple adoption includes the obligation to support the child (*obligation alimentaire*), although a nonresident biological parent must support the child if the stepparent cannot.

Other Options for Stepparents

There are some ways in which stepparents can take on parenting roles that are less than full legal parenthood, and do not include adoption. In the United States, it is possible for a stepparent to be *in loco parentis*,

---

Box 13.2 Legal options for stepparents

- *In loco parentis* (US)
- **Parental Responsibility** (England)
- **Guardianship**/parenting order (New Zealand and Australia)
- Simple adoption (France)

or to have **de facto** parenthood. This is not defined by law, but by the intent of the stepparent to be in a parenting role and is often identified post facto, or at the time that, for example, a stepfamily separates. *In loco parentis* can be terminated at any time by either a stepparent or a child, and is an example of a **derivative situation**—it exists only so long as the stepparent is married to the biological parent.

In England, stepparents can take on the status of **Parental Responsibility**. In order to have this status, a stepparent (or other person) has to have lived with the child for at least three years, and to have had a *Residence Order* granted. These options are discussed further later in the chapter.

In Australia and New Zealand, a stepparent can obtain a *Parenting Order* or *Guardianship* in relation to a child. This confers parental responsibility, and stays in existence until the child is 18 years old. France, as mentioned earlier, has simple adoption that leaves intact the relationship with biological parents and families.

All of these options are of lesser legal status than adoption, but they represent some concessions toward the realities of stepfamily life. They also recognize the fact that most children stay in contact with their nonresident parents. They vary in their stability, and most are vulnerable when a stepfamily breaks up, which means that children may lose relationships that are emotionally and psychologically important to them.

Proposals for Change in the United States

In the United States several suggestions have been made that might improve the situation for the stepparent–stepchild relationship. One is a call to strengthen de facto parenting status (Mason, Harrison-Jay et al. 2002), which appears to have resulted in a new legal doctrine called 'de facto parentage' that permits nonbiological parents to establish their parental rights in relation to their children and seek custody or access. Conversely, the biological parent is able to seek child support from a de facto parent if he or she is the primary residential parent of the child.

To establish de facto parentage, the nonbiological—in this case step— parent must prove the following:

1. that the biological parent consented to and supported the parenting relationship of the stepparent;
2. that the stepparent and the child lived together in the same household;
3. that the stepparent assumed the obligations of parenthood without expectation of financial compensation; and
4. that the stepparent has been in a parental role for sufficiently long to have established a dependent relationship with the child.

A second form of parenthood for stepparents in the US is *parenting by estoppel*. This holds more formal legal status than de facto parentage. The parent is required to have lived with the child for at least two years, and have taken financial and other responsibilities for the child. A stepparent who holds parentage by estoppel can apply for custody should he or she separate from the child's biological parent.

There has been a considerable amount of opposition to the establishment of these '*functional*' parenting roles by nonrelated adults (see, for example, www.uiowa.edu/~ilr/issues/ILR_94-2_Rohlf.pdf). The arguments in opposition are based firmly on the belief that formal, biological, or adoptive parents have primary and absolute rights (the doctrine of **Parental Rights**). These functional parenting roles, such as de facto or estoppel, have been applied in many cases to same-sex parents who separate. A recent discussion of formal and functional parenting in the US context is that by Laufer-Ukeles and Blecher-Prigate (2013). Although written in legal language, it has comprehensive coverage on the issues that exist for stepparents in the United States now.

In summary, some ways of enabling stepparents to hold second-order legal positions in relation to their stepchildren have been developed. Other countries have also put in place parenting statuses that confer a degree of legal parenthood on stepparents. Two laws, the Parental Rights Law and the tenet of Parenthood as an Exclusive Status, inhibit the possibilities of ongoing or legal parenting status for stepparents in the United States.

Policy Issues

The power of law in regulating stepfamily relationships is both constricting and constricted. The complexities of stepfamilies mean that making laws that work for all is impossible. However, there are some ways in which law and policy might change in order to improve the presently unsatisfactory situation that exists.

A key turning point in stepfamilies is the *point at which they end*. At present, it is almost universal that when parents part, the stepparent's rights and responsibilities end. Their position is derivative from the relationship between the parents. Not only does this situation remove a key source of material support for children, it can also mean the loss of a relationship that has become close and nurturing for the child. It is important to have in place mechanisms that mean that the relationship can endure if that is appropriate.

Fine (1997) has defined two factors needing to be addressed by law:

1. Clarification of the legal rights and responsibilities for stepparents.
2. Development of a sensitive standard to determine the quality of the relationship.

Clarification of legal rights and responsibilities of stepparents would validate what is often the case—they are genuinely parenting their stepchildren. The recognition of this situation legally would confer stability to the relationship, and enable perceived and actual commitment. It is important, too, to emphasize that with rights go responsibilities and the responsibilities of stepparents to nurture and support their stepchildren need to be recognized along with rights. However, as we have indicated earlier, there are some risks in conferring rights and responsibilities too easily, as partners of mothers may come and go from the family without making commitments or becoming parenting figures to the children.

One solution to this, suggested by Fine and others, is the system in England whereby stepparents can gain the status of Parental Responsibility through the awarding of a Residence Order. A Residence Order can be conferred if the stepparent is married to the children's mother, thereby signaling commitment, or through having lived with the child for three years. This arrangement has the considerable advantage of giving the family and in particular the stepparent time to establish stability and commitment.

Residence Orders and Parental Responsibility would also address the question of legalizing more than two parenting figures. Parental Responsibility is defined as: 'all the rights, duties, powers, responsibilities and authority which by law a parent has in relation to a child and his property' (Children Act 1989, section 5.3 (i)). Having Parental Responsibility status, then, enables legal relationships with three adults. Furthermore, it requires the permission only of the resident legal parent.

The development of standards to determine the quality of the relationship applies to the assessment of the quality of the relationship between stepparent and stepchild. In practice this is difficult, as it depends on the stage in the relationship that it is assessed, and it calls for considerable resources to do it. It becomes, however, particularly relevant when a stepfamily dissolves and decisions are being made about the ongoing relationship the stepparent and child might have.

In addition, and particularly relevant to stepfamilies in the twenty-first century, we need mechanisms to address a third factor: laws that *enable a child to have multiple parenting relationships* that confer rights and responsibilities on more than two parenting figures. As we have seen above, the tenet of Parenthood as an Exclusive Status in the US severely limits the ability for stepparents to have a recognized role in the lives of their stepchildren since it restricts the number of legal parents a child can have to just two. Research findings are clear that children can accumulate parenting figures to their advantage (see Chapters 7 and 8).

In summary, policy issues for stepfamilies arise from the legal anomalies that exist. The clarification of legal rights and responsibilities, the assessment of the relationship that exists between stepparent and stepchild, and the development of legal mechanisms by which a child might have more than two legal parenting figures, are some of the ways in which the actual situations for stepfamilies might be recognized.

Chapter Summary

The difficulties in institutionalizing the legal status of stepparents in relation to stepchildren are considerable. Several factors contribute to the situation. First, there is the tension between biological and social families, where the law heavily favors biological parents—especially in the US but also in other countries. This is exemplified by the existence of the doctrine of Parental Rights, and the tenet of Parenthood as an Exclusive Status. Second, there are both advantages and disadvantages to conferring legal status on the stepparent–stepchild relationship. There is the question of timing; conferring a legal parenting status on stepparents early in the formation of families, given the relative instability of stepfamilies, may not be wise. All families are vulnerable to structural change, and we have discussed in earlier chapters that the likelihood of multiple transitions following parental separation and divorce is considerable. The dilemma for the law is how to ascertain the stability of the stepfamily couple sufficiently accurately to justify conferring legal status on the relationship. One suggestion is to follow the English model of Residence Orders and Parental Responsibility.

Finally, the law is challenged to develop mechanisms by which it can enable a child to have more than two parenting figures. This would require the removal of the tenet of Parenthood as an Exclusive Status, and would reflect more accurately the day-to-day of increasing numbers of children.

Key Terms

- Simple adoption
- *In loco parentis*
- Parenting orders
- Guardianship
- Parenting by estoppel
- Derivative law
- Parenting Responsibility
- Residence Order
- Functional parenting roles

Discussion Questions

1. What do you think are the most compelling reasons for and against legalizing the stepparent–stepchild relationship?

2. What model or models do you suggest would work best for allowing more than two legal parents in a child's life?
3. How might the stepparent–stepchild relationship be assessed in order to determine its suitability for being formalized?

Exercise

Talk to someone who grew up in a stepfamily, or a stepparent you know. Discuss the legal relationships between stepchildren and stepparents. Are there ways in which they would like them to be different? If so, what do they recommend?

Additional Readings and Web Resources

Atkin, B. (2008). Legal structures and stepfamilies—the New Zealand example. In J.Pryor (Ed.), *The International Handbook of Stepfamilies: Policy and Practice in Legal, Research, and Clinical Environments* (pp. 522–544). Hoboken, NJ: John Wiley & Sons.

Laufer-Ukeles, A. & Blecher-Prigat, A. (2013). Between function and form: toward a differentiated model of functional parenthood. *George Mason Law Review*, 484 (2) (Winter), 419–484.

Malia, S. (2005). Balancing family members' interests regarding stepparent rights and obligations: a social policy challenge. *Family Relations*, 54 (2), 298–319.

Malia, S. (2008). Family and probate law in the U.S. How relevant is it to stepfamilies? In J. Pryor (Ed.). *International Handbook of Stepfamilies: Policy and Practice in Legal, Research, and Clinical Environments* (pp. 545–572). Hoboken, NJ: John Wiley & Sons.

www.thecustodyminefield.com/mobile/stepparentpr.html

www.nowellmeller.co.uk/cms/documents/FL3.pdf

www.uiowa.edu/~ilr/issues/ILR_94–2_Rohlf.pdf

Chapter 14

Overview and Conclusions

The answer to the question 'what next after the family?' is ... quite simple: the family!

(Beck-Gernsheim 2002)

Objectives of this Chapter

- To summarize the main themes of the book.
- To introduce the concepts of family practices and pedi-focal families.

Introduction

Perhaps more than any other family form, stepfamilies represent the contours of family life today. They are fluid and changing, flexible and adaptable; they have the capacity to nurture their members well, and they also have the capacity to be toxic and dysfunctional. They are, in company of perhaps the majority of modern families, incompletely institutionalized. Their place in society has been, and remains, ambivalent. Stigma lingers, and the legal system drags its feet in legitimizing stepfamily relationships. Yet stepfamilies are increasingly ubiquitous. They are not going to disappear—the ongoing trend in separation and divorce, cohabitation, and single parenting ensures that stepfamilies are permanently with us. It is crucial, then, that rather than lamenting their existence as some do, we endeavor to understand and support for their sake, and for the sake of the societies in which they exist.

Stepfamilies can be seen to occupy a midpoint on a continuum between nuclear first families, and those especially unstable families formed through the processes of multiple transitions and multipartner fertility. As such, they represent a timely opportunity to think forward rather than looking backward, to focus on how the diverse families of the twenty-first century can both be understood and have their well-being fostered. They deserve our best efforts to help them flourish. They represent a family form that has a long history, and that represents the leading edge of family formation and functioning. They have the capacity for stability and for offering sustenance to their members; in this book we have considered ways in which these capacities might be encouraged.

Yet understanding and supporting stepfamilies is as complex as they themselves are. Ganong and Coleman (2004) discuss the contrast between **deficit-comparison** approaches to stepfamilies, where the focus is on ways in which they fail, and **normative-adaptive** approaches. The latter encourages us to come to grips with their complexities and to identify aspects of stepfamily functioning that can enhance their well-being. For example, we can learn much in the West from cultural approaches in other societies. We can work with step-grandparent relationships to foster support for children. We can encourage stepfathers to claim their stepchildren and to become fathering allies with nonresident fathers. And we can support stepfamilies in enabling children to have nourishing relationships with multiple parenting figures.

All of this calls for efforts beyond the usual in making sense of research, and translating it into policy and practice. This book has identified many of the challenges in doing this, and points to areas where research and knowledge are much needed. At the same time, its message is that celebrating stepfamily life with a full awareness of its diversity is both necessary and worthwhile.

In this book, we have identified several dichotomies in regard to stepfamilies:

- social versus biological families;
- selection versus environment;
- change versus continuity;
- family versus household.

What we know so far about stepfamily dynamics is that neither pole of these dichotomies reflects accurately the situations they are in. Stepfamilies are both social and biological—usually they include a biological and a social parent; their well-being reflects features of both selection and environmental effects; they balance change and fluidity with continuity, and they function both as families across households, and the group within the household.

In the following section we will discuss some of the overarching themes that arise from previous chapters.

Fluidity of Stepfamily Households

Stepfamilies are markedly more fluid in their composition and shape than first families. In Chapter 1 we showed the ways in which stepfamily households have to be like accordions—expanding and contracting as those in the household come and go. This accordion quality is evident from week to week as children come and go to nonresident parent households, and over longer periods of time as membership changes—siblings move in and out of the household, especially in adolescence when they may choose to live with another parent.

Boundary ambiguity is another aspect of fluidity. Individual members of a stepfamily may have different perspectives on who is a member of the family (psychological ambiguity) and even who 'lives' in the household (physical ambiguity). The latter might be especially evident if children spend close to equal amounts of time in their parents' homes, and it is not clear which, if either, is their main residence.

The Importance of Time

The physical establishment of a stepfamily household is only the beginning of a process of establishing relationships. These take time, and we have seen that there are differing trajectories in, for example, the development of the stepchild–stepparent relationship (see Chapter 7). There is an understandable tendency for adults in stepfamilies to want instant love and acceptance in their new family. This does not often happen and, especially where older children are involved, it takes time for new relationships to become stabilized. It takes time, too, before it is evident who belongs to the stepfamily, what its membership is, who is 'in' and who is 'out'. Some evidence suggests that those families who take the process slowly are most likely to function well, and that agreeing to disagree about membership is helpful in the early stages. Andrew Cherlin, in his book *The Marriage Go-Round*, advocates slowing down. He says: ' "Slow down." If you are a lone parent, take your time finding a new live-in partner. See the traffic light of singlehood as yellow rather than green' (Cherlin 2009, p. 11). The same advice might be given to parents in new stepfamilies. Slow down, take your time in deciding how to define your family. Let your children adapt in their own time to your new partner, let their relationship develop naturally.

Cultural Diversity

Media depictions of stepfamilies tend to convey the image of White married couples living stepfamily life in the context of European attitudes to families. The reality of stepfamilies is that they are culturally diverse, bringing to their families disparate attitudes to family life that have an impact on how stepfamilies function and how they are accepted in different cultural milieus. For example, the fluidity of families and households in Black American culture make it comparatively easy for Black children to adapt, and to thrive, in stepfamilies. This is in contrast to those in White American culture where idealized views of marriage and family clash with the realities of stepfamily living. Black and Pacific/Polynesian family attitudes more easily allow the involvement of multiple parenting figures in children's lives—a facet of stepfamilies that exists increasingly as nonresident parents stay involved with their children. Although it is not easy to adopt the values and attitudes of cultures that are not ours, it might help White and Asian stepfamilies to adapt to the dynamics of their households if they could 'borrow' some other cultural approaches. The applicability of aspects of Black culture to White stepfamilies is discussed further later in the chapter.

Stepkinship

Stepfamilies bring with them a group of kin that are not available in first families. These additions can be both welcome and vexatious. They contribute to the difficulties of deciding who is family and who is not, and to the fluidity of membership. The two main dimensions of this feature of stepfamilies are *multihousehold kin* and *intergenerational stepkin*.

Stepfamilies exist across households, because biological parents no longer live in the same house. Children's families, both biological and step, are not in the same place. Stepsiblings and stepparents may live in other households, as parents repartner, bringing an array of stepkin into children's lives. These are potentially both enriching and overwhelming. Children's relationships with those in other houses vary in both closeness and importance.

Stepfamily formation also brings with it step-grandkin, people whose relationships with step-grandchildren have not been examined to any great extent by researchers. They vary from distant, possibly unknown adults in children's lives to close supporters and confidants.

Allan, Crow et al. (2011) have described step-kinships as *emergent* in stepfamilies. They describe the *constructed* nature of relationships that grow over time, and as being liable to change. They distinguish three categories.

1. Relationships *in name only*: these are stepkin with whom there is no interaction. An example is the new partner of a father who is absent in a child's life. This person might be formally seen as a stepmother but has no real relationship with the child.
2. *Mediated relationships*: these are contingent on the existence of the partnership that creates the tie. They include relationships with visiting step-grandparents and stepsiblings living outside the household. They are not relationships that have their own life and identity; they exist only because of the relationship between adults. They are not likely to be seen as 'family'.

3. Stepkin *regarded as family*: these are stepkin who are agreed upon as family members, and who are part of family routines and day-to-day life. A common example of a stepkin relationship that is regarded as family is that between a stepparent and a young stepchild in the same household.

Child Effects

Although we implicitly acknowledge that the relationships between adults and children generally are bidirectional in their influences, it is seldom that the impact of children on adults is explicitly described. We know that, in stepfamilies, children have a more powerful effect on the relationships with adults than they do in first families. For example, levels of adolescent well-being *cause*, rather than are caused by, levels of involvement by nonresident fathers (Hawkins, Amato et al. 2007). And as we saw in Chapter 2, levels of adolescent stepchild externalizing behavior cause stepfather negativity rather than the other way around. This is another example of the differences between stepfamily and first-family dynamics, differences that need to be borne in mind, especially by therapists.

In the remainder of this chapter, we will discuss two frameworks that take somewhat different perspectives on families, in ways that enable more accurate understanding of the reality of stepfamily living.

Family Practices and Family Displays

One of the fundamental issues that bedevils many aspects of studying families and stepfamilies is how to define a family. Definitions can be based on biological relationships, legal ties, whether or not people live in the same household, and whether or not they love each other. We have seen that the notion of **fictive kin** works in many instances, as families include both biological and nonrelated members of the family. We have seen too that the law struggles with how to define families, as do demographers and indeed researchers. The tension between the American ideal of family life and the reality of the experiences of family members is summed up by John Gillis who distinguishes the *families we live by* from the *families we live with* (Gillis 1997).

One way to approach the question 'What is a family?' is to change the emphasis from what a family *is*, to what families *do*. This leads to the consideration of **family practices** (Morgan 1996). The concept of family practices resonates with much that is typical of stepfamilies— fluidity, diversity, and multifacetedness.

Morgan suggests that rather than consider the word 'family' as a noun, we think of it as an adjective, or even as a verb. The adjectival use of it is described by Morgan: 'Family is something that people do, and in doing create and recreate the idea of family' (Morgan 2011, p. 177). And family practices are described: 'Practices are often little fragments of daily life which are part of the normal taken-for-granted existence of practitioners. Their significance derives from their location in wider systems of meaning' (Morgan 1996, p. 190).

The concept fits with stepfamilies in several of its aspects. It emphasizes that a sense of family identity, of what a particular family means, is based on practices that build up a shared sense of meaning. This takes time and accords with the notion of taking the development of the stepfamily slowly.

There are clear similarities here with implicit rituals (Chapter 11). Implicit rituals are routines that over time take on their own meaning that is important to those who take part. Practices are linked to a wider meaning that grows toward definition of the family—in this case, a stepfamily.

Family practice links, too, with the fluidity of stepfamilies. Finch, an English family sociologist, describes it thus:

> The emphasis on families as constituted by "practices, identities, and relationships" means that the fluidity of family life is not defined by shifting membership so much as by the continually evolving character of the relationships—how individuals talk to each other, act towards each other, and the assumptions on which their relationships are conducted.
>
> (Finch 2007, p. 69)

Finch also suggests that such family relationships and practices have a component of commitment and stability that calls for '**display**'. Active demonstration of relationships and confirmation that they work and are *family* relationships is important in order to sustain them and to confer stability and legitimacy. Relationships, she suggests, 'need to be displayed in order to have social reality'. In other words, in a society where relationships and their statuses are often indistinct, it is important to show that they exist, and that they matter.

A key aspect of display is that relationships not only exist in the minds of those involved, they are also seen and understood by others to be family relationships. For stepfamilies this might be especially important as members engage, negotiate, and come to an understanding of who is 'family'. Display makes these dynamics visible to outsiders, and confers identity to the stepfamily itself.

In summary, the fluid, diverse, and negotiated nature of stepfamily relationships lend themselves to being considered in the framework of family practices, and display of family relationships. Like rituals, they

---

VIGNETTE

'Doing' and 'displaying' family

Glen lived with his Dad and his stepmom, and visited his nonresident Mom regularly. He had four biological grandparents— his Dad's parents and his Mom's parents—and he also had step-grandparents—his stepmom's parents. He became close to Clara, his step-grandmother, as he saw her often and they enjoyed doing things together. When Grandparents Day came around at school, he took Clara along and proudly introduced her as his step-grandmom. Not only did Glen and Clara 'do' family, they also displayed their relationship to his friends and teachers in a way that made it clear that he regarded Clara as 'family'.

---

are ways in which the stepfamily can, over time, come to incorporate a stable set of relationships that are seen and accepted both by stepfamily members themselves and by those who observe them.

Lessons from Black Families: The Pedi-focal Family

A consistent message throughout this book has been the constraints on stepfamilies caused by the focus on nuclear families as the gold standard for family form and functioning. This constraint leads to ambiguity of roles, lack of institutionalization, stigma, and legal shortfall in supporting the reality of stepfamily life.

In Chapter 2 we discussed cultural differences in the approach to families and therefore stepfamilies. In this section the conceptualization of families as being pedi-focal is addressed. Pedi-focal means, as it suggests, a primary focus on children, and in particular on their well-being, and is a core focus of Black families.

As we observed in Chapter 2, Black families are characterized by the likelihood that one or both biological parents are absent from the home, and by ambiguity of roles and permeability of family and household boundaries. The family unit is defined, then, as 'including all those involved in the nurturance and support of an identified child, regardless of household membership' (Crosbie-Burnett & Lewis 1993, p. 244).

The application of this to stepfamily functioning and form is in the support for cooperation rather than hostility among children's parenting figures. This is relevant to the idea of father allies (Chapter 6), and to the reality of children having multiple parenting figures. This means a shift of focus from adults, and the legal and biological relationships in families, to the well-being of children, and the identification and legitimizing of the adults involved in their lives.

Crosbie-Burnett and Lewis identify other aspects of Black families that are relevant to stepfamily living. One is intergenerational flexibility and flexible gender roles; Black grandfathers, for example, take on major caring roles for grandchildren in contradiction of traditional male roles, and bringing the caring role of grandparents to the fore. We have seen in Chapter 9 that intergenerational step relationships are increasing. Yet in Western White families the inclusion of stepkin in children's lives is against the norm of the nuclear family, and individuals struggle with boundary ambiguity issues.

The permeability of household and family boundaries in Black culture also resonates with the realities of stepfamilies. Crosbie-Burnett and Lewis describe the 'functional linkages of households for the betterment of all members' (p. 245). In Chapter 2 we introduced the concept of othermothers; similar to this is the practice of informal adoption that also exists in Black culture. Both of these elements enable children and family members to adapt relatively easily to parenting figures outside the immediate biological or legal family.

The identification of key adults in the lives of children might, too, be applied to legal thinking when divorce takes place and when stepfamilies are being considered. We have discussed in Chapter 13 the difficulties facing lawmakers in legitimizing stepfamily relationships, a perspective that focuses on the children and their needs rather than on the competing positions of parents, which might illuminate ways to foster relationships that matter to children's well-being.

Chapter Summary

Deficit approaches to stepfamilies focus on their problems. A normative-adaptive approach, however, illuminates ways in which stepfamily life can be normalized and enhanced. Characteristics such as family fluidity, diversity, and wide kinship structures can be viewed as adaptive in supporting the stability and well-being of stepfamilies. In turn, stepfamilies epitomize many aspects of future family structures that do not conform to the traditional nuclear family. Efforts to understand and support their functioning, then, will spill over into support for other family forms.

The concept of family practices allows a focus on what families do, rather than on their structures. It encompasses notions of family meaning, the importance of time, and fluidity of family membership. Similarly, the pedi-focal focus of Black families offers a framework that bypasses household composition and encourages a concentration on those adults who parent and support children.

Taken together, the concepts of family practices and of pedi-focal families radically change the focus on the nuclear family as a unit. Both bring to the consideration of stepfamilies elements that more closely resemble their reality than do Western first-family models. They are consonant with the desirability of constructing stepfamily relationships over time, and they suggest ways in which legal and social structures might recognize the complexities of stepfamily relationships and respond to them appropriately.

It may take a long time before changes such as these take place. They are, though, permeating upward to some extent as the lived lives and realities of stepfamilies exert their influence. Practice, research, policy and law could profit from thinking more widely about stepfamilies, taking full account of the diversity described in this book, and working from perspectives that are outside the constraints of traditional norms and relationships.

Key Terms

- Deficit comparison
- Normative-adaptive
- Multi-household kin
- Intergenerational stepkin
- Emergent relationships
- Constructed relationships
- Bi-directional influences
- Families we live by versus families we live with
- Family practices
- Family display
- Pedi-focal families

Discussion Questions

1. Discuss the impact of using 'family' as a verb on policy approaches to stepfamilies.
2. What are the implications of bi-directional influences for interventions with stepfamilies?
3. What do you think is the single most important piece of advice to give those contemplating forming a stepfamily?

Exercise

Look at the abstracts of ten recent academic papers about stepfamilies. Do they take a deficit or a normative-adaptive approach in their hypotheses and research questions?

Additional Readings and Web Resources

Crosbie-Burnett, M. & Lewis, E. A. (1993). Use of African-American family structures and functioning to address the challenges of European-American postdivorce families. *Family Relations*, 42 (3), 243–248.

Finch, J. (2007). Displaying families. *Sociology*, 41 (1), 65–81.

Morgan, D. H. J. (2011). *Rethinking Family Practices*. Basingstoke, England, Palgrave Macmillan.

Glossary

Accordion families are those stepfamily households that expand and contract rather like a piano accordion. Each house does this depending on how many children are in it at any one time.

Accumulation suggests that children can add parents to their lives and benefit from relationships with more than one parent of the same sex (e.g. nonresident father and stepfather).

Additive hypothesis predicts that children will benefit from relationships with both parents of the same sex, and that a close relationship with both is better than with just one or the other.

Ambiguous loss is the loss felt by children when their parent is not dead, but is not readily available to them.

Attenuation hypothesis proposes that family transitions are some of many challenges faced by African-American families and so do not have the impact that they do for White children.

Authoritative parenting is a style that encompasses warmth and monitoring, and encouragement of autonomy.

Avoidance in communication involves strategies such as withdrawing, and using few negative verbal and nonverbal approaches.

Behavioral Family Interventions (BFI) are those that encourage appropriate positive and negative reinforcement of children's behavior by parents.

Bidirectional effects implies causality in both directions, from adult to child and from child to adult.

Boundary ambiguity is a conceptual framework that helps in understanding stepfamily dynamics. It exists when family members are not clear, or disagree about, who is in and who is out of the family.

Civil union is the legal status for same-sex couples that falls short of conferring all the benefits of marriage.

Collectivism is the practice or principle of giving a group priority over each individual.

Control groups do not receive the intervention that is being evaluated in an evaluation study.

Cooperative parenting is where divorced parents work together to coparent their children with little conflict, and shared views of how the children should be parented.

Deficit-comparison approach to stepfamilies focuses is on ways in which they fail.

Derivative situation refers to a relationship between a stepparent and stepchild that exists only so long as the stepparent is married to the biological parent.

Direct influences act through the interactions between grandparents and grandchildren, rather than through the middle generation.

Display is a term suggested by Janet Finch indicating the active demonstration of relationships and confirmation that they work and are family relationships.

Domestic partnerships are low-level legal agreements that confer only some of the legal rights of marriage.

Familism is a cultural belief that the family, including extended family, takes priority over the individual.

Family practices is a term that changes the emphasis from what a family is, to what families do.

Family well-being is thought of as a multidimensional concept encompassing different domains, and as an amalgamation of different types of well-being—physical, social, economic, and psychological.

'Father ally' indicates a cooperative relationship between stepfathers and nonresident fathers that is built on the recognition that children are damaged by conflict.

'Feeling like family' was described by participants in a study as including support, openness, comfort, caring, and sharing.

Fictive kin refers to people regarded as family members, who are not biologically or legally related.

Gatekeeping involves usually mothers taking primary responsibility for care and discipline of their children, and not allowing their new partner to be involved in decisions regarding the children.

Guardianship in relation to a child confers parental responsibility, and stays in existence until the child is 18 years old.

Heterosexism is the belief that only heterosexual unions are acceptable and natural.

Hierarchical families are those in which there is a line of power downward between generations, by means of which grandparents have a strong influence in families.

Homophobia is the fear and dislike of homosexuality.

Indirect influences are those that are via the support that grandparents give to the middle generation—their adult children.

Inherited step-grandparenthood occurs when a person's adult child forms a partnership with someone who already has children.

Intentionality is a strategy used by gay and lesbian families by choosing family members and friends who are supportive, with whom to spend time.

Intergenerational effect refers to the finding that if adults had lived in stepfamilies in their childhood, they were more likely themselves to form a stepfamily.

Interhouse conflict is that between ex-spouses and parents in a stepfamily.

Intrahouse conflict refers to conflict between biological and stepparents in a stepfamily.

Irrelevance hypothesis predicts that neither parent of the same sex (stepparent and nonresident parent) is beneficial for a child as neither will be sufficiently invested in the child to promote well-being.

Kinscripts are a form of racial socialization whereby family history and cultural norms are conveyed between generations, especially by grandparents.

Later-life step-grandparenthood is a pathway that occurs when an individual forms a partnership with someone who already has grandchildren.

In loco parentis, or **de facto parenthood**, is not defined by law, but by the intent of the stepparent to be in a parenting role.

Long-term step-grandparenthood is when remarriage or repartnering starts before step-grandchildren are born on this path to step-grandparenthood. The step-grandchild is usually the child of a stepchild whom the step-grandparent has helped to raise.

Loss hypothesis suggests that children do not benefit from relationships with either nonresident parents or stepparents.

Middle ground encompasses areas of agreement where joint action is easy, and does not need discussion because of shared understandings.

'Motherhood mandate' suggests that all women in all families are to a greater or lesser extent expected to be self-sacrificing, to put the needs of children and partners before their own, and to nurture children whether or not they are their own.

Multifragmented stepfamilies are those formed from multiple divorces or deaths, and subsequent transitions.

Multipartner fertility is an increasingly common phenomenon in which either parent has biological children from relationships with more than one other partner.

Normative-adaptive approaches encourage a focus that identifies aspects of stepfamily functioning that can enhance their well-being.

Othermothers are women who actively mother both biological and nonbiologically related children, especially in Black communities.

Parallel parenting is a style in which divorced parents have a business-like relationship and avoid conflict with each other in order to parent satisfactorily. They do not necessarily parent in the same ways.

Parental responsibility is a legal status in which a stepparent (or other person) has to have lived with the child for at least three years before acquiring it.

Parental rights give to biological parents who are fit, fundamental rights to make all decisions regarding their children.

Parenthood as an Exclusive Status ensures that children cannot have more than two legal parents.

Parentification is when children are put, or put themselves, into the position of caring for their parents emotionally and sometimes physically.

Patchwork stepfamilies are those in which at least two types of children live (biological, stepsiblings, half siblings).

Paternal claiming in reference to a stepfather is 'readiness to nurture, provide for, protect and see a stepchild as though the child were his own'.

Pedi-focal is a term used in regard to Black families indicating a primary focus on children and in particular their well-being, and on permeability of family boundaries rather than the inflexible boundaries that are common in White families.

Permissive parenting is a style that encompasses the features suggested by children's views of the stepparent role—warm and supportive, but not in a disciplining role.

Primacy of biology hypothesis predicts that the child's tie with their biological nonresident parent will be of most benefit to them in comparison with a stepparent of the same sex.

Primacy of residence hypothesis suggests that the parent who lives with the child will be most salient for their well-being.

Problem-focused strategies address a problem in proactive ways by making changes in the environment and the people involved.

Quasi-parenting roles are those where grandparents help to raise their grandchildren or do it single-handed, when parents are unable to do so.

Random assignment means that as couples enter a program they are directed to control or intervention groups without consideration of their characteristics.

Reciprocity is a key aspect of extended family life in which members are expected to exchange both emotional and material support.

Redefinition is a strategy to name relationships and individuals in ways that affirm the family as a unit (in the case of stepfamilies headed by same-sex parents).

Redundancy hypothesis suggests that children need positive ties to only one parenting figure in order to thrive.

Relational ambiguity is a term used in reference to same-sex parents. Gay communities are accepting of a wide variety of relationships, including nonmonogamous relationships and relationships of short duration. Those that form stepfamilies need to find different modes of commitment and stability because of the presence of children.

Selection effects are defined as the nonrandom incidence of people with particular characteristics in a situation or group.

Simple adoption exists in France, and creates a legal relationship between a stepparent and a stepchild while leaving the relationships with the biological parents intact.

Social Interaction Learning Theory (SIL) is based on the assumption that parenting skills are a vital interface between the context in which families live, and the well-being of children.

Stem families are the coexistence of three generations in one household (especially in Japan).

Substitution suggests that children substitute one parenting figure for another. For example, a stepfather may replace a nonresident father in their lives.

Turning point is described as 'a transformative event that alters a relationship in some important way, either positively or negatively'.

References

Adler-Baeder, F. (2006). What do we know about the physical abuse of stepchildren? A review of the literature. *Journal of Divorce & Remarriage*, 44 (3/4), 67–81.

Adler-Baeder, F., Russell, C., Kerpelman, J., Pittman, J., Ketring, S., Smith, T., & Stringer, K. (2010). Thriving in stepfamilies: exploring competence and wellbeing among African American Youth. *Journal of Adolescent Health*, 46, 396–398.

Alexandre, G. C., Nadanovsky, P., Moraes, C. L., & Reichenheim, M. (2010). The presence of a stepfather and child physical abuse, as reported by a sample of Brazilian mothers in Rio de Janeiro. *Child Abuse and Neglect*, 34 (12), 959–966.

Allan, G., Crow, G., & Hawker, S. (2011). *Stepfamilies*. Basingstoke, England: Palgrave Macmillan.

Allen, E. S., Baucom, D. H., Burnette, C. K., Epstein, N., & Rankin-Esquer, L. A. (2001). Decision making power, autonomy, and communication in remarried spouses compared with first-married spouses. *Family Relations*, 50 (4), 326–334.

Amato, P. R. (1994). The implications of research on children in stepfamilies. In A. Booth & J. Dunn (Eds.), *Stepfamilies: Who benefits? Who does not?* Hillsdale, NJ: Lawrence Erlbaum.

Amato, P. R. (2000). The consequences of divorce for parents and children. *Journal of Marriage and Family*, 62, 1269–1287.

Amato, P. R. (2012). The well-being of children with gay and lesbian parents. *Social Science Research*, 41, 771–774.

Amato, P. & Gilbreth, J. G. (1999). Nonresident fathers and children's well-being: a meta-analysis. *Journal of Marriage and the Family*, 61, 557–573.

Ambert, A. M. (1986). Being a stepparent: live-in and visiting stepchildren. *Journal of Marriage and Family*, 48, 795–804.

Anderson, E. R. (1999). Sibling, half-sibling, and stepsibling relationships in remarried families. *Monographs of the Society for Research in Child Development*, 64 (4), 101–126.

Anyan, S. & Pryor, J. (2002). What is a family? Adolescent perceptions. *Children & Society*, 16, 1–12.

Aquilino, W. S. (2006). The noncustodial father–child relationship from adolescence to young adulthood. *Journal of Marriage and Family*, 68 (November), 929–946.

Attar-Schwartz, S., Tan, J.-P., Buchanan, A., Flouri, E., & Griggs, J. (2009). Grandparenting and adolescent adjustment in two-parent biological, lone-parent, and step-families. *Journal of Family Psychology*, 23 (1), 67–75.

Baham, M. E., Weimer, A. A., Braver, S. L., & Fabricious, W. V. (2008). Sibling relationships in blended families. In J. Pryor (Ed.), *The International Handbook of Stepfamilies: Policy and Practice in Legal, Research, and Clinical Environments* (pp. 175–207). Hoboken, NJ: John Wiley & Sons.

Barber, B. & Lyons, J. (1994). Family processes and adolescent adjustment in intact and remarried families. *Journal of Youth and Adolescence*, 23 (4), 421–436.

Barnett, M. A., Scaramella, L. V., Neppl, T. K., Ontai, L. L., & Conger, R. D. (2010). Grandmother involvement as a protective factor for early childhood social adjustment. *Journal of Family Psychology*, 24 (5), 635–645.

Barrett, A. E. & Turner, R. J. (2005). Family structure and mental health: the mediating effects of socioeconomic status, family process, and social stress. *Journal of Health and Social Behavior*, 46 (2), 156–169.

Baumrind, D. (1971). Current patterns of parental authority. *Developmental Psychology, Monograph*, 4 (Pt. 2), 1–103.

Baxter, L. A., Braithwaite, D. O., & Nicholson, J. (1999). Turning points in the development of blended families. *Journal of Social and Personal Relationships*, 16 (3), 291–313.

Beck-Gernsheim, E. (2002). *Reinventing the Family: In Search of New Lifestyles.* Cambridge, England: Polity Press.

Bengston, V. L. (2001). Beyond the nuclear family: the increasing importance of multigenerational bonds. *Journal of Marriage and Family*, 63 (1), 1–16.

Beninger, C. (2011). Stepfamilies in Namibia: a study of the situation of stepparents and stepchildren and recommendations for law reform. Windhoek, Namibia: Legal Assistance Centre.

Berg, E. C. (2003). The effects of perceived closeness to custodial parents, stepparents and nonresident parents on adolescent self esteem. *Journal of Divorce & Remarriage*, 40 (1/2), 69–86.

Berger, L. M. (2000). Gay stepfamilies: a triple-stigmatized group. *Families in Society*, 81 (5), 504–516.

Biblarz, T. J. & Savci, E. (2010). Lesbian, gay, bisexual, and transgender families. *Journal of Marriage and Family*, 72 (3), 480–497.

Black, D., Gates, G. J., Sanders, S., & Taylor, L. (2000). Demographics of the gay and lesbian population in the United States: evidence from available systematic data sources. *Demography*, 37 (2), 139–154.

Block, C. E. (2002). College students' perceptions of social support from grandmothers and stepgrandmothers. *College Student Journal*, 36 (3), 419–432.

Bos, H. & Sandfort, T. G. M. (2010). Children's gender identity in lesbian and heterosexual two-parent families. *Sex Roles*, 62, 114–126.

Boss, P. (1999). *Ambiguous Loss: Learning to Live with Unresolved Grief.* Cambridge, MA: Harvard University Press.

Braithwaite, D. O. & Baxter, L. A. (2006). "You're my parent but you're not": dialectical tensions in stepchildren's perceptions about communicating with the nonresidential parent. *Journal of Applied Communication Research*, 34 (1), 30–48.

Bramlett, M. D. & Mosher, W. D. (2002). Cohabitation, marriage, divorce, and remarriage in the United States. National Center for Health Statistics. *Vital Health Statistics*, 23 (22), 1–103.

Bray, J. H. & Berger, S. M. (1993). Developmental issues in Stepfamilies Research Project: family relationships and parent–child interactions. *Journal of Family Psychology*, 7, 76–90.

Brown, S. (2006). Family structure transitions and adolescent wellbeing. *Demography*, 43 (3), 447–461.

Brown, S. & Manning, S. L. (2009). Family boundary ambiguity and the measurement of family structure: the significance of cohabitation. *Demography*, 46 (1), 85–101.

Brown, S. L. & Rinelli, L. N. (2010). Family structure, family processes, and adolescent smoking and drinking. *Journal of Research on Adolescence*, 20 (2), 259–273.

Browning, S. & Artelt, E. (2012). *Stepfamily Therapy: A Ten-Step Clinical Approach*. Washington, DC: APA Books.

Brownridge, D. A. (2004). Male partner violence against women in stepfamilies: an analysis of risk and explanations in the Canadian milieu. *Violence and Victims*, 19 (1), 17–36.

Buchanan, C. M. & Maccoby, E. E. (1996). *Adolescents after Divorce*. Cambridge, MA: Harvard University Press.

Bullard, L., Wachlarowicz, M., Forgatch, M., Degarmo, D., DeLeeuw, J., Snyder, J., & Low, S. (2010). Effects of the Oregon model of Parent Management Training (PMTO) on marital adjustment in new stepfamilies: a randomized trial. *Journal of Family Psychology*, 24 (4), 485–496.

Bumpass, L. L. & Lu, H. (2000). Trends in cohabitation and implications for children's family contexts in the United States. *Population Studies*, 54, 19–41.

Bumpass, L., Raley, R. K., & Sweet, J. (1995). The changing character of stepfamilies: implications of cohabitation and non-marital child bearing. *Demography*, 32, 425–436.

Burton, L. M. & Hardaway, C. R. (2012). Low-income mothers as 'othermothers' to their romantic partners' children: women's coparenting in multiple partner fertility relationships. *Family Process*, 51 (3), 343–359.

Carlson, M. J. & Furstenberg, F. F. (2006). The prevalence and correlates of multipartnered fertility among urban U.S. parents. *Journal of Marriage and Family*, 68 (3), 718–732.

Carlson, M. J. & Furstenberg, F. F. (2007). The consequences of multi-partnered fertility for parental involvement and relationships. http://crcw.princeton.edu/workingpapers/WP06-28-FF.pdf

Cartwright, C. & Seymour, F. (2002). Young adults' perceptions of parents' responses in stepfamilies: What hurts? What helps? *Journal of Divorce and Remarriage*, 37 (3/4), 123–141.

Cherlin, A. J. (1978). Remarriage as an incomplete institution. *American Journal of Sociology*, 84 (3), 634–649.

Cherlin, A. J. (2009). *The Marriage-Go-Round: The State of Marriage and the Family in America Today*. New York: Alfred A. Knopf.

Church, E. (1999). Who are the people in your family? Stepmothers' diverse notions of kinship. *Journal of Divorce & Remarriage*, 31 (1/2), 83–105.

Clawson, J. & Ganong, L. (2002). Adult stepchildren's obligations to older stepparents. *Journal of Family Nursing, 8,* 50–73.

Claxton-Oldfield, S. (2000). Deconstructing the myth of the wicked stepparent. *Marriage & Family Review,* 30 (1/2), 51–58.

Claxton-Oldfield, S. (2008). Stereotypes of stepfamilies and stepfamily members. In J. Pryor (Ed.), *The International Handbook of Stepfamilies: Policy and Practice in Legal, Research, and Clinical Environments* (pp. 30–52). Hoboken, NJ: John Wiley & Sons.

Claxton-Oldfield, S., O'Neill, S., Thomson, C., & Gallant, B. (2005). Multiple stereotypes of stepfathers. *Journal of Divorce & Remarriage,* 44 (1/2), 165–176.

Coltrane, S., Gutierrez, E., & Parke, R. (2008). Stepfathers in cultural context: Mexican American families in the United States. In J. Pryor (Ed.), *The International Handbook of Stepfamilies: Policy and Practice in Legal, Research, and Clinical Environments* (pp. 100–124). Hoboken, NJ: John Wiley & Sons.

Cooksey, E. C. & Craig, P. H. (1998). Parenting from a distance: the effects of paternal characteristics on contact between nonresidential fathers and their children. *Demography,* 35 (2), 187–200.

Crohn, J. M. (2006). Five styles of positive stepmothering from the perspective of young adult stepdaughters. *Journal of Divorce and Remarriage,* 46 (1/2), 119–134.

Crosbie-Burnett, M. (1984). The centrality of the step relationship: a challenge to family theory and practice. *Family Relations,* 33 (3), 459–463.

Crosbie-Burnett, M. & Giles-Sims, J. (1994). Adolescent adjustment and stepparenting styles. *Family Relations,* 43, 394–399.

Crosbie-Burnett, M. & Lewis, E. A. (1993). Use of African-American family structures and functioning to address the challenges of European-American postdivorce families. *Family Relations,* 4 (3), 243–248.

Curtis-Clark, A. (2012). A qualitative study of Maori experiences of stepfamily living. PhD thesis, University of Auckland.

Cutrona, C. E., Russell, D. W., Burzette, R. G., Wesner, K. A., & Bryant, C. M. (2011). Predicting relationship stability among midlife African American couples. *Journal of Consulting and Clinical Psychology,* 79 (6), 814–825.

D'Andrea, A. (1983). Joint custody as related to paternal involvement and paternal self esteem. *Conciliation Courts Review,* 21, 81–87.

Daly, M. & Wilson, M. (1998). *The Truth about Cinderella: A Darwinian View.* New Haven, CT: Yale University Press.

Day, R. D., Jones-Sanpei, H., Smith Price, J. L., Orthner, D. K., Hair, E. C., Anderson Moore, K., & Kaye, K. (2009). Family processes and adolescent religiosity and religious practice: view from the NLSY97. *Marriage & Family Review,* 45, 289–309.

Doodson, L. & Morley, D. (2006). Understanding the roles of non-residential stepmothers. *Journal of Divorce and Remarriage,* 45 (3/4), 109–130.

Doyle, M., O'Dwyer, C., & Timonen, V. (2010). "How can you just cut off a whole side of the family and say move on?" The reshaping of paternal grandparent–grandchild relationships following divorce or separation in the middle generation. *Family Relations,* 59 (5), 587–598.

Drew, L. M. & Silverstein, M. (2007). Grandparents' psychological wellbeing after loss of contact with their grandchildren. *Journal of Family Psychology*, 21 (3), 372–379.

Dunn, J. & Deater-Deckard, K. (2001). *Understanding Children's Views of Support Following Parental Separation and the Formation of Stepfamilies.* London: Joseph Rowntree Foundation.

Dunn, J., Deater-Deckard, K., Pickering, K. K., O'Connor, T. G., Golding, J., & ALSPAC Study Team (1998). Children's adjustment and pro-social behavior in step-, single-parent, and non-stepfamily settings: findings from a community study. *Journal of Child Psychology and Psychiatry*, 39, 1083–1095.

Edwards, R., Gillies, V., & Ribbens McCarthy, J. (1999). Biological parents and social families: legal discourses and everyday understandings of the position of stepparents. *International Journal of Law, Policy and the Family*, 13 (1), 78–105.

Elder, G. H. (1998). The life course as developmental theory. *Child Development*, 69, 1–12.

Erera-Weatherley, P. I. (1996). On becoming a stepparent: factors associated with the adoption of alternative stepparenting styles. *Journal of Divorce and Remarriage*, 25 (3/4), 155–173.

Ermisch, J. & Francesconi, M. (2000). The increasing complexity of family relationships: lifetime experience of lone motherhood and stepfamilies in Great Britain. *European Journal of Population*, 16, 235–249.

Espinosa, G., Elizondo, V., & Miranda, J. (2003). *Hispanic Churches in American Public Life: Summary of Findings.* Notre Dame, IN: University of Notre Dame.

Falke, S. I. & Larson, J. H. (2007). Premarital predictors of remarital quality: implications for clinicians. *Contemporary Family Therapy*, 29, 9–23.

Ferri, E. & Smith, K. (1998). *Stepparenting in the 1990s.* London: Family Policy Studies Centre.

Finch, J. (2007). Displaying families. *Sociology*, 41 (1), 65–81.

Fine, M. A. (1997). Stepfamilies from a policy perspective: guidance from the empirical literature. *Marriage & Family Review*, 26 (3–4), 249–263.

Fisher, P. A., Leve, L. D., O'Leary, C. C., & Leve, C. (2003). Parental monitoring of children's behavior: variation across stepmother, stepfather, and two-parent biological families. *Family Relations*, 52, 45–52.

Fleming, R. (1999). *Families of a Different Kind.* Wellington, New Zealand: Families of Remarriage Project.

Flouri, E., Buchanan, A., Tan, J.-P., Griggs, J., & Attar-Schwartz, S. (2010). Adverse life events, area socio-economic disadvantage, and adolescent psychopathology: the role of closeness to grandparents in moderating the effect of contextual stress. *Stress*, 13 (5), 402–412.

Fomby, P. & Cherlin, A. J. (2007). Family instability and child wellbeing. *American Sociological Review*, 72 (2), 181–204.

Forgatch, M., Degarmo, D., & Beldaves, Z. G. (2005). An efficacious theory-based intervention for stepfamilies. *Behavioral Therapy*, 4, 357–365.

Fulcher, M., Sutfin, E. L., & Patterson, C. J. (2008). Individual differences in gender development: associations with parental sexual orientation, attitudes, and division of labor. *Sex Roles*, 58, 330–341.

Funder, K. (1996). *Remaking Families: Adaptation of Parents and Children to Divorce*. Melbourne: Australian Institute of Family Studies.

Furstenberg, F. F. & Kaplan, S. (2004). Social capital and the family. In J. Scott, J. Treas & M. Richards (Eds.), *The Blackwell Companion to Sociology*. Malden, MA: Blackwell.

Ganong, L. (2008). Intergenerational relationships in stepfamilies. In J. Pryor (Ed.), *The International Handbook of Stepfamilies: Policy and Practice in Legal, Research and Clinical Environments* (pp. 394–422). Hoboken, NJ: John Wiley & Sons.

Ganong, L. & Coleman, M. (2004). *Stepfamily Relationships: Development, Dynamics, and Interventions*. New York: Kluwer Academic/Plenum.

Gelles, R. J. & Harrop, J. W. (1991). The risk of abusive violence among children with nongenetic caretakers. *Family Relations*, 40, 78–83.

Giles-Sims, J. & Finkelhor, D. (1984). Child abuse in stepfamilies. *Family Relations*, 33, 407–413.

Gillis, J. (1997). *A World of Their Own Making: Myth, Ritual and the Quest for Family Values*. Boston, MA: Harvard University Press.

Ginther, D. K. & Pollak, R. A. (2004). Family structure and children's educational outcomes: blended families, stylized facts, and descriptive regressions. *Demography*, 41 (4), 671–696.

Goldberg, A. E. (2007). (How) does it make a difference? Perspectives of adults with lesbian, gay, and bisexual parents. *American Journal of Orthopsychiatry*, 77 (4), 550–562.

Golish, T. D. (2003). Stepfamily communication strengths: understanding the ties that bind. *Human Communication Research*, 29 (1), 41–80.

Golombok, S. & Badger, S. (2010). Children raised in mother-headed families from infancy: a follow-up of children of lesbian and single heterosexual mothers, at early adulthood. *Human Reproduction*, 25 (1), 150–157.

Golombok, S., Perry, B., Burston, A., Golding, J., Murray, C., Mooney-Somers, J., & Stevens, M. (2003). Children with lesbian parents: a community study. *Developmental Psychology*, 39 (1), 20–33.

Goodnight, J. A., D'Onofrio, B. M., Cherlin, A. J., Emery, R. E., Van Hulle, C. A., & Lahey, B. B. (2013). Effects of multiple maternal relationship transitions on offspring antisocial behavior in childhood and adolescence: a cousin-comparison analysis. *Journal of Abnormal Child Psychology*, 41, 185–198.

Gorrell Barnes, G., Thompson, P., Daniel, G., & Burchardt, N. (1998). *Growing Up in Stepfamilies*. Oxford: Clarendon Press.

Graham, R. (2010). The stepparent role: how it is defined and negotiated in stepfamilies in New Zealand. PhD thesis, Victoria University of Wellington, New Zealand.

Green, R.-J. (2004). Risk and resilience in lesbian and gay couples: comment on Solomon, Rothblum, and Balsam (2004). *Journal of Family Psychology*, 18 (2), 290–292.

Green, R.-J. & Mitchell, V. (2002). Gay and lesbian couples in therapy: homophobia, relational ambiguity, and social support. In A. S. Gurman & N. S. Jacobson (Eds.), *Clinical Handbook of Couple Therapy* (3rd ed., pp. 546–568). New York: Guilford Press.

Gross, P. (1987). Defining post-divorce remarriage families: a typology based on the subjective perceptions of children. *Journal of Divorce*, 10, 205–217.

Gunnoe, M. L. & Hetherington, E. M. (1995). *Custodial parents, non-custodial parents, and stepparents, and adolescent adjustment in enduring stepfamily systems*. Washington, DC: Child Trends.

Hadfield, K. & Nixon, E. (2012). Comparison of relationship dynamics within stepmother and stepfather families in Ireland. *The Irish Journal of Psychology*, 33 (2–3), 100–106.

Halford, K., Nicholson, J., & Sanders, M. (2007). Couple communication in stepfamilies. *Family Process*, 46 (4), 471–483.

Hamer, J. & Marchioro, K. (2002). Becoming custodial dads: exploring parenting among low-income and working-class African-American fathers. *Journal of Marriage and Family*, 64 (1), 116–129.

Hanson, T. L. (1999). Does parental conflict explain why divorce is negatively associated with child welfare? *Social Forces*, 77, 1283–1315.

Harknett, K. & Knab, J. (2007). More kin less support: multipartner fertility and perceived support among mothers. *Journal of Marriage and Family* (1), 237–253.

Hawkins, D. N., Amato, P. R., & King, V. (2007). Nonresident father involvement and adolescent wellbeing: father effects or child effects? *American Sociological Review*, 72 (6), 990–1010.

Heard, H. E. (2007). The family structure trajectory and adolescent school performance. Differential effects by race and ethnicity. *Journal of Family Issues*, 28 (3), 319–354.

Henry, C. S., Ceglian, C. P., & Ostrander, D. L. (1993). The transition to stepgrandparenthood. *Journal of Divorce & Remarriage*, 19, 25–44.

Hetherington, E. M. & Jodl, K. M. (1994). Stepfamilies as settings for child development. In A. Booth & J. Dunn (Eds.), *Stepfamilies: Who Benefits? Who Does Not?* (pp. 55–79). Hillsdale, NJ: Lawrence Erlbaum.

Hetherington, E. M., Henderson, S. H., & Reiss, D. (1999). Adolescent functioning in stepfamilies: family functioning and adolescent adjustment. *Child Development, Monograph* (64), 1–222.

Higginbotham, B. & Skogrand, L. (2010). Relationship education with both married and unmarried stepcouples: an exploratory study. *Journal of Couple and Relationship Therapy*, 9, 133–147.

Hofferth, S. L. (2006). Residential father family type and child well-being: investment versus selection. *Demography*, 43 (1), 53–77.

Juby, H., Billette, J.-M., Laplante, B., & Le Bourdais, C. (2007). Nonresident fathers and children: parents' new unions and frequency of contact. *Journal of Family Issues*, 28 (9), 1220–1245.

Kiernan, K. E. (1992). The impact of family disruption in childhood and transitions made in young adult life. *Population Studies*, 46, 213–234.

King, V. (2006). The antecedents and consequences of adolescents' relationships with stepfathers and nonresident fathers. *Journal of Marriage and Family*, 68, 910–928.

King, V. (2007). When children have two mothers: relationships with nonresident mothers, stepmothers, and fathers. *Journal of Marriage and Family*, 69 (December), 1178–1193.

King, V. (2009). Stepfamily formation: implications for adolescent ties to mothers, nonresident fathers, and stepfathers. *Journal of Marriage and Family*, 71 (4), 954–968.

Kinniburgh-White, R., Cartwright, C., & Seymour, F. (2010). Young adults' narratives of relational development with stepfathers. *Journal of Social and Personal Relationships*, 27 (7), 890–907.

Kreider, R. & Ellis, R. (2011). Living arrangements of children 2009. *Current Population Reports* (pp. 70–126). Washington, DC: US Census Bureau.

Kurdek, L. (2001). Differences between heterosexual-nonparent couples and gay, lesbian and heterosexual-parent couples. *Journal of Family Issues*, 22 (6), 727–754.

Kurdek, L. (2006). Differences between partners from heterosexual, gay, and lesbian cohabiting couples. *Journal of Marriage and Family*, 68 (2), 509–528.

Laufer-Ukeles, A. & Blecher-Prigat, A. (2013). Between function and form: toward a differentiated model of functional parenthood. *George Mason Law Review*, 484 (2), (Winter), 419–484.

Leake, V. S. (2007). Personal, familial, and systemic factors associated with family belonging for stepfamily adolescents. *Journal of Divorce and Remarriage*, 47 (1/2), 135–155.

Leon, K. & Angst, E. (2005). Portrayals of stepfamilies in film: using media images in remarriage education. *Family Relations*, 54 (January), 3–23.

Lucier-Greer, M. & Adler-Baeder, F. (2012). Does couple and relationship education work for individuals in stepfamilies? A meta-analytic study. *Family Relations*, 61 (5), 756–769.

Lussier, G., Deater-Deckard, K., Dunn, J., & Davies, L. (2002). Support across two generations: children's closeness to grandparents following parental divorce and remarriage. *Journal of Family Psychology*, 16 (3), 363–376.

Lynch, J. M. (2004). The identity transformation of biological parents in lesbian/gay stepfamilies. *Journal of Homosexuality*, 47 (2), 91–107.

Lynch, J. M. & Murray, K. (2000). For the love of children: the coming out process for lesbian and gay parents and stepparents. *Journal of Homosexuality*, 39 (1), 1–23.

McCreary, L. L. & Dancy, B. L. (2004). Dimensions of family functioning: perspectives of low-income African American single-parent families. *Journal of Marriage and Family*, 66 (3), 690–701.

McLanahan, S. & Sandefur, G. D. (1994). *Growing Up with a Single Parent*. Cambridge, MA: Harvard University Press.

McLloyd, V. C., Cauce, A. M., Takeuchi, D., & Wilson, L. (2000). Marital processes and parental socialization in families of color: a decade review of research. *Journal of Marriage and Family*, 62, 1070–1093.

Malia, S. (2005). Balancing family members' interests regarding stepparent rights and obligations: a social policy challenge. *Family Relations*, 54 (2), 298–319.

Malkin, C. M. & Lamb, M. E. (1994). Child maltreatment: a test of sociobiological theory. *Journal of Comparative Family Studies*, 25, 121–133.

Manning, W. D., Stewart, S. D., & Smock, P. J. (2003). The complexity of fathers' parenting responsibilities and involvement with nonresident children. *Journal of Family Issues*, 24 (5), 645–667.

Marsiglio, W. (2004). When stepfathers claim stepchildren: a conceptual analysis. *Journal of Marriage and Family*, 66 (1), 22–39.

Marsiglio, W. & Hinojosa, R. (2007). Managing the multifather family: stepfathers as father allies. *Journal of Marriage and Family*, 69 (August), 845–862.

Martinez, C. R. & Forgatch, M. (2002). Adjusting to change: linking family structure transitions with parenting and boys' adjustment. *Journal of Family Psychology*, 16 (2), 107–117.

Mason, M. A., Harrison-Jay, S., Svare, G. M., & Wolfinger, N. (2002). Stepparents: de facto parents or legal strangers? *Journal of Family Issues*, 23, 507–522.

Monte, L. M. (2011). Multiple partner maternity versus multiple partner paternity: what matters for family trajectories. *Marriage & Family Review*, 47, 90–124.

Moore, M. (1999). Is living in a stepfamily related to positive outcomes for African American adolescents? *Perspectives* (Fall), 47–56.

Morgan, D. H. J. (1996). *Family Connections*. Cambridge, England: Polity Press.

Morgan, D. H. J. (2011). *Rethinking Family Practices*. Basingstoke, England: Palgrave Macmillan.

Nicolson, J. M., Fergusson, D. M., & Horwood, L. J. (1999). Effects on later adjustment of living in a stepfamily during childhood and adolescence. *Journal of Child Psychology and Psychiatry*, 49 (3), 405–416.

Nicolson, J. M., Sanders, M., Halford, K., Phillips, M., & Whitton, S. (2008). The prevention and treatment of children's adjustment problems in stepfamilies. In J. Pryor (Ed.), *The International Handbook of Stepfamilies: Policy and Practice in Legal, Research, and Clinical Environments* (pp. 485–521). Hoboken, NJ: John Wiley & Sons.

Nozawa, S. (2008). The social context of emerging stepfamilies in Japan. In J. Pryor (Ed.), *The International Handbook of Stepfamilies: Policy and Practice in Legal, Research, and Clinical Environments* (pp. 79–99). Hoboken, NJ: John Wiley & Sons.

Nozawa, S. (2011). The social and structural aspects of difficulties in stepfamilies. Paper presented at the US Japan Stepfamily Conference, Meiji Gakuin University.

Osborne, C. (2012). Further comments on the papers by Marks and Regnerus. *Social Science Research*, 41, 779–783.

Oswald, R. F. (2002). Resilience within the family networks of lesbians and gay men: intentionality and redefinition. *Journal of Marriage and Family*, 64 (2), 374.

Pallock, L. L. & Lamborn, S. D. (2006). Beyond parenting practices: extended kinship support and the academic adjustment of African-American and European-American teens. *Journal of Adolescence*, 29, 813–828.

Papernow, P. (2008). A clinician's view of 'stepfamily architecture'. In J. Pryor (Ed.), *The International Handbook of Stepfamilies: Policy and Practice in Legal, Research, and Clinical Environments* (pp. 423–454). Hoboken, NJ: John Wiley & Sons.

Patterson, C. J. (2000). Family relationships of lesbians and gay men. *Journal of Marriage and Family*, 62 (4), 1052–1069.

Planitz, J. M., & Feeney, J. A. (2009). Are stepsiblings bad, stepmothers wicked, and stepfathers evil? An assessment of Australian stepfamily stereotypes. *Journal of Family Studies*, 15 (1), 82–97.

Pryor, J. (2004). *Resilience in Stepfamilies*. Wellington, New Zealand: Ministry of Social Development.

Pryor, J. (2006). *Beyond Demography: History, Ritual and Families in the Twenty-first Century*. Wellington, New Zealand: New Zealand Families Commission.

Pryor, J. (2008a). *The International Handbook of Stepfamilies: Policy and Practice in Legal, Research, and Clinical Environments*. Hoboken, NJ: John Wiley & Sons.

Pryor, J. (2008b). Child-nonresident relationships in stepfamilies. In J. Pryor (Ed.), *The International Handbook of Stepfamilies: Policy and Practice in Legal, Research, and Clinical Environments* (pp. 345–368). Hoboken, NJ: John Wiley & Sons.

Pryor, J. & Rodgers, B. (2001). *Children in Changing Families: Life after Parental Separation*. Oxford: Blackwell Publishers.

Raley, R. K. & Wildsmith, E. (2004). Cohabitation and children's family instability. *Journal of Marriage and Family*, 66 (1), 210–219.

Regnerus, M. (2012). How different are the adult children of parents who have same-sex relationships? Findings from the New Family Structures Study. *Social Science Research*, 41, 752–770.

Rigg, A. & Pryor, J. (2007). Children's perceptions of families: what do they really think? *Children & Society*, 21, 17–30.

Rivers, I., Poleat, V. P., & Noret, N. (2008). Children of same-sex parents in the United Kingdom. *Developmental Psychology*, 44 (1), 127–134.

Robertson, J. (2008). Stepfathers in families. In J. Pryor (Ed.), *The International Handbook of Stepfamilies: Policy and Practice in Legal, Research, and Clinical Environments* (pp. 125–150). Hoboken, NJ: John Wiley & Sons.

Robitaille, C. & Saint-Jacques, M.-C. (2011). Social stigma and the situation of young people in lesbian and gay stepfamilies. *Journal of Homosexuality*, 56, 421–442.

Rohlf, L. (2009). The psychological parent and de facto parent doctrines: how should the Uniform Parentage Act define "parent'? *Iowa Law Review*, 94, 691–725.

Ruiz, S. A. & Silverstein, M. (2007). Relationships with grandparents and the emotional well-being of late adolescent and young adult grandchildren. *Journal of Social Issues*, 63 (4), 793–808.

Schrodt, P. & Braithwaite, D. O. (2011). Coparental communication, relational satisfaction, and mental health in stepfamilies. *Personal Relationships*, 18, 352–369.

Seltzer, J. A. & Bianchi, S. M. (1988). Children's contact with absent parents. *Journal of Marriage and Family*, 50, 663–677.

Serpell, R., Sonnenschein, S., Baker, L., & Ganapathy, H. (2002). Intimate culture of families in the early socialization of literacy. *Journal of Family Psychology*, 16 (4), 391–405.

Smith, M., Robertson, J., Dixon, J., Quigley, M., & Whitehead, E. (2001). *A Study of Stepchildren and Stepparenting*. London: Thomas Coram Research Unit Institute of Education.

Smith, T. A. (1991). Family cohesion in remarried families. *Journal of Divorce & Remarriage*, 17 (1/2), 49–66.

Soliz, J. (2007). Communicative predictors of a shared family identity: comparison of grandchildren's perceptions of family-of-origin grandparents and stepgrandparents. *Journal of Family Communication*, 7 (3), 177–194.

Solomon, S. E., Rothblum, E. D., & Balsam, K. F. (2004). Pioneers in partnership: Lesbian and gay male couples in civil unions compared with those not in civil unions and married heterosexual siblings. *Journal of Family Psychology*, 18 (2), 275–286.

Stack, C. B. & Burton, L. M. (1993). Kinscripts. *Journal of Comparative Family Studies*, 24 (2), 157–168.

Stewart, S. D. (1999). Nonresident mothers' and fathers' social contact with children. *Journal of Marriage and Family*, 61, 894–907.

Stewart, S. D. (2001). Contemporary American stepparenthood: integrating cohabiting and nonresident stepparents. *Population Research and Policy Review*, 20, 345–364.

Stewart, S. D. (2007). *Brave New Stepfamilies: Diverse Paths Toward Stepfamily Living*. Thousand Oaks, CA: Sage.

Stewart, S. D. (2010). Children with nonresident parents: living arrangements, visitation, and child support. *Journal of Marriage and Family*, 72 (5), 1078–1091.

Sweeney, M. M. (2007). Stepfather families and the emotional wellbeing of adolescents. *Journal of Health and Social Behavior*, 48 (1), 33–49.

Sweeney, M. M. (2010). Remarriage and stepfamilies: strategic sites for family scholarship in the 21st century. *Journal of Marriage and Family*, 72 (3), 667–684.

Sweeting, H., West, P., & Richards, M. (1998). Teenage family life, life-styles and life chances: associations with family structure, conflict with parents, and joint family activity. *International Journal of Law, Policy and the Family*, 12, 15–46.

Szinovacz, M. E. (1998). Grandparents today: a demographic profile. *Gerentologist*, 38, 37–52.

Tasker, F. & Golombok, S. (1997). *Growing up in a Lesbian Family: Effects on Child Development*. New York: Guilford Press.

Teachman, J. (2008). Complex life course patterns and the risk of divorce in second marriages. *Journal of Marriage and Family*, 70 (2), 294–305.

Teachman, J. & Tedrow, L. (2008). The demography of stepfamilies in the United States. In J. Pryor (Ed.), *The International Handbook of Stepfamilies* (pp. 3–29). Hoboken, NJ: John Wiley & Sons.

Tillman, K. H. (2008) "Non-traditional" siblings and academic outcomes of adolescents. *Social Science Research*, 37 (88–108).

van Eeden-Moorefield, B., Pasley, K., Crosbie-Burnett, M., & King, E. (2012). Explaining couple cohesion in different types of gay families. *Journal of Family Issues*, 33 (2), 182–201.

Ventura, S. J. (2009). Changing patterns of nonmarital childbearing in the United States (18). US Department of Health and Human Services, Center for Disease Control and Prevention.

Wainright, J. L., Russell, S. T., & Patterson, C. J. (2004). Psychosocial adjustment, school outcomes, and romantic relationships of adolescents with same-sex parents. *Child Development*, 75 (6), 1886–1898.

Wang, Q. & Zhou, Q. (2010). China's divorce and remarriage rates: trends and regional disparities. *Journal of Divorce & Remarriage*, 51 (4), 257–267.

Weaver, S. E. & Coleman, M. (2005). A mothering but not a mother role: a grounded theory study of the nonresidential stepmother role. *Journal of Social and Personal Relationships*, 22 (4), 477–497.

White, L. & Gilbreth, J. G. (2001). When children have two fathers: effects of relationships with stepfathers and non-custodial fathers on adolescent outcomes. *Journal of Marriage and Family*, 63, 155–167.

White, L. & Riedmann, A. (1992). When the Brady Bunch grows up: step/half- and full sibling relationships in adulthood. *Journal of Marriage and Family*, 54, 197–208.

Whitton, S., Nicholson, J., & Markman, H. (2008). Research on interventions for stepfamily couples. In J. Pryor (Ed.), *The International Handbook of Stepfamilies: Policy and Practice in Legal, Research, and Clinical Environments* (pp. 455–484). Hoboken, NJ: John Wiley & Sons.

Whitton, S., Stanley, S., Markman, H., & Johnson, C. A. (2013). Attitudes toward divorce, commitment, and divorce proneness in first marriages and remarriages. *Journal of Marriage and Family*, 75 (April), 276–287.

Wollney, I., Apps, J., & Henricson, C. (2010). *Can government measure family wellbeing? A literature review*. London: Family and Parenting Institute.

Wu, L. L. & Martinson, B. C. (1993). Family structure and the risk of a premarital birth. *American Sociological Review*, 58 (April), 210–232.

Yorgason, J. B., Padilla-Walker, L., & Jackson, J. (2011). Nonresidential grandparents' emotional and financial involvement in relation to early adolescent grandchild outcomes. *Journal of Research on Adolescence*, 21 (3), 552–558.

Zvab, A. (2007). New ways of parenting: fatherhood and parenthood in lesbian families. *Levijaza sociologija*, 38 (1–2), 43–55.

Subject Index

Yee sau for 2

Author Index